WORLD CRISIS AND BRITISH DECLINE, 1929–56

Roy Douglas

Reader
University of Surrey

MACMILLAN

First published 1986

Published by
THE MACMILLAN PRESS LTD
Houndmills, Basingstoke, Hampshire RG21 2XS
and London
Companies and representatives
throughout the world

Typeset by
Vine & Gorfin Ltd,
Exmouth, Devon

Printed in Hong Kong

British Library Cataloguing in Publication Data
Douglas, Roy, *1924–*
World crisis and British decline, 1929–56.
1. Great Britain—History—20th century
I. Title
941.082   DA566
ISBN 0-333-40578-1 (hardcover)
ISBN 0-333-40579-X (paperback)

Contents

List of Cartoons

Acknowledgements

The author wishes gratefully to acknowledge those who have helped in the production of this book. First he would like to thank his wife, and Dr Michael Burstall of the University of Surrey, who have read and criticised the manuscript, and whose comments have proved of enormous value. He would also like to thank the proprietors of copyrights in the various manuscripts listed in the bibliography, and the very helpful librarians of the institutions indicated.

The author has tried to keep notes to a minimum. Those statements which the reader may be disposed to query, and which are not covered by notes here, will mostly be found in the appropriate volume of the author's four books covering the period 1938–1948 which are listed opposite the title-page.

ROY DOUGLAS

1 A Kind of Stability

The world of early 1929 appeared to have recovered from the 1914 war, in the sense in which a man may be said to have recovered from the amputation of a limb. His life is no longer in imminent danger, he has adjusted himself to the loss, and he is going about his activities in the way in which he expects to continue for a long time to come.

The countries of western Europe exerted an influence utterly disproportionate to their size and population. Their empires comprised about 45 per cent of the land mass of the world, and a similar proportion of its population. The British Empire, larger than the others combined, covered rather more than a quarter of the globe. India, which then included also Pakistan, Bangladesh and Burma, carried about three-quarters of the total population of that Empire. In Asia and beyond, the British Empire included Australia, New Zealand, Malaya, Ceylon, parts of the archipelago joining Asia to Australia, and Hong Kong. A large part of Africa, many of the West Indian islands, and various territories in other parts of the world, also came within the Empire. Europe was the only continent in which – outside the British Isles themselves – Britain had few possessions: Gibraltar, Malta and Cyprus, all of them acquired and held essentially for strategic reasons. Substantial 'Mandates' had been acquired at the end of the First World War: over former German or Turkish possessions for which, at least in theory, Britain was accountable to the League of Nations. There were also various Protectorates which were under local rulers, but in which British interests were safeguarded by 'unequal treaties'. In many places lying outside the Empire – countries like Egypt and Persia, for example – British influence was strong. Much even of the territory lying formally within the British Empire was for practical purposes independent so far as internal government was concerned – although it was not until 1931 that the Statute of Westminster formally acknowledged that the United Kingdom Parliament would not legislate for these 'Dominions' unless requested by them to do so. Independent or not, the whole British Empire looked to Britain for a lead in matters of defence and foreign policy.

1

Britain's great organ of defence was the Navy – still, by most tests, the strongest in the world. The navy, which cost the taxpayer about £55 millions a year, was the essential link of the Empire, and – as wartime experience had shown – the vital means of ensuring supplies of food and other goods to the home islands. 'Showing the flag' in foreign waters was an acknowledged means of emphasising, in a friendly but firm manner, that British sea power was not to be trifled with. The other British forces together roughly balanced the Navy in cost, and the number of men serving in them was three or four times the number of sailors; but their international importance was far less. Nobody expected the British army to match up to the army of – say – France, or saw any reason why it should do so. In so far as soldiers were required for defence of the overseas Empire, they were to a large extent local levies, stiffened by British officers and troops. Conscription had been in force for a little under three years of the 'Great War', but it had been abandoned with relief at the end, and nobody thought of reintroducing it in the peaceful world of 1929. Why should Britain wish to have a great army on a continental scale? Soldiers returning from the war were determined that neither they nor their sons should repeat the experiences of the Western Front. Pacifists who hated all war on principle, realists who denied that war was worth what it cost, military officers who had no wish to train conscripts, taxpayers anxious to reduce their burdens, enthusiasts for civil liberties who feared that large armies must always be a threat to those liberties – they all agreed with the ex-soldiers' views for their disparate reasons.

Britain's economic position was less secure than in 1914, but by no means alarming. Historians have argued about at just what point Britain began to decline relative to other countries: perhaps about the middle of the nineteenth century. The war had given the United States the dubious benefits of being the universal creditor. Yet the British economy was still, to all appearances, very strong. Overall exports of merchandise and bullion were considerably exceeded by imports – £1292 millions against £926 millions in 1929[1] – but the difference was met, and exceeded, by large revenues from overseas investments, shipping and other services, which totalled £517 millions in the same year. Thus there was usually a healthy balance available for new investment overseas.

The recent memories of the First World War, and the 'lessons' which should be drawn therefrom, dominated political thinking in the 1920s – and, indeed, for long afterwards. The 1914 war had come as a bolt from a clear sky, in the sense that there was no living tradition of anything remotely comparable. The European wars after 1815 had been, for the most part, fought by professional soldiers, and the casualty lists – or at least the lists of casualties resulting from enemy action – had been astonishingly light. The American Civil War had been the one conflict in which huge numbers of people had perished on both sides. The 1914 War not only produced huge casualty lists, but a great proportion of those casualties had been sustained in apparently futile trench warfare. When war ended there was a tremendous reaction in the direction of a rather simplistic semi-pacifism. Not many people, perhaps, were prepared to go to the extreme of saying that all war at all times is evil; but a lot doubted the wisdom of fighting the recent war, and more still were determined at all costs to avert another. Many people on the 'right' were deeply conscious that much of the established order had already been destroyed in the 1914 conflict, and the remainder was in jeopardy should war recur. They reflected on the Bolshevik victory in Russia, and how close similar elements came to victory elsewhere at the end of the war. Many on the 'left' who had always hated war for humanitarian and idealistic reasons, felt abundantly confirmed in their judgement by recent experience.

The leaders of the various political parties in Britain symbolised these attitudes. At the General Election of May 1929 the Conservatives, headed by Stanley Baldwin, were rather narrowly defeated by Labour, headed by Ramsay MacDonald, with the Liberals, headed by David Lloyd George, holding (at least in theory) the balance of power. Baldwin was an industrialist with a deep hatred of war. MacDonald, the incoming Prime Minister, and Philip Snowden, his Chancellor of the Exchequer, had both acquired wartime notoriety for their pacifist opinions. Lloyd George was alternately blessed and reviled for his wartime leadership; but nobody reading his memoirs can doubt his deep sense of the horror of war. The views of such political opponents of war were shared by businessmen who were aware of the disruption which it caused to their affairs; by workers who believed in the international brotherhood of their own class; by ex-soldiers who found their wartime 'enemies' more, agreeable as individuals than the allies whom they met; by people who were appalled at the lies and half-truths which had been ciculated everywhere to encourage the necessary war hysteria; by people counting the cost in human, economic or diplomatic terms . . . and, above all, by parents whose overriding concern was that their own children should not become 'cannon-fodder' in some future conflict.

Yet 'lessons of history' are seldom unambiguous; and other people drew 'lessons' with very different overtones. Many ex-soldiers had pleasant memories of the deep friendships forged in the tribulations of conflict. People on the allied side could derive the lesson that Germany must be 'kept down'; people on the other side could derive the lesson that Germany had been cheated of victory. Had not Russia admitted total defeat at Brest-Litovsk in March 1918, and were not Germans fighting almost exclusively on enemy soil in the west at the moment of armistice in November? Thus diametrically opposite 'lessons' might very readily be drawn from the First World War. When Britons swore every Armistice Day that they would not 'break faith' with the wartime dead, did this mean that they would ensure at all costs that no others had to suffer the same experience; or did it mean that they would themselves be ready, if required, to repeat the sacrifice?

The immediate aftermath of war had also set indelible marks on the attitudes of people living in 1929. The settlement emerging from the Paris Peace Conference included several distinct instruments, of which the Treaty of Versailles, concluded in June 1919, is the most famous. New frontiers were drawn, to the disadvantage of the defeated 'Central Powers' – Germany, Austro-Hungary, Turkey and Bulgaria. Germany was required to admit that the war was all her fault, and to pay reparations. The former German colonies, and various non-Turkish portions of the Ottoman Empire, were set under Mandates of various allies. The armed forces and weapons of the defeated enemy were severly limited both in number and character. Several areas on the edges of Germany were to hold plebiscites to decide their futures. The Austro-Hungarian Empire had already ceased to exist when the armistice sounded; the peace treaties recognised three new sovereign states established on its ruins, and awarded great tracts of territory to four neighbours.

Like any settlement in which there are many participants, the post-1918 arrangements were in many ways a makeshift compromise between conflicting interests. Much more than in the 1815 settlement, they were also a compromise between radically different principles. During the war both sides had appealed to disaffected ethnic minorities within the enemy lands, and the victorious allies were compelled to grant considerable acknowledgement to ethnic considerations in devising the new frontiers. Unfortunately there were many parts of Europe where ethnic groups were so inextricably mixed that it would have been impossible to draw boundaries on purely ethnic grounds, even if other considerations had not entered the calculations. The allies, and particularly the French, were anxious that new frontiers should be militarily defensible. Italy, Romania, and Serbia – reborn as Yugoslavia

– demanded territorial favours which were sometimes difficult to defend on strictly ethnic lines, but were essentially spoils of war. The restoration of Poland and the establishment of Czechoslovakia necessarily involved drawing frontiers which were by no means purely ethnic. In various places historic associations affected the design of frontiers. Economic considerations sometimes ran counter to all others; for it was generally considered that countries should be potentially autarkic, and therefore contain a balance of different kinds of production, There was the overriding rule *vae victis* – woe to the vanquished! In no circumstances must the defeated enemy be left in a better position than he had been before the war. Thus it happened that almost any frontier established by the peace treaties could later be challenged on at least one of the conflicting principles which had influenced the peace settlement. It also followed that some states – broadly speaking the former Central Powers – were at heart 'revisionist', and hoped that some time the boundaries would be drawn differently; while other states – broadly speaking the former allies – were fearful of any revision and anxious to avert it. While the peace treaties were being drawn up, the Allies also established the League of Nations. It was intended that the League would possess real 'teeth', and would serve as effective arbiter in future disputes. The League was the particular idea of President Wilson of the United States; but his compatriots refused to join, and would accept no obligation to maintain the settlement. For practical purposes this meant that Britain, France, Italy and Japan were guarantors of the peace treaties and pillars of the League of Nations. In Britain the League came under savage attack both from critics on the 'left' who regarded it as a 'burglars' union', set up to preserve ill-gotten gains, and by critics on the 'right', especially in the services, who disliked the idea that national interests should ever be sacrificed to some international body; but the great centre ground of politics, including most leading figures in all three political parties, tended to applaud the League's apparent idealism, and to regard it as the best hope for preserving peace.

One series of events which marked the war and its immediate aftermath also coloured everybody's thinking in the years which followed. The Russian Bolshevik Revolution of November 1917 was perceived both by its authors and by its enemies as the spark designed to ignite a world revolution in the not-very-distant future. 'Either the Russian revolution will create a revolutionary movement in Europe, or the European Powers will destroy the Russian revolution', declared Trotsky.[2] The Russian revolutionaries tried to set off a European, if not world, revolution; and the European Powers in their turn tried to suppress the Russian revolution; but within a few years it was evident that neither objective was likely to be achieved for a very long time, and a kind of reluctant mutual toleration slowly developed. In 1920 socialist movements throughout the world were invited to join the 'Communist International', or 'Comintern', under Russian sponsorship. Those who accepted the invitation, known henceforth as communist parties, followed very closely indeed the perceived wishes and interests of the Soviet Union. Informed opponents of communism during the 1920s were not much afraid of military attack from the Soviet Union, which was currently in no condition to attack anybody; but they were deeply apprehensive of internal subversion organised by the Comintern and operated by the various national communist parties. Even this risk soon began to abate. In many countries communist parties were illegal but, whether legal or not, most of them were very small in 1929. In the British House of Commons there had never been more than a single Communist MP at any one time. (There would be two from 1945 to 1950, but that was the maximum.) In the French Chamber, where the popular strength of small parties was more accurately reflected, there were sixteen in 1929. Only the German Communist Party, which held just under one-eighth of the seats in the Reichstag, seemed to pose any serious challenge.

Perhaps the last clear echo of wartime hatreds was the bitter dispute between France and Germany over reparations in 1923. This led to the total collapse of the mark, and French occupation of the Rhur – to which event a large mass of British opinion reacted by a wave of pro-German and anti-French feeling. 'I am wondering whether it was worth giving up four years of one's life to overthrow Germany in order to set up France',[3] wrote one young ex-service MP. In the following year the United States devised the Dawes Plan, revised five years later as the Young Plan. The overall effect was to reduce the burden of reparations on Germany and spread them over a very long period. Germany could now discharge her reparations to the European allies, particularly France – who, in their turn, could pay their war debts to the United States. Russia owed huge debts to everybody, but these had been repudiated by the Bolsheviks, and the chances of reclaiming them were zero, whoever might rule in Russia.

These financial settlements – not really satisfactory to anybody, but tolerable to all – were paralleled by other serious and apparently hopeful efforts to resolve dangerous international differences. In 1925 a series of agreements was reached at Locarno. France concluded treaties with Poland and with Czechoslovakia, each providing that if Germany made an unprovoked attack on one, the other party would go to her aid. Britain guaranteed France against attack by Germany, and Germany against attack by France. The combination against any likely aggressor seemed so overwhelming that peace was apparently assured.

The matter of international armaments remained one of deep concern, and behind that concern lay widely-held, but unproven, theoretical assumptions. Many people regarded an 'armaments race' not so much as a symptom of deteriorating international conditions, but rather as a major cause of that deterioration, and a likely prelude to war. It was also commonly believed that armament manufacturers deliberately – and sometimes successfully – sought to engineer wars. Germany was still in the largely disarmed condition prescribed by the peace treaties. The victorious allies had promised to disarm themselves as soon as this might safely be done; but they had also appointed themselves judges of when that moment might arrive. Britain really was disarming – but very slowly. Defence estimates issued early in 1929 proposed slight reductions on those of the previous year for each of the three Services: an overall reduction of about £2 millions, or about 2 per cent of the total defence spending. In most other places there was a tendency to increase armament spending. In the previous four years the expenditure of France and Russia had nearly doubled while in Italy, Japan, the United States and Germany the increases had lain between 10 and 20 per cent.[4]

From time to time the question of general disarmament was seriously raised. In 1925 the League of Nations established a Preparatory Commission in anticipation of a general Disarmament Conference. That Preparatory Commission soon ran into great difficulties. At its first meeting, in 1926, the Commission decided that it was not practicable to set limits on the 'ultimate war strength' of a country; and from that point attention became concentrated on limiting particular kinds of armaments. It soon became apparent that each country had its own 'favourite' kinds of armaments, which were deemed necessary for security; and, while it might be willing to disarm in other ways, no nation was likely voluntarily to forego those particular armaments. Thus it gradually became evident that any Disarmament Conference which might be held would be unlikely to record those dramatic achievements which at one time had seemed possible.

Although deep anxieties about possible future wars were vexing people in 1929, the concern was long-term rather than immediate, and a dispassionate observer could be excused for thinking that material conditions were improving so generally that nobody was likely to behave in a manner which could give rise to war. Statistics all pointed to prosperity and rising standards.[5] Between 1921 and 1929, populations were rising and mortality – especially infant mortality – was falling nearly everywhere in Europe. Production figures were improving dramatically. In the same period the annual output of hard coal in Britain, France, Germany and Italy all rose between 40 and 100 per cent; the output of steel from 50 to over 200 per cent. Where recent technology was involved, improvements were more spectacular still. Taking the four countries together, electrical output more than doubled, and the number of motor vehicles in use multiplied nearly fourfold.

Other statistical trends were less reassuring. It had long been the practice of governments to impose trade barriers against each other – sometimes in order to levy revenue, sometimes to protect indigenous producers, but all such barriers hampered international commerce and distorted internal demand. By the late 1920s tariffs between major European states were on the whole higher than they had been pre-war, although this tendency was to an extent compensated by the opposite trend in North America.[6] With the rise in prosperity during the 1920s, trade barriers became in a sense more visible. Between 1925 and 1929 the proportion of government revenues deriving from import levies rose sharply in many places: in France from 6.3 per cent to 10.8 per cent; in Germany from 12.5 per cent to 16.5 per cent; in Russia from 5.5 per cent to 14.1 per cent; in Italy from 4.5 per cent to 10.4 per cent.[7] Manifestly some people were contriving to surmount the trade barriers, or import duties could never have been collected; but it is also evident that many external producers were excluded altogether from markets which would otherwise have looked hopeful. In 1931 – admittedly at a time when import duties had begun to rise sharply – Belgium, Sweden and Switzerland were among the few continental countries with less than 30 per cent *ad valorem* import duties; France and Germany stood at 38 and 41 per cent respectively; while most countries of central and Eastern Europe were far above that level.[8]

To make matters worse, the peace settlement had considerably increased the number of sovereign states in Europe. The three great empires of the centre and east had yielded ten successors – not counting other tracts of territory which had been lost to outsiders. Each asserted the right to regulate commerce according to its own whim. Whatever the ethnic or political advantages of the new arrangements, these were counterbalanced by grave economic disadvantages when the new countries of Europe proceeded to erect trade barriers with even more enthusiasm than did the old countries. In 1927 France and Germany had tariff indices of 23.0 and 20.4 respectively while the corresponding values for Czechoslovakia and Poland were 31.3 and 53.5.[9] Such new barriers broke established trade links, and fostered acrimony in various ways. People who had once traded freely in areas where new frontiers had been established, resented the impediments. But instead of pressing for abolition of barriers they were more likely to demand retaliatory barriers from their own governments. To make matters a great deal worse, most of the new countries contained different ethnic groups with conflicting economic interests. In Czechoslovakia, as we shall see, the predominantly agricultural Czechs had different interests from the predominantly industrial German-speaking inhabitants. Barriers devised to favour one group could prove ruinous to another. This had a deeply disruptive effect in the following decade. As with armaments, so also with trade barriers. There were various attempts to secure reduction through international agreements. In 1927 the League of Nations summoned an International Economic Conference, which approved the view that 'the time has come to put an end to the increase in tariffs and to move in the opposite direction'. Such brave words, however, were not followed by dramatic actions, either unilateral or through agreements. Once a trade barrier is imposed, powerful interests rapidly build up behind it; and those interests fight vigorously for its retention.

There were other baleful statistics in the late 1920s which would also soon become much worse. Unemployment had been an intermittent problem for working people in urban areas from time immemorial; but it was usually associated with trade recessions, and more or less disappeared when general prosperity returned. In Britain before 1914 it usually ranged from about 2 per cent to about 6 per cent or so of the industrial working class. In 1921 the figures suddenly shot up to 17 per cent. That level was not maintained for long, but thereafter no annual figures fell below 9 per cent, and in 1929 they stood at 11 per cent. The incidence varied enormously from place to place: it tended to be low in the south and high in the regions of the old heavy industries; but many towns depended on the activities of one or two firms, and quite accidental local considerations could prescribe that unemployment was negligible in one town, while it might approach or exceed half of the work-force in another not many miles away. Mass unemployment was a matter of deep political concern. Both the Liberal and Labour Parties made the conquest of unemployment a major issue at the 1929 General Election, advocating what would today be called Keynesian remedies, such as energetic programmes of public works, with deficit financing. It is important to remember that unemployment was not just a problem for the working class: high unemployment usually indicated empty order books, and extensive bankruptcies.

Comparative figures for other countries are not always easy to provide. Many countries did not keep official figures, and those who did often defined unemployment in different ways. In Germany, for example, different criteria might set the 1929 figures as low as 4.3 per cent or as high as 13.1 per cent.[10] Most European countries appear to have had unemployment values far below double figures; in France, to take an extreme case, it was negligible. In the United States unemployment followed something like the pre-1914 British pattern; the official figures for 1929 set it at 3.2 per cent.

If all these different, and sometimes conflicting, indications of conditions in the developed world of the late 1920s could be drawn together, then one might say that the outlook for future peace and prosperity all round seemed fairly good. Grave problems certainly remained, but there was no good reason for thinking that they were insoluble. The language which was generally being used did not imply violence or war. True, Benito Mussolini, head of the Italian Government since 1922, had made some disturbing speeches in the past year or so; while the theoretical writings of Josef Stalin, who was in the process of consolidating his power in the Soviet Union, were more disturbing still. Such utterances, however, were apparently designed for the propaganda among the 'faithful', with no immediate relevance to action. As for Germany, Adolf Hitler's National Socialists, or Nazis, held only about a dozen seats in the Reichstag.

The one condition on which this generally optimistic view depended was that no sudden calamity should intervene and invalidate the calculations which ordinary people and governments alike were making for the present and the foreseeable future. The longer the general framework of existing political and economic conditions persisted, the more likely it was that the rough edges could be removed without the need to restructure the whole edifice from its foundations. Gradually the ex-enemy would be brought into the comity of nations on a footing of equality with everybody else. The somewhat odd frontiers drawn after 1918 would either become accepted as permanent or else rectified quietly without too much fuss. Meanwhile technology would continue to bring rising prosperity to all. The economic barriers set up by self-conscious nationalism would gradually be removed as that nationalism became less self-conscious.

2 The Great Depression

The prospect of preserving the world order established at the end of the First World War, and of preserving Britain's position within that order, turned to a very large extent upon the maintenance of economic stability. For a long time there seemed a fair chance that this would happen, but on 24 October 1929 the financial world was horrified to learn of the 'Wall Street Crash' – an exceedingly widespread collapse of prices on the New York stock market. Some people argue today that signs existed long before October 1929 which showed that all was not well with the American economy, and that disaster was bound to come sooner or later. Scholars still discuss how far the crash was the 'cause' of other economic evils which followed swiftly afterwards. Such arguments are important, but they must be left firmly out of the present story. What matters here is that the drama which commenced on the New York Stock Exchange in the autumn of 1929 was followed by a long series of economic disasters, affecting all nations and all classes. This was the beginning of the Great Depression; and its consequences, direct and indirect, would prove almost limitless.

It very soon became apparent that speculative investors in the United States were by no means the only sufferers. The *Annual Register* for 1929 reflects that:

> The stock market crash had instant repercussions: [American] shopkeepers who feared that the Christmas trade would be less than anticipated cancelled orders right and left . . . By the end of the year it was estimated that about 3,000,000 wage earners, or perhaps 8% of the total, were out of work.[1]

That figure, 8 per cent, represents more than double the unemployment figures recorded in the United States during the previous year.

From America the tidal wave swept on to Europe. At first it was far from clear whether the world was entering some minor and temporary recession, or a serious depression. For Britain at least, perhaps the clearest index of what was happening, and when, is provided by the

11

unemployment figures. Down to the end of 1929 there was nothing to show that there was any trouble at all, for these figures were no higher than for the corresponding months of 1928. By March 1930, however, unemployment was three points up on the same month of the previous year; by July it was seven points up, and still rising. Every month of 1930 showed an increase on the previous month, and in most months the gap between corresponding months in 1929 and 1930 widened as well. By December 1930 the figure stood at over 20 per cent, and was still rising. Bad as matters had been in the post-war recession of 1921, they were considerably worse at the end of 1930. Other indices confirmed the seriousness of the depression. In 1930 exports were down by more than 20 per cent on the previous year, imports were down by more than 14 per cent.[2]

Other advanced economies followed a similar pattern, though not all at exactly the same time. Unemployment got worse; businesses failed; exports and imports both declined substantially. The significance of such matters in human terms varied substantially from place to place. In predominantly agricultural, more or less self-sufficient, countries, neither industrial unemployment nor declining international trade was a major threat to society; but in industrial countries for which external trade was essential, they represented catastrophe. No large country was more highly industrialised, or more dependent on external trade, than Britain, who produced only half the food her population required. For Britain, trade on a huge scale, and a high level of employment in manufacturing and extractive industry, was essential for very survival.

Britain, as we shall see later, was not the worst sufferer from the Depression, for the country entered the 1930s at a high level of general prosperity by comparison with most others, and could live for a time on accumulated fat. In this period Britain ranked as a Free Trade country. Barriers to foreign trade were a good deal less than those of most other countries, although in the previous decade and a half a number of important measures had been enacted which eroded the strict Free Trade position occupied before the war. There had been two serious attempts in living memory to strike at the root of Free Trade. Joseph Chamberlain's 'Tariff Reform' campaign of 1903, and Stanley Baldwin's announcement twenty years later in favour of tariffs, had both been emphatically repudiated by the electorate, and by common consent had played the major part in destroying the governments with which they were associated. It would be wrong to say that the mass of voters in Britain around 1929 were Cobdenite Free Traders; but they were certainly not disposed to embark on major experiments in the

Protectionist direction. As the situation worsened during 1930, however, so also did people become increasingly willing to consider fiscal changes which they would have rejected in more prosperous times: more out of panic and despair, no doubt, than out of any deep conviction that the advocates were right. Yet the situation was very far from straightforward in either the Protectionist or the Free Trade camp, and there were many cross-currents.

Agriculturalists had long complained about cheap foreign food; but the one kind of import duty which no government was likely to introduce in the foreseeable future was a tax which would seriously increase the price of food to the domestic consumer. Agriculture was of diminishing importance in the economy; 'stomach taxes' were anathema to the voters; and manufacturers could plainly see that any large rise in food prices would necessarily be reflected in higher costs of production, which would be likely to drive them out of business. The Conservative Party, currently in opposition, was traditionally disposed to favour Protection, and its roots were deepest in rural areas; but when their leader and recent Prime Minister Baldwin spoke to an agricultural audience in June 1930 he could offer them no more substantial favours than guaranteed prices for home-grown wheat, restrictions on 'dumping' of oats and import duties on foreign barley. No doubt farmers who reared livestock which required grain for fodder regarded such proposals with apprehension.

There was also a drift towards Protectionism among industrial interests in the course of 1930; but again Protectionists spoke with conflicting voices. As Winston Churchill had pointed out long before, the finished products of one industry are the raw materials of another. The man who calls for protective duties against his foreign competitors usually insists with equal concern on free trade in the raw materials and machinery which he uses in production.

One of the most popular forms of protectionism advocated in 1930 was what was known, rather confusingly, as 'Empire Free Trade'. Let Britain, who was mainly an industrial country, and the other countries of the British Empire, who were mainly primary producers, admit Free Trade between themselves and set tariff walls against outsiders. This notion was not very different from the original idea of 'Tariff Reform'. 'Empire Free Trade' had a strong emotional appeal. Nearly every British family had relatives or close friends in the self-governing Dominions. In an uncertain world people were uneasily conscious that the Empire countries were the closest friends which Britain had – whether 'friendship' was seen in the everyday sense of mutual sympathy and affection, or in the diplomatic sense of common interest. The Empire Free Trade movement had powerful support from Lord Beaverbrook of the *Daily Express* and Lord Rothermere of the *Daily Mail*. In the course of 1930 a fascinating power-struggle was waged, in which the two 'Press Lords' sometimes co-operated and sometimes fought each other, while each tried to push the Conservative Party into supporting Empire Free Trade. The party leadership, who were well aware of the difficulties into which firm commitment to any kind of fiscal policy might plunge them, stubbornly refused to move any further or faster than they could help.

Empire Free Trade was not the only candidate as an alternative fiscal policy. Various forms of domestic protectionism were proposed. Considerable attention was attracted to the proposals which the French Foreign Minister, Aristide Briand, set before the League of Nations in favour of a European Federal Union, which would involve political and presumably economic unification, and which would include the United Kingdom. Nobody was very clear just how this would work, but it seemed to imply some sort of common external tariff. Briand's plans did not receive particularly enthusiastic welcome either in his own country or elsewhere; but his authority as an international statesman was considerable, and it did represent another possible direction in which protectionists might move.

Thus the Free Traders could, to an extent, console themselves by listening to the internecine battle between their opponents; but they were also well aware of the profound difficulties of their own opponents. The Labour Party, which formed the government, was not very firmly committed on the fiscal issue, but included some strong Free Traders in its ranks. Most influential of these was the Chancellor of the Exchequer, Philip Snowden. Furthermore, the Labour Government had no over-all majority, and depended for survival on the toleration of the Liberals who were – in theory at least – totally committed to Free Trade. Yet in the course of 1930 there were signs of doubt among supporters of both parties. Sir Oswald Mosley, the future Fascist leader, who was still a member of the Labour Party in those days – issued a manifesto, supported by sixteen other MPs of his party, calling for a protective tariff. The Economic Committee of the Trade Union Congress declared that Britain should join some 'economic group' which maintained Free Trade between its own members, even though this might also imply tariffs against outsiders. Among the Liberals E. D. Simon, one of the party's leading lights in Manchester, of all places, expressed his own hesitations to the Liberal Summer School.

Arguments over tariffs also raged in the United States. During the election campaigns of 1928 the victorious Republicans had proposed increases in agricultural tariffs, plus some readjustment of industrial tariffs. From these proposals sprang the 'Smoot-Hawley' tariffs, which were hammered out by Congress in the gloomy atmosphere of 1930. The proposals began to assume a scale far beyond that originally envisaged, as various interests who sought tariffs for their own purposes began to co-operate with each other in 'log-rolling' tactics. The measure which eventually passed was not only much more extensive than had first been envisaged, but it also seemed essentially arbitrary in character: prescribed by obscure and possibly nefarious political deals, rather than the product of anybody's conception of the general good of the United States. There was considerable international protest at the new tariffs. President Hoover contended that the over-all effect would not be very great; but it looked otherwise on the eastern side of the Atlantic, where exporters were having difficulty enough already. What matters in such circumstances is not so much what has actually happened as what people think has happened. The general message taken was that America had 'gone protectionist', and therefore others began urgently to consider raising their tariff barriers as well. Indeed, existing pressures in the United States after the Smoot-Hawley tariffs had been passed, were for more protection rather than less.[3]

If the position in Britain and the United States was bad, in Germany it was appalling. One assessment set the unemployment figure even at this stage at close to five millions. In Britain and the United States, those workers who contrived to keep their jobs found themselves better off, because prices were falling; in Germany even those who remained in employment suffered a severe drop in living standards. Economic misery was matched by political chaos. At the General Election of September 1930 there were eleven parties each with a dozen or more representatives, and no single party held as many as a quarter of the total. The Nazis, who had only won twelve seats a couple of years earlier, became second party of the state with 107; while the Communists advanced from 54 to 77. Both of those parties believed in revolutionary solutions, and were perfectly willing to allow the state to collapse in ruins, in order to rebuild from their own preferred foundations. Thus they had no interest in making the economy work as well as possible, and every interest in refusing to co-operate with anybody. Any government which sought to reform the existing society was bound to cause distress somewhere, and both revolutionary parties were eager to make every ounce of political capital from that situation. In that sort of

Reichstag, ordinary democratic procedures were unworkable. So the 'centrist' Chancellor, Heinrich Brüning, sought and secured large powers to govern by decree. This created a most dangerous precedent, which others would later follow. The Social Democrats, fearful lest Brüning should collapse and give way to the Nazis, were compelled to give tacit support to measures they intensely disliked. The communists, who had no such scruples, saw the chance of damaging their Social Democratic rivals, and were willing from time to time to work with the Nazis and other forces of the 'far right' to encompass Brüning's political destruction.

The wider scene did not suggest that countries living under dictatorships – whether of the 'right' or the 'left' – were faring significantly better than others. The Fascist Government of Italy experienced the same sort of steeply rising unemployment as did the democracies, and great pressure was applied to produce drops in wages, prices and rents. The Soviet Union was more or less insulated from the rest of the world, but had economic troubles of its own. Exceedingly rapid land nationalisation was achieved in the early part of the year. This produced enormous internal turmoil, and the secret police became more and more in evidence to establish their own kind of control.

Early in the new decade there were again signs of improvement in the United States. 'By February 1931', one American author writes:

The Press, business, labor, nearly everyone again hailed the signs of recovery. In the first quarter, industrial output was up 5%, payrolls 10%, stock prices 11%. The crisis, said the *New York Times* on March 23rd., had passed bottom, and the country was on its way up. At the end of the month 120 cities announced the closing down of relief activities because they were no longer needed.[4]

There were faint signs of an answering trend in Britain. Unemployment figures for March, April and May 1931 each registered a small drop on the preceding month; though perhaps this was no more than the normal seasonal movement. In this slightly better atmosphere the British Government approached seven European countries with the object of securing a general reduction of tariffs. The response of the Europeans was uniformly disappointing,[5] and the relaxation of the Depression did not last long. This time the trouble started in Europe rather than the United States. The story of these events may appear peripheral to our main study, but the indirect effect which it exerted on future attitudes both in continental Europe and in Britain would be difficult to exaggerate.

On 20 March 1931, the world learnt with astonishment that Germany and Austria had agreed to form a Customs Union..The negotiations had been conducted in conditions of the utmost secrecy, and no doubt there were various considerations – political as well as economic´– at work. It seemed possible, though far from certain, that the proposed Customs Union would violate the 'Geneva Protocol' of 1922, under which reconstruction loans had been granted to Austria. Whether the proposal was legal or not, the French were determined to wreck it. The British Government was inclined, on balance, to dislike the Customs Union idea, but did not regard it as an unmixed curse, and in any case was sceptical whether the parties could bring it to fruition, even if left to themselves. Foreign Secretary Arthur Henderson was therefore disposed to play things coolly, and on a British proposal the matter was remitted to the International Court at The Hague, for a decision on the question of legality.

Before the matter had even been formally discussed by the League, the French began to withdraw short-term loans from the great Austrian bank, Kreditanstalt. It seems possible, though not certain, that the French Government was actively encouraging these withdrawals. Kreditanstalt was almost the lifeblood of Austria, financing three-quarters of Austrian industry and owning a great deal of it.[6] On 11 May came the announcement that Kreditanstalt was in difficulties.

The French now offered to 'save' Kreditanstalt by purchasing 150 million Treasury bonds for Austria, but the terms were exceedingly onerous, and could not fail to rankle deeply with the Austrian and German people. The Austrian Government was required to submit the economic and financial condition of the country to investigation by the League of Nations, consenting in advance to set into effect whatever measures the League might propose, and to renounce all idea of the Customs Union. Austria was saved from the necessity of accepting these appalling terms by a short-term loan from the Bank of England. This gave a brief respite, and Kreditanstalt was preserved from total destruction, but the situation remained precarious for a long time to come.

Meanwhile, the financial and political situation in Germany was deteriorating rapidly. The French behaviour in response to the Customs Union proposal produced a predictable reaction. On 17 May the regional elections for Oldenburg delivered a 37 per cent Nazi vote, a matter which attracted a great deal of international comment and concern. The French response, however, was not to allow matters to settle down, but rather to repeat in Germany what they had already begun in Austria. Foreign credits were rapidly withdrawn from the German Reichsbank, which was compelled to announce that its reserves were close to the legal limit of 40 per cent of the printed currency.

Anguished meetings took place between leading figures of the German and British Governments. Brüning warned that his country might be forced soon to invoke that clause of the 'Dawes Plan' which authorised her to suspend payment of reparations. Whether the Chancellor realised it or not, matters had long passed the point where there was any real doubt that this would have to happen. The operative question, one might say, was whether the Allies were prepared to make some kind of gesture in Germany's favour, or whether the country should be allowed to dissolve in chaos – in which case the shock waves would be felt far beyond the borders of the Reich. President Hoover wisely decided to make a virtue out of a necessity, and on 20 June 1931 announced that the United States was prepared to suspend for one year its own demands for reparations and reconstruction debts, provided that others would do likewise. The British Government promptly announced that it was willing to follow the American lead, and there was immediate steadying of the money market. Unfortunately the French were less obliging, and proceeded to haggle. In the end, however, a conference was summoned, and for the time being collapse was averted.

Long before this the idea of an Austro-German Customs Union, which had precipitated all the recent trouble, had virtually vanished from the scene. Early in September the two governments formally announced that it had been abandoned. A few days later the Hague Court pronounced on the matter of legality, declaring that the proposed arrangement would contravene the Geneva Protocol. That decision, already far too late to affect anybody's action, was reached by the highly unconvincing majority of one vote, with Britain, the United States and Japan all voting in the minority.

With this, one might say, the direct consequences of the Austro-German Customs Union proposals came to an end. Alas, the force of stability had everywhere been the losers. The German and Austrian Governments had originally sought the Customs Union, partly as a device to strengthen their economies, and partly to throw a sop to the forces of extreme nationalism. They had signally failed in both respects. Their economies were in a much worse condition than they had been at the start, while extreme nationalists in both countries could now pose as patriots who deplored their respective governments' surrender to the forces of international coercion.

The French had achieved their immediate objective of defeating the Customs Union; but that objective had been only part of a much deeper quest for security against renascent German nationalism, which had signally failed. In winning the battle, the French had lost the war. It was to be expected that many Germans who were far from being Nazis would resent bitterly the economic methods of the French, and would see the decision at The Hague as less than impartial. The British and the Americans were both angered by French behaviour, and a good deal less sympathetic with French apprehensions than they had formerly been. No doubt the French, for their part, bitterly resented the way in which the Anglo-Saxons got the Austrians and Germans off the hook which had been carefully prepared for them. Above all, the whole episode further destabilised the world economy, and totally destroyed whatever chances might have existed for an early recovery from the depressed conditions of 1930. The willingness of investors to advance money turns very largely upon confidence, and confidence had been shaken to the core. If Kreditanstalt and the Reichsbank could be set in such dire and immediate peril, what financial institution in the world was really secure? In Germany and Britain, in the United States and Italy, unemployment figures rose with the decline in investors' confidence, and were between 50 and 100 per cent higher than even the appalling figures of the previous year – and they continued to rise. In some countries, like Czechoslovakia, the volume of unemployment nearly trebled. Even France, hitherto immune from the Depression, began to show perceptible unemployment. In many countries welfare provisions were minimal, and unemployment became associated with grave primary poverty, as well as the frustrations of enforced idleness. In all social classes there was a deep feeling of insecurity, for there was no sign of any end to the Depression.

Not long before the Austro-German Customs Union saga came to an end, Britain found herself in the middle of a crisis which for the time being subsumed all interest in the difficulties facing other countries. That crisis, and its aftermath, were to have the most profound implications at home and abroad, both in the short and in the long term, for in nothing was British influence greater than in the extremely sensitive matter of finance and trade.

Government receipts from taxation and other sources were declining rapidly as the Depression advanced, while demands on public spending rose. This was particularly true in the matter of unemployment benefits. These were granted under a contributory insurance scheme, which had been devised on the assumption of far lower unemployment levels than currently prevailed. Contributions were dwindling because there were fewer employed workers to pay then, while demands were increasing. On several recent occasions, the government had sought and received large loans to bridge the gap. That kind of expedient worked well enough if there was prospect of recovery in the foreseeble future, but the date of recovery began to seem more and more remote. As 1931 progressed there were growing fears of a huge Budget deficit; and in the context of declining confidence in financial institutions which had hitherto seemed impregnable, this apprehension could very easily turn to general panic.

Early in 1931 a Committee on National Expenditure was set up to examine the situation. This committee – usually known as the May Committee, from the name of its Chairman – issued its Report on 31 July. The committee indicated that there would probably be a shortfall of £120 millions by the date of the next Budget. At a time when the income and expenditure of British governments usually balanced at a little over £800 millions, this was seen as an appalling sum. The May Committee proposed economies of a little under £100 millions. Such measures would certainly be extremely unpalatable, and it would be difficult for any government to carry them through – least of all a government without an over-all majority, and one which was coming under growing pressure from its own supporters. Whatever economies were to be made, those who suffered from them would inevitably complain – probably sincerely – that the cuts were unfair, and the political problems would be enormous.

Long before the May Report came out there had been deep discussions between the Government and the Liberals, about possible support which might be given to provide a working majority, but this prospect inevitably set up tensions within both parties. A section of the Labour Party would certainly be profoundly critical of any deal concluded with a 'capitalist' party, and would much prefer that Labour should be out of office altogether. Several important members of the Liberal Party had already repudiated the Party Whip several weeks before the crisis broke, preferring to make common cause with the Conservatives to turn the government out rather than do a deal with Labour to keep it in. The one man who might conceivably be able to carry the arrangements through on the Liberal side was David Lloyd George; and he became suddenly and dangerously ill just before the May Committee produced its report. As the crisis proceeded his health improved, and he was able to keep a finger in the pie, but Lloyd George was at no stage well enough to assume office himself.

The story of the debates within the Labour Government after the May

Report was published has been told many times.[7] Suffice here to say that the Cabinet set up an Economy Committee which proposed reductions in expenditure and increases in taxation going some way, but by no means all the way, to bridge the gap. The Cabinet accepted some, but not all, of the proposed economies. On 24 August, in circumstances which are still not clear in all respects, the Government fell, and was replaced by a 'National Government'. This was originally conceived as a genuine all-Party Government, which would carry through the necessary, but unpopular, measures and would then break up. In the original Cabinet of ten there were four Labour, four Conservative and two Liberal members. Almost immediately the Labour participants were repudiated with great emphasis by their own party. Arthur Henderson, Foreign Secretary in the old administration and the most senior Minister to be omitted from the new administration, became Leader of the diminished Labour Party. Parliament was recalled to endorse the new Government and to approve a Budget containing substantial tax increases and expenditure cuts – notably, a 10 per cent reduction in unemployment benefit, and pay reductions for teachers and various other public servants. The various cuts were uneven, and some bitter criticism came from those who suffered worst. This led to the so-called 'mutiny' of the Fleet at Invergordon – an event which deeply shocked many observers both in Britain and abroad. The government relented its most savage cuts, but – perhaps in part as a result of these upheavals – world financial pressure compelled the passage of emergency legislation taking Britain off the Gold Standard – an event which had a deeply traumatic effect in a great many places.

Stability was briefly restored, but again trouble blew up from an unexpected quarter. Investors, and particularly overseas investors, had greeted the arrival of the National Government with relief; now they began to wonder how long the government would last, and what its successor would be like. By the beginning of October Ministers were edging towards the view that the best way of ensuring confidence was by the Government calling an immediate General Election in the hope of securing a convincing majority.[8] It was one thing to decide that a General Election might prove a useful expedient, a different thing to secure agreement on the programme with which it should confront the country. By far the deepest dispute was on the matter of tariffs. Cabinet Minutes are usually rather coy about Ministerial disputes, but on this occasion they record that 'it was not found possible to reconcile these differences'.[9] In any ordinary circumstances, a government in fundamental discord on such an important matter would have collapsed at that point. In the special circumstances of 1931, however, the consequences of disruption would be incalculable, not only for Britain but for the rest of the world as well. In the end a sort of compromise was achieved. The Prime Minister would issue a kind of blanket appeal for support; but this would amount to little more than a call for what was described as a 'doctor's mandate' – that is, the electors should give Parliament and Government a free hand to deal with the situation as best they could. The parties issued their separate manifestos, and in a number of constituencies there were contests between different candidates who were supporters of the Government.

The General Election of October 1931 gave the National Government by far the biggest majority anybody has recieved in modern times: 554 MPs against 61 for all other groupd combined. The Conservative Party alone held 473 seats – well over three-quarters of the House of Commons. Neither the known disagreement over tariffs nor the astonishing call for a 'doctor's mandate' appears to have done the government any harm. There was a visible disposition on the electors' part to throw any decision, whether on fiscal or other matters, on the government, hoping that they would somehow come up with the 'right' answer to the awful and perplexing problems posed by the Great Depression. This frame of mind was surely not very dissimilar from the growing inclination of continental Europeans to abandon democratic government altogether in the hope that some dictator might have the 'right' answer.

By that General Election the familiar pattern of British politics was altered beyond recognition. There was no credible 'alternative Government'. The official opposition, the Labour Party, was not only exceedingly small, but had lost all its acknowledged leaders. Some had departed to the National Government, and were reviled as traitors by their erstwhile followers. Others, like Arthur Henderson, did not defect, but were defeated at the election. Sir Oswald Mosley, who a year earlier had seemed likely to be the next leader of the Labour Party, had gone off in a very different direction, and soon appeared as leader of the new British Fascist movement. The Independent Labour Party (ILP), which currently represented the 'left', was in process of seceding from the Labour Party altogether. Only one significant figure of the recent Labour Government survived – George Lansbury, an old-style socialist with pacifist opinions, who became the Party leader in default of anybody with stronger credentials. About half of Lansbury's followers were nominees of a single Trade Union – the Mineworkers. Lacking office, and lacking any prospect of office in the foreseeable future, the Labour Party was in no position to offer constructive and useful criticism. The Liberals – technically more numerous than Labour in that Parliament – had broken into three groups. The Party's official leadership, headed by Sir Herbert Samuel, sat in the Government, but had strong reservations in favour of Free Trade; another group, the Liberal Nationals, headed by Sir John Simon, gave the government unconditional support; while a 'family group' of four, headed by Lloyd George, sat on opposition benches.

From the circumstances of the General Election, and the composition of the resulting House of Commons, it was virtually certain that a major attack would be made on Free Trade, although it was by no means clear from which particular Protectionist direction the attack would come. Within a fortnight of polling, a very marked increase in imports was observed,[10] evidently caused by the anticipation that protective tariffs would soon be applied, and it was now or never. Special legislation against 'abnormal imports' was rushed through Parliament, and even before the year was out there were signs that Britain and other countries were exchanging shots in what could well become a general 'tariff war'.[11]

The City Waits
Banks are heavily laden with deposits which are inaccessible and useless, while industry and the unemployed, both of whom desperately need the money, are busking outside.
Daily Express, London, 13 December 1930.
The London Express News and Feature Service

3 The Darkening Skies

In the early 1930s several exceedingly important processes, all to a greater or lesser degree related to the impact of the Great Depression, were taking place in different parts of the world: events which to a considerable extent interacted upon each other.

It will be recalled that, in the early days of the National Government, the possibility of levying protective import duties had been raised, but no decisive action had been taken. There was disagreement within the government as to whether tariffs were desirable or not; the protectionists themselves were not united as to the kind of protection they required; and the issue was considered one which would prove politically damaging to anyone who raised it. At the close of 1931, however, the Cabinet began to brace itself for action in the matter. A Cabinet Committee was set up under the chairmanship of Neville Chamberlain, who had recently succeeded Snowden as Chancellor of the Exchequer. The Conservatives, who formed a majority of the Committee, declared in favour of a system of protective tariffs. There were two Free Traders on the Committee: Sir Herbert Samuel, chairman of the Liberal MPs, and Snowden. Both of them produced dissenting reports. Sharp splits appeared in the Cabinet.[1] The 'official' Liberals and Snowden refused to countenance erosion of Free Trade; the Liberal Nationals, headed by Foreign Secretary Sir John Simon, and most of the 'National Labour' members, were prepared to follow the majority recommendation. The normal outcome of such a split would be the secession of the minority from the Cabinet; but in this case they were persuaded to remain, on the understanding that they would be free to express their dissent in public, and to vote against the Bill which would be presented to Parliament. Of course, nobody doubted that the measure would be passed.

The measures thus enshrined in the new Import Duties Act were scarcely a 'scientific' tariff, in the sense of a tariff designed to produce some long-term structural changes in the economy. In fact they looked surprisingly like a stopgap compromise between different kinds of Protectionists, all hoping to get the principle of Protection accepted and thereafter to mould its character to their own liking. The legislation,

"WI' MACDONALD, SIR DONALD, SAM (HERBERT), SAM HOARE, JIM THOMAS.
STAN' BALDWIN, OLD UNCLE PHIL SNOWDEN AND ALL."

Some Members of the National Government, 1931
Ramsay MacDonald (Labour) (Prime Minister); Sir Donald Maclean (Liberal); Sir Herbert Samuel (Liberal); Sir Samuel Hoare (Conservative);
J. H. Thomas (Labour); Stanley Baldwin (Conservative); Philip Snowden (Labour).
Punch, London, September 1931

which received Royal assent at the beginning of March, imposed a 10 per cent *ad valorem* tax on most kinds of imported goods, but made a very important qualification. As an Imperial Economic Conference was to be held later in the year at Ottawa, Empire goods would be – for the time being at any rate – exempt from the Act's provisions. An Advisory Committee was established under the chairmanship of the same Sir George May who had presided over the May Committee of 1931, and was charged to recommend additional duties in appropriate cases. The implementation of the Advisory Committee's proposals was to be by executive action. In fact the Cabinet – and not least the Prime Minister – were astonished at the speed with which the Advisory Committee brought out its first schedule, and with the length of that list.[2] They were furthermore convinced that there could have been no adequate examination of individual items by the Advisory Committee. Yet the Ministers were hoist with their own petard. Their object in recommending establishment of the Advisory Committee in the first place had been to ensure that the resulting new duties did not look too 'political'; the Cabinet now felt themselves obliged to rubber-stamp the Committee's proposals. The overwhelming majority in the House of Commons, avid for Protection, inevitably endorsed them too. So the Advisory Committee's new duties took effect without close investigation anywhere – in the Committee itself, in the Cabinet or in Parliament.

Even after all this, Britain still remained very much one of the 'low tariff' countries of the world. As a very large proportion of imported food came from the Empire, domestic food prices were kept from rising too much. As with the Smoot-Hawley tariffs in the United States, the deepest consequences were psychological and international. Formal abandonment of Free Trade by Britain was bound to encourage further measures of 'Protection' throughout the world. It is impossible to quantify the effect of British 'Protectionism' upon others, although there can be no doubt that it had a substantial influence. The Economic Section of the League of Nations established that the volume of international trade had declined in 1932 to less than half of what it had been three years earlier.[3] No doubt, this was partly the result of general poverty; but trade restrictions made the situation worse. The import duties controversy was also to have important consequences on imperial relations before the year was out, and these consequences, in their turn, would have significant repercussions on British politics – as will be seen later.

The furore over the Import Duties Act was at its height when a crisis in the Far East became acute: a crisis whose roots lay partly, but not entirely, in the Great Depression. That crisis was to have profound indirect consequences on Britain's world position, and on many other matters as well.

Over a long period great numbers of Japanese peasants living in parts of Honshu island had developed a sort of 'cottage industry' in silk production. As one recent writer has observed, that industry was 'to many thousands of households . . . what made all the difference . . . between hard living and downright penury'.[4] One of the early effects of the Depression was to cut dramatically the demand for silk in the exceedingly important American market. In the course of 1931 this situation was made worse by crop failures within Japan, and then by a Chinese embargo on Japanese imports. Soon there was actual starvation.

Relations between China and Japan had been bad for many years, and the situation was complicated further by the fact that neither government had much control over its own army. Manchuria was a particularly sensitive region in this running dispute. Technically a province of China, in practice its status was most dubious. Across Manchuria ran a railway which the Japanese were authorised by treaty to protect and contol, but China deeply resented the arrangement. Land-hungry peasants began to look wistfully at the prospect of settling in Manchuria. On 18 September 1931 Japanese soldiers suddenly seized a number of points in Manchuria. The incident itself, reflected a writer in the very influential American journal *Foreign Affairs* shortly afterwards, 'was unimportant: a gunmen's fight in New York or a riot of unemployed in London would produce as many casualties'.[5] Yet it proved the spark which would start a conflagration.

Three days later, on 21 September, the Chinese Government formally appealed to the League of Nations. The Japanese at first appeared willing to withdraw on reasonable terms; later they showed signs of growing truculence, with the arrival in office of a new government disposed towards a 'forward' policy. What caused immediate international concern was the possible bearing of Article 16 of the Covenant of the League of Nations on the dispute. This Article provided that if any member of the League should resort to war in disregard to its obligations, this would constitute an act of war against all other members of the League 'which hereby undertake immediately to subject [the aggressor] to the severance of all trade and financial relations'. There was also provision for military action in certain cases. It was by no means clear that the Japanese action constituted a 'resort to war' in an area where 'incidents' were endemic. Furthermore, the two countries were not technically at war in the ordinary diplomatic sense; the Chinese

Government had not attempted yet to invoke Article 16, and there was hope that it would never had need to do so.

For the time being nobody was committed, either legally or morally, to do anything more dramatic than to investigate the latest stage of a convoluted Far Eastern quarrel which had existed for a very long time, and to make some kind of recommendation at the end. While the League of Nations was deliberating, the Chinese intensified their trade boycott against Japan, which set considerable further strains on the Japanese economy. There were also anti-Japanese demonstrations in Shanghai, which were countered by Japanese shelling of Chinese areas in that very cosmopolitan town. Newsreels were screened on cinemas throughout the western world, and this appears to have played an important part in mobilising popular opinion against Japan. Diplomatic initiatives followed, and an agreement over Shanghai and its vicinity was soon reached. This, however, would not prove the end of the story.

In Britain the Shanghai incident led to some dramatic changes of thought at the highest levels. Britain had many valuable possessions in and near the Pacific, and the British were one of the three great naval powers in the area – the others being the Japanese and the Americans. At one point in the crisis there appeared a substantial possibility that British and other naval vessels lying nearby might become involved in action against the Japanese. Even when the Shanghai trouble abated, the possibility that some other incident might arise out of the blue at any moment in the Far East could not be discounted. The League of Nations' Covenant was seen to have implications very different from those originally envisaged. Most people had assumed that if any serious fighting arose which activated the celebrated Article 16, this would bring all League members out against the aggressor, with inevitable consequences which would entail little sacrifice in the military sense. Careful study of the situation in the Far East had a very chilling effect on this euphoric view. The model of a simple 'police' action, whose upshot was a foregone conclusion, was by no means valid; and operations could prove very costly, not to say precarious. In March 1932 the British Chiefs of Staff circulated a Memorandum to the Cabinet, suggesting that substantial improvements were necessary for defence in the Far East. More dramatic still, the 'Ten year Rule' – that is, the diplomatic and military assumption that no major war would occur in the forthcoming decade – was no longer warranted, and must be abandoned forthwith. A few days later the Cabinet accepted the views of the Chiefs of Staff.[6] It is surely striking to observe that the consideration which drove people to that conclusion related almost exclusively to the Far East, and not to the darkening skies of Europe.

We may today discern features in the Far Eastern dispute, already apparent in the spring of 1932, which disclosed fundamental weaknesses both in international arrangements and in Britain's system of defences, which went far beyond the contents and the risks of that particular problem. Right down to the middle of 1931 Britain's defence policy and her foreign policy had appeared to be parts of a consistent whole. The British navy, largest in the world, seemed well able to protect territories and interests which Britain already possessed, and there was no question whatever of her seeking to acquire more. The army was minuscule and the air force small, for nobody seriously contemplated engagement in a major war: the view officially enshrined in the 'Ten Year Rule'. Foreign policy centred on support for the League of Nations and other devices designed to achieve international conciliation and stabilisation. Much attention had been given to the possibility that Germany might at some point seek to reverse the military decision of 1918; far less attention had been given to the possibility that international disturbance would arise through action of one of the major ex-allies. The overriding reason why Britain was in no position to act against Japan without great cost and great risks was that successive British Governments had for decades taken it for granted that Japan was their firm friend; so British forces had been organised accordingly.

When excitement over the Shanghai incident had died down, the Sino-Japanese struggle in Manchuria was resumed. In September 1932 the Japanese had secured such effective control that they felt able to recognise the 'independence' of the province, under a puppet adminis-tration of their own. Again there was much honest confusion over facts, but investigations were carried out by the League of Nations. At last, on 24 February 1933, the General Assembly of the League declared the Japanese occupation of Manchuria to be unjustified, and called for a resumption of Chinese suzerainty. In the following month Japan retorted by declaring the intention of leaving the League.

The real problem was what 'sanctions', if any, should be directed against Japan. War was universally ruled out. None of the countries which traded extensively with Japan had any enthusiasm for economic sanctions. The one possible kind of disciplinary action available was some sort of blockade on arms and war materials. Much of the vital discussion took place in the British Cabinet, for it was widely assumed that any lead in such matters would come from Britain. Simon, the Foreign Secretary, was anxious to do what could be done: a statement not equally true of all his colleagues. No new legislation was required, for under existing law arms could not be exported without government licence. A sort of compromise emerged. There would be a general embargo for a fortnight; meanwhile contact should be made with other arms-exporting countries to see whether they would join in the embargo. The response was not encouraging. The United States Government had no lawful authority to prohibit arms exports, and it would take at least a couple of months to get legislation through Congress. Other countries had other problems. The Dutch, for example, who were having much trouble in the East Indies, would not agree to participate if oil was included in the embargo. So it soon became apparent that if the British embargo were continued the Japanese would get what they required from other sources, and the only practical effect would be to lose orders for British firms: not a popular course of action at a time when unemployment was in the region of 22 or 23 per cent of the total workforce. The Service Departments adduced a further argument against embargo. Britain's strategic position in the Far East, both on land and sea, was precarious, so no action should be taken which involved any risk of war. The argument ran backwards and forwards, but in the end the British embargo was withdrawn.[7] Nothing could disguise the fact that the League had received a most serious rebuff. Whether particular individuals or governments were at fault, or whether it was by the nature of things impossible to coerce a recalcitrant Great Power through existing international machinery, was open to doubt. In either event the outlook was not encouraging. If Japan could get away with it, why not others?

The Japanese crisis was still far from settled when world attention swung to events in Germany. In the spring of 1932 a new Presidential election was due. For the past seven years the President of the Reich had been Paul von Hindenburg, who had acquired massive prestige as the country's predominant military figure throughout the war. As Head of State Hindenburg wielded very considerable real powers, notably in choice of a Chancellor and in his authority to take emergency action at times of peril. He was 84 years old, and in all ordinary circumstances it would have been unthinkable that a man of such an age would seek a further septennium of office. These, however, were very far from ordinary times. Hitler was bound to be a candidate, and a great many people concluded that Hindenburg was the only man who could beat him. So the old man was prevailed upon to stand for a second term of office, as a non-party candidate. More astonishing still, he received support ranging from the 'right-wing' Nationalist Party to his sometime enemies, the Social Democrats – still the largest party in Germany. Polling took place in two stages, but on the second count, on 10 April, Hindenburg won an over-all majority. He secured 19.4 million votes, against 13.4 million for

Hitler and 3.7 million for the Communist, Thälmann. The world had to derive what consolation it could from such figures. The Nazis, with 36.7 per cent of the total despite the incredible coalition ranged against them, had approximately doubled the percentage recorded at the Reichstag elections two years earlier. What had produced this massive upsurge? Two factors appear to have been of particular importance. Unemployment, which was bad enough in 1930, had increased greatly since then, and stood at about 30 per cent of the total workforce; while the Nazis had recently received massive injections into their party funds.

Whatever small relief might have been drawn from Hindenburg's re-election was soon dissipated. For a long time there had been close co-operation between Hindenburg and his Chancellor, Brüning, but Brüning's influence upon the President was beginning to wear thin. When the Chancellor sought Hindenburg's authority for decrees banning the Nazi quasi-military organisations, the SA and SS, the President at first agreed, but later insisted that he would only accede to the request if other private armies were banned as well. This lead to Brüning's resignation at the end of May, and the establishment of a new government under the Catholic aristocrat Franz von Papen. Papen had a considerable gift for political intrigue, and was a 'born survivor'; but judgement was not his strongest attribute, and he soon ran himself and everybody else into the very situation which Brüning had striven with all his might to avert over the previous two years. Within days a new General Election was decreed.

The Nazis emerged from the contest by far the largest party, with 230 seats – nearly 100 more than their nearest rivals, the Social Democrats. The Communists made gains, though these were less spectacular, and received eighty-nine seats. Thus there were 319 deputies openly opposed to parliamentary democracy, against 292 for all other parties combined. These appalling results compelled von Papen and Hindenburg to consider radical changes in the character of the existing government. Approaches were made to Hitler to see where he was prepared to enter a new coalition, but he refused. By this time the Chancellor had antagonised most political groups for one reason or another, and on 12 September a vote of no confidence in the von Papen Government was carried through the Reichstag by a vast majority. The Reichstag was dissolved, thus setting in motion a new General Election, which was fought over a period of nearly two months.

The poll, on 6 November, was just a little more encouraging than that of three months earlier in one respect at least. The Nazis fell from 230 seats to 195. This decline was particularly noticeable in the economically advanced areas, and in places where the Nazis had a share in local government.[8] The picture also had a dark side. The gradual shift of 'left' votes from Social Democrats to Communists continued; and the Communists gave every sign of being far more interested in improving their position *vis-à-vis* the Social Democrats than in keeping out the Nazis. The gap between the two socialist parties was slight: 120 Social Democrats, 99 Communists. The election was followed by a renewed period of intense political activity; but at the begining of December von Papen resigned and was succeeded by the putatively non-political General Kurt von Schleicher.

These German events took place against the background of what had seemed at its inception one of the most hopeful initiatives of the Depression period: the World Disarmament Conference. It has been seen that the idea of such a Conference had attracted much attention and support over several years, and when the Conference was eventually convened in February 1932 it really did look like a world-wide movement for peace. Every substantial country in the world was participating – not only those belonging to the League of Nations, but also the two great countries which were outside the League – the United States and the Soviet Union.

The Conference soon ran into the sort of problem which great gatherings often do encounter: to every participant, his own immediate perceived interest was of greater importance than success of the whole venture, while considerations of domestic politics tended to override all others. In June President Hoover of the United States took a very strong initiative in advocating specific measures of disarmament of the powers assembed at the Conference. Hoover's appeal made world headlines, but it was soon overtaken by other events, and in the end nothing came of it. The Americans, like the British, felt enthusiasm for almost any idea which appeared likely to produce some kind of agreement on something between European Powers and, at the time of Hoover's appeal, were looking forward with benign interest to another meeting – this time at Lausanne – where the matter of German reparations was about to be considered.

At the Lausanne Conference the European Powers did reach agreement. Existing reparation claims of the European Allies against Germany were to be abrogated in favour of a lump-sum payment. The amount involved might theoretically reach a figure of around £150 millions; but there were various escape clauses which made actual payment of any money at all highly unlikely. If something like the Lausanne agreement could have been reached a couple of years earlier, much good might have been done through removing for ever the folly of reparations by means of an international understanding. In 1932, however, the agreement proved an unqalified disaster. The Americans were furious. The arrangements had been described in diplomatic circles at the time as a 'gentlemen's agreement'. That term, innocuous enough in England, had a highly pejorative meaning in vernacular American usage, for it implied a dishonest arrangement to frustrate the legitimate claims of a third party. That, in American eyes, was exactly what had happened at Lausanne. The Europeans were seen to have been attempting to get each other off various hooks at the expense, not of themselves, but of the United States. Whatever else Lausanne may have achieved, it did nothing to improve relations between Americans and Europeans, or to discourage isolationism in the United States.

In Germany, the effect of Lausanne was far worse, for the agreement was concluded not long before the first General Election of 1932. Most Germans had considered reparations a monstrous injustice from the start, and felt no gratitude to the allies for the new agreement. They were much more disposed to blame von Papen for having given technical acknowledgment to the reparations debt, than to praise him for having effectively extinguished it. Nothing could have averted a massive swing towards the Nazis at that election; but there can be little doubt that criticisms of the German Government's part at Lausanne made that swing a good deal stronger than would otherwise have been the case.

After Lausanne and that appalling German election, attempts to reach international agreement on the disarmament question were fouled up by the vagaries of German domestic politics, and the desperate plight in which German moderates found themselves. The Nazi menace was universally recognised, and about the only hope of holding it at bay was for politicians of the Republic to be seen by their domestic electorate as 'good nationalists'. The question of *Gleichberechtigung* – a term usually translated as 'equality of rights' – was raised. This highlighted a problem which had been rumbling on for a long time. The Germans contended that the allies had played false by their own promises. At Versailles, it was argued, Germany had been forcibly disarmed. Around that time the allies had announced their own intention to disarm, but they had failed to do so. Most of them, but particularly France, were currently rearming. On these grounds the Germans declared that they would only continue to participate in the Conference if it was agreed that they would be on the same footing as everybody else when it came to an end. In other words, the limitations imposed on kinds or quantities of armaments at Versailles should be abrogated, and replaced by new agreements freely negotiated by Germany at the Disarmament Conference. Many people in Britain felt considerable sympathy with such arguments.

All this appalled the French. The population of France was only about two-thirds that of Germany, the proportion of men of military age a good deal smaller. So long as the terms of Versailles were not too flagrantly violated, France was secure. But Versailles was meant to last for ever, and any arrangements which might emerge from the Conference were likely to apply only for a limited number of years. So why should France forego the permanent security which Versailles gave her, in favour of new arrangements offering less security, and that only for a limited period? To many Frenchmen it looked very much as if 'equality of rights' meant in practice that Germany would be able to rearm and again threaten France. These suspicions were enhanced by another demand which the Germans made as part of their claim for *Gleichberechtigung* – that they should receive 'specimens' of arms which were currently prohibited to them. What use were such 'specimens' to Germany, demanded the French, unless the Germans proposed to make copies from them – either secretly and illegally in peacetime, or in great quantities in time of war?

And so, for entirely different reasons, large numbers of ordinary people in both France and Germany were not disposed to make great sacrifices in order to ensure success for the Conference. Yet it was plain that if either, or both, of them withdrew, there would be little point in other countries proceeding, and the whole venture would collapse. Matters would then be incomparably worse than if the Conference had never been called. Leading statesmen in all countries were probably conscious of this risk, and sought to keep the Conference going if they could. On 11 December a compromise was devised: agreement on a form of words which included the emotive terms 'equality' and 'security' within the same sentence. The two Governments agreed to return to the deliberations. In both countries a bitter and furious opposition prepared to destroy the authors of the agreement, who were cursed for abandoning the interests of their respective nations.

In France the critics' main target was Premier Edouard Herriot, a Radical with strong pan-European ideas. He was bitterly attacked in the Chamber – ostensibly on a quite different matter from the Disarmament Conference – and in mid-December was driven from office. Another Radical, Joseph Paul-Boncour, succeeded him. Within the space of fourteen months thereafter there would be five French Governments, all headed by Radicals and all without real stability. What the French call the 'decadence' of their country had begun.

In Germany the target of opponents of the Disarmament Conference compromise was Chancellor Kurt von Schleicher. Like Herriot in France, von Schleicher had fallen foul of critics on other grounds as well. He had prepared a policy of land reform which was bitterly condemned by people like the President's son, Otto von Hindenburg, as 'rural bolshevism'. On 28 January 1933 von Schleicher was driven out. Two days later the old President invited Adolf Hitler to assume the office recently vacated, and that offer was accepted.

The Cabinet which Hitler formed was not predominantly Nazi. Von Papen was Vice-Chancellor. Hugenberg, leader of the Nationalist Party, appeared an indispensable element of the government. Baron von Neurath, Foreign Minister under the two previous Chancellors, remained in that office. The new government sought a working majority in the Reichstag, and on 5 March yet another General Election was held. There was much street violence; many socialist and communist organs of the Press were banned, as also were some organs of the Catholic 'Centre'. A few days before polling the Reichstag was destroyed by fire. Communists were blamed, and the Communist Party was suppressed. Despite all this Opposition candidates, including Communists, were able to stand, and the electors could record their votes in secret. A quite exceptional poll was recorded – 89 per cent of the electorate. The Nazis surged from 195 delegates to 285, but still fell short of an over-all majority.

Their opponents, however, were largely demoralised. In the new Reichstag an Enabling Act was passed giving the government far more power to rule by decree than its predecesors had possessed. Authority was given to legislate, to tax, and to conclude international treaties. By around midsummer the remaining parties – Social Democrats, Nationalists, and the various groups of the Centre – had either been absorbed by the Nazis or proscribed. The Nazis themselves admitted that 18 000 people were already in concentration camps, and some evidence suggested that the true figure was far higher than that.

It requires little imagination to visualise the shocked horror with which opinion in the democratic countries reacted to such events. The anger was reinforced by grim speculations about the Nazis' likely international programme. Not many people outside Germany had yet read Hitler's *Mein Kampf*; but those who had done so attempted to warn others about what seemed to lie in store. Some observers drew conclusions from what they could see in Germany. Sir Horace Rumbold, British Ambassador in Berlin, foretold that if current trends continued, the likely upshot would be 'a European war in four or five years' times'.[9] Sir Robert Vansittart, Civil Service head of the Foreign Office, began a long series of impressive memoranda, warning Ministers of the egregiously evil character of Nazism. Yet the fact that important men were making such assessments did not give anyone power to intervene. Hitler, indeed, had no guaranteed security of tenure. Unless he could deliver visible and speedy results which would give his country some relief from the economic misery which plagued it, and from the deep sense that it was being wronged by other nations, then Hitler would assuredly be swept aside, just as earlier governments had been swept aside. There were many people waiting for this to happen, some of them within the Nazi Party itself.

Although the atmosphere at the Disarmament Conference was gloomy, the Conference was still in existence, and another attempt was being made to secure international collaboration on important problems. A World Economic Conference, foreshadowed at Lausanne, was to open in London in June 1933. It received wide terms of reference, ranging from consideration of war debts through problems of international currency management to possible reductions of tariffs and trade barriers. At a time when the world was in the depths of an economic depression of unparalleled magnitude, which all agreed had been caused at least in part by trading and financial barriers between states, one might have expected that everyone would approach the Conference with deep concern for its success. There was one important sign which seemed to provide encouragment. Early in the year the Democrats had won both Presidential and Congressional elections in the United States, and Franklin D. Roosevelt was now in office. The Democrats were, traditionally, the low-tariff party, and the new Secretary of State, Cordell Hull, believed in what the Conference sought to achieve. 'If any nation should obstruct and wreck this great Conference on the short-sighted notion that some of it favoured local interests might temporarily profit . . . that nation will merit the execration of mankind', he told the delegates. Others approached the matter in a different spirit. 'I have a horrible time in front of me with this awful World Conference coming on in June', wrote Neville Chamberlain in a private letter a month before it opened, 'And it is difficult to see how anything valuable can come out of it.'[10] Such prophecies tend to be self-serving. Behaviour of the Europeans in general suggested that their overriding interest in the Conference was not to destroy trade barriers but to clear their liabilities on war debts. Great interests had grown up behind the tariffs and other restrictions. Those interests feared external competition, and were full of plausible arguments against any suggested reductions. The Conference soon decided that trade liberalisation could only be achieved through bilateral discussions; and these, in their turn, soon ran into the sands. And so, very soon, did the World Conference itself run into the sands. MacDonald had originally expected that it would last into the following year; but towards the end of July it was adjourned *sine die* amid a general feeling of frustration and futility. Chamberlain's prophecy had fulfilled itself indeed.

If Britain's Chancellor of the Exchequer had little enthusiasm for the International Conference which was his special responsibility, the same was most certainly not true for the Foreign Secretary in relation to the Disarmament Conference. Cabinet minutes are full of evidence for the concern – one might almost say obsession – which Sir John Simon felt about it. Yet by the end of June 1933 matters were close to a breakdown, and proceedings were adjourned until mid-October. The crucial problem was how to bring about measures of disarmament on which the French and Germans might eventually agree. French apprehensions over security had been deep enough in December 1932, but the arrival of Hitler in office in Germany the following month made them much deeper. As for the German Government, evidence does not suggest that they actively desired a breakdown, but they were probably not much disturbed at the prospect, and were certainly concerned that if it did take place the blame should appear to lie with France.[11]

In September a new plan for disarmament emerged from France, and by the latter part of the month the British Government was beginning to evince sympathetic interest. The idea was that the Conference should be followed by what became known as a 'Convention' period of eight years, divided into two equal phases. In the first phase a system of international inspection should be established, designed to ensure that the agreed measures of disarmament were carried out. During this phase there should be no rearmament. In the second phase, the actual disarmament procedure should be carried out. The Germans reacted strongly against these proposals, arguing that the effect would be to deny them the 'equality' promised by the agreement of the previous December; instead, they were to have a further four years of 'probation', during which their armament would still be restricted to the limits imposed at Versailles. The British, the Italians, and the Americans, all foresaw grave and possibly fatal trouble on that score; but after much argument they lined up behind the French proposal, and eventually agreed that it should be submitted, not by the French delegate but by Simon, on 14 October.

The general drift of the new proposals was already known long before the meeting, and the Germans were well prepared. At the Conference Neurath made a savage personal attack on Simon, and the same evening Hitler delivered three vital announcements. Germany would leave the Disarmament Conference. She would also leave the League of Nations. There would be an immediate election-cum-plebiscite in the Reich.

The Conference had now lost its whole point. Without German participation, no useful agreements could possibly be achieved between the other powers. Yet there was an enormous amount of emotional capital stored up in that Conference, and a very long time would elapse before it enthusiasts could admit to themselves that it was dead. Throughout 1934, and well into 1935, many people continued to speak as if it were merely in recess. In truth the Disarmament Conference had been a disastrous failure, counter-productive on a massive scale. For years the British Government had known perfectly well that the Germans were violating the disarmament clauses of the peace treaties.[12] They had kept silent because they feared that public intimation of that knowledge would vitiate the Conference's chances of success. When a conference designed to produce disarmament failed, the inevitable result would be large-scale rearmament, for the world had received plain intimation that agreement was impossible. In just the same way failure of the World Economic Conference led infallibly to more trade barriers rather than less.

Meanwhile the Nazis exploited to the full the priceless advantage which the situation afforded them for domestic propaganda. On 12 November 95 per cent of the voters gave the approbation required of them on the question of German foreign policy, while about 92 per cent voted for Nazi candidates – the only ones permitted to stand in the 'General Election'. These figures suggest that some of those brave people who could not be cajoled or terrorised into supporting the Nazis were nevertheless responsive to a 'patriotic' appeal. It is tempting to treat the results as ridiculous, and in a sense they certainly are. There is plenty of evidence that both coercion and downright fraud were rife.[13] Yet it would also be wrong to assume, as opponents of Nazism frequently did, that the German people were writhing unwillingly under Hitler's rule, which they earnestly desired to cast off. One of the most telling claims which the Nazis made during the campaign was that unemployment had already dropped by well over two millions since Hitler took office. The accuracy of such figures may be disputed, and there was a disturbing link between public works operated with the object of relieving unemployment and preparations for war; but there can be no doubt that unemployment in Germany had already improved immensely, and the Nazi Government was winning a great deal of public support for its success in that direction. It is also true that vast numbers of Germans, probably the overwhelming majority, had deeply and consistently resented the Versailles arrangements right from the beginning, and rejoiced to see a government in their own country behaving with truculence towards the victors.

While the German elections were in progress some important political activities took place in Britain. There had been much internal criticism of British foreign policy from very different political standpoints, and many people on the 'left' were disposed to set a large share of blame on Simon for the collapse of the Disarmament Conference. This discussion was in full swing when a by-election took place in East Fulham – a rather down-at-heel London suburb with a long Conservative record. The Labour candidate won the seat on a massive swing of votes. Within a month four other by-elections held in widely scattered parts of the country all produced huge swings to Labour, and a spate of local elections did the same. Such voting, one might say, was no more than the ordinary swing of the political pendulum against a government which had won a distorted majority in freak conditions three years earlier. Scholarly research has since established that the campaigns were fought overwhelmingly on domestic issues,[14] and there can be little doubt that most voters were far more concerned about social conditions at home than about international conferences.

Politicians, however, have a marked propensity to believe that matters which currently interest them are also of deep interest to the public at large, and the accident that the Labour Party appeared to be taking a pacifist line at the time may have encouraged observers to think that this view was widespread among the voters at East Fulham and elsewhere. Stanley Baldwin, leader of the Conservative Party and probably the most powerful man in the government, seems to have drawn the conclusion that there was a deep current of pacifism in Britian which no politician or government could ignore. Certainly he showed a preoccupation with the East Fulham result which amounted almost to obsession. Baldwin had a similar preoccupation with the destructive power of bomber aircraft, epitomised in his remark, 'The bomber will always get through'. This preoccupation, indeed, was very widespread in the 1930s, and goes some way towards explaining many political attitudes.

If general disarmament was now out of the question, the main burden of resistance to German designs lay with France, for the French army was by far the strongest in Europe. Very soon, however, the credit of the

French Government – and, indeed, of French politicians as a race – was profoundly shaken by the 'Stavisky scandal' which broke at the end of 1933. A disreputable financier was shown to have a large number of French politicians in his pay. The current Prime Minister, the Radical Camille Chautemps, was among those on whom suspicion rested, and he was driven from office. For a brief space another Radical, Edouard Daladier, took over; but there was extensive rioting in Paris and he in turn resigned. On 9 February 1934 a new government, well to the 'right' of its predecessor, took over under the leadership of Gaston Doumergue, a former President of the Republic who has brought from retirement. Perhaps the most famous member of the new government was the Foreign Minister, Louis Barthou. 'Bristly and foxy, I should think a nasty old man at heart'[15], was the judgement of one British Minister on Barthou.

The atmosphere of instability prevailed in other places as well as the Great Powers. Poland had long cultivated the friendship of France, for the famous 'Polish Corridor' acquired after 1918 split the Reich in two, and was deeply resented in Germany. On 26 January 1934 there came a sudden announcement that Poland had concluded a ten-year non-aggression pact with Germany. At best, France's 'eastern policy' required some radical re-thinking. The world had hardly recovered from the news when trouble blew up in another acknowledged danger-spot. Hitler's seizure of power in Germany was predictably followed by a sympathetic movement in Austria, and there were many complaint from Chancellor Dollfuss against both propaganda and terrorism inspired by the Reich. Dollfuss's strongest ally was undoubtedly Benito Mussolini, who had been head of government in Italy for a dozen years, and had much reason of his own for wishing to keep Hitler's Germany well within bounds. Yet the Austrian Government suddenly encountered a different challenge to its existence, for in February 1934 there was virtual civil war in Vienna. Great tenement blocks, fortified by machine-gun nests manned by a revolutionary socialist body, the Schutzbund, were reduced by artillery, with many casualties. The Austrian Nazis were curiously silent during these proceedings, obviously on instructions from the Reich; but they plainly prepared to profit from the situation at the expense of both contestants.

Thus stood the world situation, barely a year after Hitler took office. Two hopeful vehicles of international agreement, the Disarmament Conference and the World Economic Conference, were in a state of collapse, and the League of Nations itself greatly weakened. The Japanese attack on Manchuria had achieved its purpose. The Nazis were in complete control of Germany, and there was no likely way of shifting them for a very long time to come without external force. The prestige of France had been gravely undermined by both internal and external events. Even in Britain, despite the Government's massive majority, there was much doubt about the future direction of foreign policy. The United States, which had begun to take renewed interest in European affairs, received sharp rebuffs for its pains, and might easily retreat again into isolation. The Soviet Union, with its deep internal problems, seemed to possess neither the power nor the will to assist anyone else. Few people today would dispute that the Great Depression had played a vital part in setting this international disintegration into motion. Yet, one might reflect, by early 1934 there were already signs that the worst phase of the Depression might be over. But an avalanche, once set into motion, does not cease just because the initial impetus is no longer applied.

4 Stresa and After

In March 1934 Ramsay MacDonald posed a very disturbing question to his Cabinet colleagues: whether they agreed that 'we take Germany as the ultimate potential enemy against whom our long-term policy must be directed'.[1] A couple of years before, that question would have been almost unthinkable; but the Foreign Secretary, Sir John Simon, supplied considerable quantities of information which suggested that the answer should be affirmative:

> German civil aviation is now the first in Europe. Germany already has in effect a fleet of 600 military aeroplanes and facilities for its very rapid expansion. She can already mobilise an army three times as great as that authorised by the Treaty and a rapid expansion of her mobilisation facilities must be expected.[2]

The Prime Minister received no clear answer from his colleagues. A large part of Britain's difficulty in the 1930s lay in the fact that it was by no means certain against whom she should prepare herself and others. The view that Germany was the principal danger was closely linked to the idea that the most vital British interest threatened was the political status quo on the European continent. Yet was this the case? The enthusiasts for Empire or the partisans of the navy could very well argue that the greatest danger was to her lines of communication, especially in the Far East, and that Japan posed a more serious threat. The Covenant of the League of Nations might require Britain to engage in war against any enemy anywhere at any time; and within a couple of years very serious attention would be given to the possibility of war against Italy. Some people still thought of the Soviet Union as the ultimate threat to Britain, while many ordinary men and women felt bitterness towards France. The one thing completely out of the question was that Britian could engage in war simultaneously against several of those possible antagonists, without the support of major allies. To those with the most superficial knowledge of strategy it was very plain that different enemies implied different organs of defence. So we return to what was really the root problem of the time: who was the perceived enemy? If the enemy could be identified, then Britain might well be able to withstand that enemy without war, through a mixture of threats, alliances and concessions. No doubt unpleasant decisions would need to be taken in any event; but if the enemy could not be identified, then neither defence policy nor foreign policy could have any clear direction, and it was likely that at some time or other Britain would find herself in the middle of an appalling crisis for which she was wholly unprepared.

Britain was not the only country which needed to make radical reappraisals of the European situation about this time. Right at the end of 1933 the Soviet Commissar for Foreign Affairs, Maxim Litvinov, made a speech which attracted considerable attention in diplomatic circles. He complained of the 'aggressive ideas' of the new German leadership, and expressed a desire for improved relations with Britain.[3] Hints began to appear that Russia was softening her long-declared contempt for the League of Nations, and might soon attempt to join. This shift of policy carried enormous implications. Communist theoreticians had long taught that all 'capitalist' countries were equally the enemy of the 'proletariat', whose interests were synonymous with those of the Soviet Union. In the closing years of the German Republic Communists had not scrupled to undermine the moral authority of the Republic itself, and of the Social Democrats in particular. If Hitler took power, so they argued, this must not be regarded as an unmitigated disaster, for the excesses of Nazism would soon compel the proletariat to recognise its true interests, and encompass the final destruction of the *bourgeois* state. When Hitler had been in power for less than a year the Soviet Government was plainly coming to realise that Nazism was a good deal more stable, and vastly more menacing to themselves, than they had thought; and the best chance of destroying it lay in alliance with others. Indeed, one might reflect that Litvinov's announcement was not the first indication that the Soviet Union might be changing fundamentally her attitude toward other states. As far back as July 1933 a Convention for the definition of aggression had been signed by the Soviet Union along with all her neighbours in Europe and several in Asia. This declared that no consideration – political, military, economic or of any other kind – gave any state authority to invade the territory of any other, with or without declaration of war. Whether the Soviet Union had had a total change of heart about her function in relation to world revolution, or whether she had found it convenient to dissemble her ambitions for the time being was, and is, a matter of deep argument. It was quite certain, however, that she was willing to co-operate, for the time being at least, with others who felt the same threats as she did.

As in the 1890s, the rising power of Germany led to moves towards a Franco-Russian alliance, representing a remarkable shift of policy on both sides. Around 1930 there had been a savage 'trade war' between the two countries. This hostility was set aside, and in January 1934 – just before the Chautemps Government fell – a commercial treaty was concluded. Nor did the marked shift to the 'right' under Doumergue, soon afterwards, in any way impair the moves toward rapprochement. In the early part of 1934 there was much discussion about a possible 'Eastern Pact' (or 'Eastern Locarno', as it was often called) in which France, Russia, Germany and various countries of Eastern Europe might join. But if Germany proved recalcitrant, could she not be omitted from the arrangements, which might then be modified into an alliance to contain German ambitions?

News from within Germany encouraged others to draw together against a common threat. On 30 June 1934 came the 'night of the long knives', during which Hitler's actual or potential rivals within the Nazi Party itself, and also his immediate predecessor in office, Kurt von Schleicher, were murdered. This provided a clear warning about the ruthless character of the Nazi dictatorship, and its utter contempt for legality. Just over a month later came even more sensational news. Chancellor Dollfuss of Austria was assassinated by Austrian Nazis. To the world at large, this seemed to have been achieved with at least connivance from the German Government. It now appears that this interpretation was wrong. The German Nazis certainly hoped that their Austrian counterparts would take over that country as well; but they planned to operate by infiltrating the government, rather than by organising a coup to destroy it.[4] Whatever the facts of the situation, reactions elsewhere were sharp. Mussolini moved Italian troops to the Austrian frontier to forestall a German takeover. For a considerable time to come the Italian dictator remained Hitler's most intransigent opponent among all the leading statesmen of Europe.

Hitler did not suffer severely from the rebuff. The German Minister in Vienna had behaved in an embarrassing and unauthorised manner just after the murder, and this gave the Chancellor a good excuse not only to dismiss the erring diplomat but also to remove a potential nucleus of opposition at home. Von Papen was appointed German Minister in Austria, which produced the double benefit of removing him from the Vice-Chancellorship and despatching him to a country where his presence might prove reassuring to Catholic co-religionists. A very few days later, a further event occurred at a peculiarly convenient moment. President von Hindenburg died on 2 August. Next day the Reichstag dutifully proposed that Hitler should combine the offices of President and Chancellor, with the title *Reichsführer*. This provided occasion for yet another set of 'elections' in Germany. Vast and predictable majorities endorsed the constitutional changes required.

Acts of violence were not the monopoly of the Nazis. On 9 October a Croat terrorist assassinated King Alexander of Yugoslavia and Foreign Minister Barthou of France. That double murder would have profound repercussions. Alexander was one of the most powerful and prestigious men in Balkan politics: an irreplaceable force of cohesion in a highly unstable country. Barthou, despite his unpopularity, had also represented a major force of cohesion. His immediate successor was Pierre Laval, whose baleful infuence would not cease until he eventually met a traitor's death. Premier Doumergue remained in office a bare month, and on 8 November was succeeded by Pierre-Étienne Flandin. With the disruption of Doumergue's government, and the removal of the 'strong man' of Yugoslavia, a grave blow had been struck against stability in France and the Balkans.

Despite such troubles, substantial changes of diplomatic orientation could be discerned in the latter part of 1934 which suggested that the European Powers were coming to recognize Nazi Germany as a common menace to them all. With this went signs that the League of Nations might be about to enjoy a revival, despite the great rebuffs sustained in the previous year. In September 1934 the Soviet Union was admitted to membership. Perhaps the departure of Germany and Japan had been no bad thing after all? The four new 'pillars of the League', Britain, France, Italy and Russia, all had good reason to fear Germany; and three of them had good reason to fear Japan as well. If the League could be changed from a debating society into an alliance, then there was good reason for hoping that both Germany and Japan might be contained.

The visible threat from Nazi Germany not only brought together governments with very different ideologies; it also prompted a growing interest in defence. In France, where belief in the Disarmament Conference had never been very strong, the defensive Maginot Line was being constructed along the Eastern frontier. The British had already begun to show concern for protection in the Far East, and now became increasingly interested in defence, particularly in the air, against Germany. In the summer of 1934 proposals were submitted to Parliament for increasing the Air Force by forty-one squadrons over a four-year period, at a cost of £20 millions. Even in 1934 money values, this programme appears modest enough; but it generated a political furore. The Labour Opposition submitted a motion of censure regretting 'a policy of rearmament . . . certain to jeopardise the prospects of international disarmament'. That resolution was, of course, defeated; but it won unanimous support from the Labour Party, and was backed by most of the Liberals and even one rebel Conservative. Clearly the nation was by no means 'sold' even on this measure of rearmament.

Yet even among those who promoted or favoured these measures of rearmament, there was often a deep inconsistency. The arms they were willing to provide were defensive in the narrow sense. There have been many gibes against the 'Maginot mind' in France; but, whatever else the Maginot Line implied, it certainly served notice to friend and foe alike that France's predominant interest was to protect French soil against German attack, not to launch an attack in support of some hard-pressed ally. The situation in Britain was similar. 'Rearmament' meant improved means for protecting the British homeland or Empire, not means for providing assistance to some third party who might be attacked. For all that, there were certainly signs that people were becoming aware of the dangers of peace, and of the need to do something about them.

The Depression was now visibly past its worst. In some countries unemployment was beginning to fall quite markedly. In Britain it had been around 22.5 per cent in 1932, and by 1934 was down to 17.7 per cent; in the United States the worst annual figure had been 24.9 per cent and in 1934 it was down to 21.7 per cent; in Germany during the same period it had fallen from 30.1 per cent to 14.9 per cent. A few countries, of which France was the most important, evinced a different pattern; and to that point it will be necessary to return. Where real improvement was visible, appalling though the figures still were, internal political stabilisation usually followed. The National Government in Britain could not hope to repeat the sensational electoral performance of 1931, but was beginning to look tolerably secure for a very long time to come. In the United States President Roosevelt was beginning to capture the imagination and enthusiasm of the people. Unfortunately the same visible economic relief also gave more and more stability to the government of Adolf Hitler; and it was also increasing the appeal which that government made to German-speaking people beyond the Reich.

The first certain evidence of this came in circumstances about which, for once, the allies could raise no moral complaint. The coal-producing Saar region had been detached from Germany at Versailles, and set under the League of Nations, with provision that a plebiscite should be held after fifteen years. The promised poll was held in January 1933 in unexceptionable conditions, and more than 90 per cent voted for a return to Germany: a change which was effected soon afterwards.

The German Government was pleased to record such a significant advance obtained by undeniably 'legal' means; but there was no disposition to eschew illegality where that seemed more appropriate. On 16 March 1935 the Nazis issued what was by far the clearest and most unambiguous challenge which the rest of the world had received to date. The military clauses of the Treaty of Versailles were formally repudiated. Specifically, conscription – forbidden under the Treaty – would be introduced; while the peace-time army, limited by the Treaty to 100 000 men, would be increased to thirty-five divisions, or about five times the permitted number.

The German announcement caused extreme alarm in France and Italy. The French at any rate had long been aware that Germany was acting in violation of the military clauses of Versailles;[5] but the new announcement gave Germany the opportunity to increase her army on a vastly greater scale than would ever have been possible on a more or less clandestine basis, and it constituted a diplomatic challenge which could only be ignored at great moral cost. So in April the heads of government and the Foreign Ministers of Britain, France and Italy all met at Stresa. Mussolini appears to have been very much the front runner in urging positive action. One account tells that he was 'boiling with anger' against Germany ; another that he telephoned Laval a few days before the Conference, indicating that his own advisors were pressing for indirect military engagements in defence of Austria. The response of the French Foreign Minister was not encouraging: 'Être prudent'.[6] Britain was in a somewhat different position from France and Italy, for the threat posed was much more remote and indirect. The Germans had said nothing about naval rearmament, which Britain would at once recognise as a vital danger to herself. Britain was certainly committed to go to war should Germany launch an unprovoked attack upon France; but her obligations in most other cases of German aggression by land were far from clear, and the Cabinet had no wish to extend them, whatever they might be. Nor was there the slightest evidence that any significant body of opinion in Britain desired that they should do so.

From the labouring mountains at Stresa there emerged one living mouse. The parties confirmed the undertakings which they had made in the past to consult together in the event of a threat to Austrian independence. Perhaps this altered Hitler's timetable a little, and pushed

Austria some way down his list of priorities. This was by far the most significant element of the 'Stresa Front'. The other mice which emerged were still-born. Formal approbation was given to the idea of an eastern pact comparable with Locarno; although by this time everybody realised that Germany would not participate, and therefore that the plan could not possibly be fulfilled. Even more pathetically, the three powers proclaimed that the German announcement over rearmament 'had undermined public confidence in the security of a peaceful order' – a statement of the blindingly obvious. Doubtless it was intended as a vague warning; but the Nazis probably took it as confirmation of the view that the three powers did not propose to do anything much about that rearmament.

It was hardly necessary to convene six of the most important men in Europe to a Conference lasting several days, if nothing more dramatic than a re-affirmation of existing policies was envisaged. Why, then, was so little done? The answer appears to be that each of the three countries had, or thought she had, another option open, which would preserve her own security without involving any risk that she would be fishing someone else's chestnuts from the fire. Within a month or two of Stresa each of them was more or less committed to a course of action which was bound to cause high embarrassment to the others.

The British option was to come to terms with Germany on naval questions. During the Manchurian crisis the government had suddenly become aware of perils in the Pacific, and they had no wish to face even graver dangers in home waters as well. So they were favourably inclined to a settlement which was likely to preserve British preponderance over Germany at sea. Hitler also had good reason to desire a settlement, for his main interest lay on the European continent, and he sought to avoid a long and exhausting naval race which would assuredly range Britain alongside his enemies. Thus the idea of an Anglo-German Naval Agreement was quickly taken up on both sides, and by early June there was a consensus that the German fleet should be limited to 35 per cent of the British, with special arrangements governing particular classes of vessels. Specifically, Germany would be immediately authorised to build up to 45 per cent of the submarine tonnage possessed by the British Commonwealth, and – after notice and 'friendly discussion' – up to 100 per cent of that tonnage. Formal agreement was concluded before the month was out. The arrangements had an easy political ride: the Opposition Parties made no serious criticism, although a few individuals protested. No doubt the French and Italians were displeased, but their anger was not particularly blatant.

The option which France took was to seek closer links with the Soviet Union. The moves which had been made in that direction during 1934 had hung fire for some time. Then, just before Stresa, things suddenly began to move again. Laval laid plans for a Franco-Russian treaty of alliance before the Council of Ministers, and indicated – even more confidentially – that, whatever might happen at Stresa, France was prepared to sign a pact with Russia thereafter.

The thinking behind the pact idea on France's side appears to have involved a mixture of international and domestic considerations. If such arrangements were concluded there would be no immediate need for military action, and there would be some hope that if fighting later became necessary it would be Russians rather than Frenchmen who would do most of it. The domestic argument was more complex. The French Communists did not at this time form a very important group in the Chamber, but they had considerably influence in the Trade Unions. They were currently engaged in an anti-militarist campaign, which could prove highly embarrassing to a government which sought to rearm against the German threat. If the French Government did a deal with Russia, then Moscow would certainly require the French Communists to call off their campaign, which would ease the situation considerably. There was also another political aspect to the matter. The French Government was considered well to the 'right' of the majority of the Chamber, and a very important factor contributing to its survival was support from the prestigious Radical, Edouard Herriot. Although in no sense a communist sympathiser, Herriot was an enthusiast for a Franco-Russian alliance, and if his support were withdrawn the government might well collapse. So the government pushed ahead with the arrangements, and on 2 May reached agreement with the Soviet Union about the form of the Treaty. Ratification, however, was postponed for a considerable time; and when that issue was raised again, much trouble was to follow.

Such arrangements might or might not add to the security of France, but they gave little encouragement to either Britain or Italy. Those countries had reason to doubt the Soviet Union's capacity to wage war beyond her own frontiers should need arise, and even more reason to wonder how, as a matter of simple geography, she could engage her armies against Germany without a common frontier. Thus a Franco-Soviet alliance seemed of dubious advantage for France, and a possible source of high embarrassment to France's allies. How seriously the Germans took the threat is a matter of speculation; but if they took it sufficiently seriously to relax pressure on France, the likely effect would be for them to direct their principal attention to Austria, and perhaps beyond.

If France and Britain took their cue from Stresa to pursue their own independent policies with scant regard for each other's susceptibilities, Italy did the same sort of thing in a much more spectacular manner. For some months before Stresa she had been embroiled in a quarrel with Abyssinia (Ethiopia), which at that time was one of the very few African countries not under European domination. In December 1934 a force of Italian colonial troops and some Abyssinian levies were engaged in a bloody conflict at the obscure water-hole at Wal Wal, situated in an undefined border-zone between Italian Somaliland and Abyssinia. This incident was the cause, or the pretext, of exaggerated Italian demands for compensation and other humiliating conditions. An offer from Abyssinia to refer the dispute to arbitration was rejected by Italy, and so Abyssinia submitted the whole matter to the League in January 1935. Futile direct negotiations between the two countries ensued, and Italy proceeded to send large numbers of troops to Italian Somaliland. Just before the Stresa Conference Abyssinia formally complained to the League of Nations.

Nobody doubted that Mussolini was contemplating some kind of action in relation to Abyssinia, but there was little to show that he had definitely made up his mind what that action was to be. There were various possibilities, ranging from more or less voluntary territorial exchanges, through some kind of Italian protectorate over part or all of Abyssinia, to outright annexation of the whole country. No doubt various kinds of bribes or threats could be applied, and it was by no means self-evident how the British or French Governments might react to the various possible courses of Italian action. The Italo-Abyssinian dispute was no doubt 'serious', and it came up for a lot of discussion in the British Cabinet well before Stresa: but so also were many other international quarrels 'serious'. There was little to suggest that this particular dispute would prove of crucial importance to the whole course of world events.

One of the most extraordinary features of the Stresa Conference is that the Italo-Abyssinian dispute appears not to have been mentioned at all in the formal sessions, and not much was said about it even in the informal 'corridor' discussions. Mussolini could be excused for thinking that neither Britain nor France was particularly exercised about what he did, provided that he did not encroach seriously into their own vital interests in Africa.

Very soon after Stresa Simon became convinced that the Italians contemplated military action against Abyssinia; but the build-up was far from complete, and in any event a major invasion was out of the question before the rainy season came to an end about September. Thus the world was presented with the spectacle of a crisis in slow motion throughout the summer.

As the Abyssinian quarrel moved gradually but inexorably towards its climax, important political change took place in Britain. On 7 June Ramsay MacDonald – whose control over events had been visibly weakening for some time – at last resigned the Premiership and was succeeded by the Conservative leader Stanley Baldwin. At the same time Sir John Simon departed from the Foreign Office, where he was replaced by the Conservative Sir Samuel Hoare. MacDonald and Simon both remained in the Cabinet, but in less critically important places. This relegation of Ministers with Labour or Liberal antecedents, and the advancement of avowed Conservatives, signalled the changing character of the National Government.

While it was plain enough that some coercive action was being prepared against Abyssinia, it was not equally plain exactly what effect Mussolini was seeking to achieve, nor what – if anything – Britain, France and the League of Nations ought to do in the matter. At one extreme they might seek to organise international resistance against anything which Italy might do – the policy which became known as 'Collective Security'. At the other extreme, they might decide to wash their hands of the whole business. In between, they might seek to achieve some sort of durable compromise between the two sides – the original sense of the word 'Appeasement'.

During the summer of 1935 it became increasingly clear that there were considerable differences of outlook both within and between the governments of Britain and France. The British were, on the whole, disposed towards action, though they vacillated between 'Collective Security' and 'Appeasement'; while the French were inclined towards inaction, vacillating between 'Appeasement' and 'Neutralism'. A variety of explanations may be given for these differences. Britain had a 'strong' government, supported by a large parliamentary majority, which seemed unlikely to be overturned at the General Election which was fast approaching. France had a 'weak' government, which could be brought down at any moment. Indeed, there was a serious political crisis in May and June, whose upshot was that Flandin was replaced as Premier by Laval, who combined this office with the portfolio of Foreign Affairs. Both countries had colonial interests in East Africa, but those of Britain were a good deal greater than those of France, and therefore Britain had the more to lose by Italian expansion. There were considerable differences in personality and outlook between the rather plodding Sir Samuel Hoare and the ultra-subtle Laval, for whom intrigues were the very lifeblood of existence. And there were differences of national attitude and tradition in politics which were so strong that no government, however big its majority, could afford to ignore, even if it sought to do so. The French, living on a very dangerous continent, were overwhelmingly concerned with their own national security, and were prepared to make or break international liaisons with scant reference to any kind of ideological considerations; while the British, relying on 22 very useful miles of water, could afford a measure of altruism. Thus the French could never look at their policy towards Italy in isolation, and always asked themselves how it might bear on their primary concern, which was Germany. Yet, despite this very marked difference of emphasis, both British and French politicians were well aware that it was highly desirable that their two countries should keep in step if possible. Some rather futile arguments ran to and fro throughout the summer, and various ideas were tentatively broached with Italy. At one stage there were hopes of a three-way deal: Britain should offer parts of British Somaliland in order to give Abyssinia access to the sea, and the Abyssinians should make substantial concessions to Italy. Then the suggestion was broached that Italy might receive a sort of League of Nations protectorate over Abyssinia. All such ideas ran into the sands. Laval was plainly dragging his feet, and the Italians refused point-blank to co-operate.

So it began to look as if the Italo-Abyssinian war which both Britain and France dreaded would take place, and in consequence the League of Nations would be compelled to decide whether to adopt economic sanctions, and perhaps even military measures, against Italy, in fulfilment of the celebrated Article 16 of the Covenant. Could economic sanctions be made effective, with countries like the United States, Japan and Germany outside the League? If sanctions were applied, and they really hurt Italy, would the Italians resort to some 'mad dog' attack on the British fleet, or Malta, or both? The idea seems far-fetched, but it was raised in Cabinet by Hoare at the beginning of December 1935, and appears to have been taken seriously in later discussions. If for any reason Britain did become engaged in hostilities against Italy in the Mediterranean, the use of French bases would be absolutely vital. It took some effort to extract assurances from France about the availability of such bases, and the assurances eventually given were not wholly satisfactory.

Despite the protracted limbering-up period to the Italo-Abyssinian war, it was only about August that a virulent Italian press campaign compelled British leaders to give serious attention to the possibility that fighting might occur between Britain and Italy. Baldwin was told bluntly by one of his most important advisers that 'we never had the smallest thought that in any circumstances could we become involved in hostilities with Italy' – consequently such funds as were available for reconstructing Britain's defences were devoted to other quarters of the Mediterranean.[7] Here was a close repetition of the problem which had arisen with Japan a few years earlier. The reason Britain was unable to deal with aggression was that her military and diplomatic dispositions had long turned on the assumption that the country concerned was a firm and permanent friend, against whom no preparations were necessary. If we are disposed today to criticise successive governments for such assumptions, the reply must be that no government anywhere could guard against all dangers which were theoretically possible; that, until very recently, there had been far more political steam behind movements to reduce Britain's armaments than behind movements to increase them; and that neither Japan nor Italy had given much prior warning of aggressive deisgns which Britain might seek to curb.

In the crisis over Abyssinia Britain made some belated preparations in order to deal with possible trouble in the area; apparently no other power in the League of Nations did even that.[8] In public, the British and French delegates to the League declared support for the Covenant, and for Collective Security. Mussolini evidently regarded this as bluff. On 2–3 October 1935 Italian troops crossed the frontier into Abyssinia on three fronts.

Almost immediately the Council of the League of Nations, and soon the League Assembly as well, denounced Italy as the aggressor, and demanded sanctions against her. In theory sanctions might have a considerable coercive effect, for something like 70 per cent of Italy's overseas trade was with League countries. Hoare – unlike considerable elements of influential British opinion – was eager for sanctions,[9] and in practice the Cabinet could be brought more or less into line when important decisions were required. A more spectacular dispute arose in the Labour Opposition. The Conferences held both by the Trades Union Congress (TUC) and by the party in the early autumn resulted in clear and overwhelming majorities for sanctions. These led to the resignations of two pacifists holding important offices: first Lord Ponsonby, leader in the Lords, then George Lansbury, leader of the party. Arthur Henderson, who would have been the natural successor, died about this time; and leadership passed to the little-known Clement Attlee.

The apparent unity of the Government over sanctions, plus the visible confusion of the Opposition, afforded a priceless occasion for calling a General Election. Predictably, the Government won a great majority, though substantially smaller than that recorded in the wholly freak conditions of 1931: 432 seats, against 154 for Labour and 20 for the Liberals.

In the immediate aftermath of the General Election plans for League of Nations sanctions against Italy went rapidly ahead. By early December, the great majority of members of the League, headed by Britain and France, were applying embargos against Italian exports, were refusing to supply arms to Italy, were imposing financial sanctions, and had joined in 'compensatory agreements' to assist any nation which suffered disproportionate losses by co-operating in the sanctions policy.[10] The crucial question, however, was the supply of strategic materials, and most particularly oil, to Italy. This was the sanction which could really bite; for the general view was that Italy's existing oil stocks would last for about two or three months, after which time she would be in real difficulties. Even on this point it looked as if substantial advances were being made, although there were serious problems. Mussolini was sedulously putting out the message that, while economic sanctions were in no sense a *casus belli*, the oil sanction could be different. In the British Cabinet there were lingering fears of a 'mad dog act' by Italy, and these reports natually played on such apprehensions. Nor was there absolute certainty that France would give full support in that event. Information from the United States suggested that every possible pressure would be set on American oil companies to co-operate,[11] although the difficulties of getting legislation through Congress were immense, and perhaps insuperable.

France was the weak link in the chain, although there was considerable reason for thinking that the weakness lay not in public opinion in France but in Pierre Laval.[12] The French Premier indicated a wish to discuss matters with a British Minister, preferably Baldwin.[13] As it happened, Sir Samuel Hoare, whose health had been rather poor of late, was proposing to travel through Paris on his way to a holiday in Switzerland, and it was felt that a brief stopover to meet Laval would be useful in the circumstances. All evidence shows that neither the Cabinet, nor the Prime Minister, nor Hoare himself, contemplated that any kind of commitment would be entered into during the meeting.[14] Hoare was to be accompanied by Sir Robert Vansittart, and this may have been of crucial importance in what followed.

Hoare met Laval in Paris on 7–8 December. Laval played on existing

British fears by declaring that his own government had information that Mussolini would regard oil sanctions as a 'military act'.[15] He further argued that Mussolini would never negotiate under threat of oil sanctions; and any proposal for peace terms must be made within the next few days to have any chance of success.[16] He made another point, perhaps even more cogent. If oil sanctions led to war, Britain must not rely on French support. Vansittart appears to have taken this very seriously, and may well have prevailed upon Hoare. At any event, Hoare and Laval decided to initial a four-page document which, while it did not formally commit either country, would prove of massive importance in the whole subsequent course of events.[17]

Under the Hoare–Laval plan Italy was to receive a large area of Abyssinia, while a further area should be set aside for Italian economic development. Emperor Haile Selassie would retain the ethnically Abyssinian 'mountain Kingdom', and would receive access to the sea – though no authority to construct a railway to the port. This was the celebrated 'corridor for camels'. To give the arrangements a further air of conspiracy, the ban on railway construction, which was included in the original French document, was omitted from the translation circulated to the British Cabinet.[18]

Hoare requested the Cabinet to consider these proposals as a matter of high urgency, but he himself continued the journey to Switzerland, instead of returning to London to defend them. This set the Cabinet in a considerable quandary: either they must endorse proposals which many of them could not be expected to like, more or less on the *argumentum ad hominem*: or else they must take the grave step of repudiating the Foreign Secretary. In the end they decided to support the Hoare-Laval proposals.[19]

At this point these deeply confidential proposals were suddenly leaked to the French Press. Reactions were immediate and explosive. All significant elements of the British Press, with the exception of the *Daily Mail*, condemned the Hoare-Laval plan with considerable anger. The American consul at Geneva reported that confidence of the smaller League Powers 'had been so shattered that it could scarcely be recaptured'.[20] What shocked the critics was not the plan itself – for not wildly different ideas had been broached from time to time during the summer – but its timing. Aggression had been committed, and had been condemned by the League: was this not a lifeline to the aggressor?

Hoare's presence at home was now urgently necessary; but to add an element of farce to high tragedy, he had contrived to break his nose badly in a skating accident in Switzerland. He was unable to return at once; and when well enough to do so was confined to his room and unable to attend Cabinet. Meanwhile feeling continued to mount; and in the end there was much acrimonious argument in Cabinet.[21] Neville Chamberlain defended Hoare; Sir John Simon and Viscount Halifax – who would later play a very large part in events – argued against him.

The plan itself came in for an even rougher passage. It was submitted to the two belligerents, and both rejected it. On 18 December Hoare resigned. Baldwin proceeded to assure the House of Commons that 'the proposals are absolutely and completely dead'. A motion of censure was, of course, moved from the Opposition benches. Baldwin had at one stage anticipated a very sharp drop in the Government's majority, but this was averted – perhaps by Hoare's own resignation. Laval survived a similar vote of censure moved in the French Chamber, but Radical support for his government was seriously undermined and he fell from office in the following month.

The Hoare-Laval episode provides a prime example of a phenomenon which would become increasingly common in the period which followed; for the British Ministers criticised were in no position to state their own best case. Critics very naturally supposed that the government as a whole was up to its neck in the arrangements, and in the end had thrown Hoare to the wolves to save themselves. In fact the responsibility of the government was a whole was very late and peripheral. Hoare himself appears to have acted largely on the advice of Vansittart – whose name could not be brought into the public debate. As for Vansittart, his overriding concern was to hold down Nazi Germany. It must have appeared monstrous to a man in his position that Britain and France were being sundered from each other, and from Italy, at a time when the best hope of keeping Nazi Germany in check lay in the three countries acting together. Was it really more important to preserve Haile Selassie's backward monarchy, in which slavery was by no means unknown, or to preserve the security of Europe?

Hoare's successor was Anthony Eden, who had been noted as a particularly eager supporter of sanctions, and who had already conceived a deep hatred for Mussolini – much deeper at that time than his animosity to Hitler. Laval was replaced at the Quai d'Orsay by Flandin – not the most prepossessing of French politicians, perhaps, but an improvement on the earlier incumbent. But the stuffing had gone from the League. The various powers went on talking about sanctions in general and oil sanctions in particular; but whereas the original concern had been to bring these into force as swiftly and effectively as possible, in order to compel Italy to relax her aggression, people now began to ask whether sanctions were likely to prove successful at all. Nor did Britain and France move closer together; there was a more or less public dispute between the British, who were eager to go ahead, and the French, who continued to drag their feet. While the argument proceeded, Mussolini won his war. In the first week of May 1936 Haile Selassie fled his country, and the Italians occupied Addis Ababa. Soon afterwards the King of Italy was proclaimed Emperor of Abyssinia, and on 15 July the League decided to end sanctions.

For a long time to come the League powers refused to recognise the Italian conquest. This did no good to Abyssinia, but produced a measure of economic loss both to the League countries and to Italy, and infuriated Mussolini. In the end the various countries drifted one by one into recognition. Henceforth, we may say, the League of Nations was more of a liability than an asset for the causes for which it had been established. Many League supporters would not admit, even to themselves, that its effectiveness had been lost beyond hope of revival, and therefore they failed to make proper alternative provisions for international security. Many people, and not least of them Anthony Eden, felt such continuing bitterness against Mussolini that they failed to recognise until too late that Nazi Germany had become an incomparably greater menace, with a far more virulent form of 'fascism'. The similarities in kind between the two systems were noted, and from this the deduction was drawn that the two must therefore become allies. The conclusion was bad in logic; but it turned out to be a self-serving prophecy.

5 Polarisation

While Britain, France and the other League Powers were arguing over sanctions against Italy, and Mussolini's forces were advancing into Abyssinia, another issue arose which carried even deeper implications. Plans for a military alliance between France and the Soviet Union, which appeared almost complete in May 1935, had hung fire for a very long time. After the fall of Laval in January 1936 the new Premier, Albert Sarraut, came under considerable pressure both from domestic critics and from the Soviet Union, to finalise the arrangements which required ratification from the National Assembly. On 27 February 1936, by a majority of more than two to one, the Chamber declared for ratification. Consent of the Senate was still necessary, but this was more or less a foregone conclusion, and on 2 March the French Ambassador told Hitler that his government considered itself already bound by the arrangements.[1]

The Nazis, and some of the government's critics in France, complained that the Franco-Russian agreement was a violation of the Locarno agreements of 1925. The argument was rather a subtle one, but it was not without force. The Nazis had always declared that Versailles was a *Diktat* by the victorious allies, which had no moral authority over Germany, and which Germany was free to transgress whenever it suited her. Locarno, however, was different, for it had been freely negotiated by a past German Government. The Locarno arrangements had included, among many other provisions, a non-aggression agreement between France and Germany. That agreement had been admittedly qualified by a French engagement undertaken at the same time, which required France to go to war against Germany in the event of an attack on either Poland or Czechoslovakia. The new treaty with Russia, the Germans argued, established a new set of circumstances, not envisaged at Locarno, where France might attack Germany. Indeed, there might be secret protocols, or confidential understandings, which extended the possibility of such action far beyond the conditions contemplated in the published treaty. Thus the treaty was inconsistent with the non-aggression agreements reached at Locarno, and if France persisted in her arrangements with Russia, then Germany was absolved from her obligations under Locarno.

The obligation which Germany had particularly in mind was the one which required her not to maintain military forces in the Rhineland – that is, the part of Germany lying between the French frontier and the Rhine, plus a few bridgeheads east of the river. The main reason for keeping the Rhineland free from German troops and fortifications was not so much to protect France from attack, but rather to permit an easy passage for French troops, should they require to go to the aid of an eastern ally. The obligation had originally been set on Germany at Versailles, but it had been repeated in the Locarno arrangements. Until 1930 the Rhineland had been occupied by French forces; but then, by agreement, they were withdrawn.

The nature of the German objection was well known to the French Government long before the Chamber was asked to ratify the Franco-Soviet Treaty.[2] It was also clear to the French that the Germans were by no means the only people aggrieved by the arrangements they were in the process of making with Russia. The Poles realised that the treaty might require Soviet troops to pass through Poland *en route* for Germany. The Belgians, who stood to gain nothing from the treaty, realised that it might be used by the Germans as grounds for re-entering the Rhineland, thereby menacing their own country.

No doubt Hitler would have remilitarised the Rhineland sooner or later on one pretext or another; but the Franco-Soviet Treaty provided him with a very good excuse. On 7 March 1936 German troops were ordered to move in. The allies were in a vastly worse position than they had been a year earlier, at the time of the German rearmament announcement. Italy, who had been prime mover for resistance in 1935, was now herself the subject of sanctions by the League powers. A couple of days earlier the French Cabinet had discussed the possibility of the new German move in the light of military advice that the Germans were already stronger than themselves.[3] Nor did their new Soviet allies encourage them to attempt force. Soviet Foreign Minister Maxim Litvinov was in an 'almost violent rage', but considered a French counter-invasion of the Rhineland imprudent 'as that would mean immediate war'.[4] So nothing was done.

In Britain, the reactions of government and what was called 'public opinion' were very different. The government reaction was rather like that of the French: they deplored what had happened, but saw no way of reversing it. By contrast, a large section of the Press, and its readers, evinced reactions ranging from positive delight to a feeling that the Germans were doing no more than 'walking into their own back garden'. Cabinet minutes recorded a strong ministerial concern 'to enlighten public opinion which was assuming that Germany was the "white sheep" and not the "black sheep"'.[5]

The 'Locarno Powers' – Britain, France, Italy and Belgium – were under a Treaty obligation to 'consult'. Tentative enquiries were even made to determine whether Italy – despite her anomalous position – might assist the others in dealing with the common problem; but the answer was inevitably a refusal while sanctions remained in force. Belgium was also aggrieved, and was disposed to blame the French for their Soviet Treaty as much as she blamed the Germans for their response. So what could Britain and France do? Military action was ruled out; while economic sanctions had even less prospect of success than they had against Italy. Very solemnly and very explicitly, the French foretold war in two years' time, and British spokesmen were disposed to accept the validity of that appalling prediction.[6] Yet what could be done? Perhaps there was no way of belling the cat; certainly nobody was prepared to undertake the risky enterprise.

In the immediate aftermath of these distressing events, France prepared for a General Election. The existing government had long been under heavy criticism for its domestic policies, and this criticism had been sharpened by the economic adversity which visited France at the very moment when other countries were gradually emerging from the Depression. France, which had seemed immune from the economic catastrophes of the very early 1930s, was now suffering from heavy unemployment. On the 'right' the government was assailed by the 'Ligues' – a miscellany of more or less fascist bodies, whose public support was probably overrated, but whose capacity for mischief was considerable. On the 'left' it faced a much more serious challenge from the 'Popular Front' of Radicals, Socialists, Trade Unionists and Communists. The growing fear of Germany, and the widespread dispute about the Government's capacity to deal with that threat, undermined the position further. On 3 May the Popular Front won a great victory, with 387 seats out of 618. That majority, however, was very mixed. The socialists had 146 seats, and were for the first time the largest party in the Chamber. The Radicals, with 116, had lost ground. There were 52 more or less independent supporters of the Popular Front. But what caused real consternation was the great advance of the Communists. A party which had mustered a dozen seats in the old Chamber now surged forward to seventy-two.

Léon Blum, leader of the Socialists, became Premier; but the Communists refused to join his Ministry, which became for practical purposes a coalition of Socialists and Radicals. Intense industrial unrest accompanied the advent of the Popular Front. Wage claims were settled in a way very favourable to the strikers. The industrial upheaval was followed by a great wave of social legislation, including the introduction of a forty-hour working week, and paid holidays. In the space of about a couple of months in the middle of 1936, many other large changes took place in domestic policy, affecting agriculture, education and public finance. Inevitably there were sharp reactions both from opponents who found the pace and direction alarming, and from enthusiasts who tried to push matters a good deal faster. For the time being there was noticeably less division on matters of foreign policy. The new government was at least as anxious as its predecessor to end sanctions against Italy, and perhaps even more anxious to reach an accommodation with Germany.[7]

The domestic turmoil in France was by no means resolved when the Spanish Civil War broke out. The situation in Spain presented political divisions comparable with those in France, but in a more extreme form. In Spain, as in France, there had been a General Election in the first half of 1936, which led to the establishment of a Popular Front Government. On 17 July came news of a military rising in Spanish Morocco, which was followed swiftly by insurrections at various points on the mainland. The insurgents included people whose ideas ranged from 'traditionalist' to fascist, and General Francisco Franco soon emerged as leader. On 23 July the rebels set up a 'Provisional Government' at Burgos, and a few days later invited the powers to grant recognition. Neither side appeared likely to achieve a swift victory, and as time went on both indulged in frequent and wanton atrocities, often completely unwarranted by considerations of military interest.

There is no principle of international law forbidding one government from assisting another in such circumstances, and the Blum administration in France was at first disposed to supply arms on request to the Spanish Government. The British Government, however, was deeply concerned about the international dangers which would be presented if some powers recognised the Madrid Government and supplied it with arms, while others later came to recognise the Burgos administration, and do the same for them. After acrimonious discussion, the French Cabinet decided to refuse military support to both sides.

Although the French Government was at least morally committed to the Madrid Government right from the start, other governments were less deeply involved. Down to the beginning of August even the Italian and Soviet Governments made no attempt to mobilise public opinion one way or the other.[8] On 2 August the French Government, perceiving the risks in the situation, took the initiative in favour of general 'non-intervention' by the powers in Spain: a move which many people wrongly considered to have been inspired by the British. Others perceived the same dangers, and by the end of August a 'Non-Intervention Committee' was planned, with representatives from all the major European powers and most of the minor ones.

Yet at the very moment when people were organising 'non-intervention', the totalitarian governments began to mobilise domestic propaganda one way or the other: the Italians and Germans in favour of the insurgents, the Russians in favour of the Spanish Government. Very soon the seconds of both sides were busily infringing the rules of non-intervention. In October the British Cabinet was regaled with a long list of proved infringements, some committed by Italy on one side and others by the Soviet Union on the other.[9] It soon became apparent that Germany and France were also assisting rival sides – though, at first, in a less blatant manner.

In Germany and Italy on one side, and in the Soviet Union on the other, no public dissent from the government view over Spain was possible. Within the democracies, however, the Spanish Civil War provided further polarisation and deep tensions. Broadly, the 'left' wanted the Spanish Government to win; while the 'right' was more split. Some favoured the government, some had little sympathy with either side, others favoured Franco. The British Cabinet gravitated more and more to the position expressed by Neville Chamberlain: 'It did not matter to us which side won so long as it was a Spanish and not a German or an Italian victory'.[10] Although the French Government was of a noticeably different political complexion from the British, they would probably not have dissented much from that judgement.

The totalitarian countries also had initial difficulties in establishing a clear-cut Spanish policy. In the early part of 1937 there was general agreement among the powers that intervention should cease; and a plan was agreed under which volunteers, real or spurious, should be stopped, and a control scheme set in operation. Then, in March, the Italians already in Spain suffered a heavy and humiliating defeat; whereafter Mussolini appears to have resolved to recapture his damaged military prestige by sending more contingents to Spain. Indeed, as 1937 advanced the military position became more and more bizarre. Neither the Spanish Government nor the insurgents appeared to be at great pains to recruit Spaniards who happened to live within their respective jurisdictions into the armed forces which were fighting on their behalf.[11] Both, apparently, had considerable doubts about the reliability and loyalty of such troops. Instead they found it convenient to use large numbers of foreigners. It soon became apparent that if the seconders of either side should withdraw support unilaterally, victory for the other would be swift and certain; while if both sides should decide to leave the business to Spaniards, the upshot would be anybody's guess.

During the spring, summer and early autumn of 1937, there were several incidents in, or related to, the Spanish Civil War which really frightened diplomats, who saw in them the seeds of general war. Yet the Powers somehow pulled back from the brink. Sometimes they talked themselves to a standstill in protracted arguments where deep issues disappeared in a mass of words: occasionally – as with the Nyon agreement of September 1937 – they patched up *ad hoc* arrangements to deal with dangerous new problems. Ill will and mistrust were general; but nobody cared to push matters to the limit. The Spanish Civil War drifted on right into 1939, with appalling suffering by the people of that unfortunate country; but by the end of 1937 a kind of stability was established. Thereafter, events began to take place elsewhere which were so important that even the long agony of Spain slipped from the centre of world attention.

Perhaps contemporaries were inclined somewhat to exaggerate the risk of the Spanish Civil War proving the spark which would set off a general conflagration. The country's geographical location posed a visible risk to France by land, and to the passage of vessels through the Mediterranean should war arise. It was widely suspected – wrongly, as it turned out – that Italy sought to establish permanent bases in the Balearic Islands. There could be little doubt that Franco's Italian and German supporters viewed Spain as a useful practice-ground to assess the value of new military techniques. Destruction of the little town of Guernica by German bombing in April 1937 was an incident which burned particularly deeply into the minds of contemporaries. Few people would have guessed during the Civil War that Franco would have sought – and still less that he would have been able – to preserve Spanish neutrality throughout the Second World War, despite blandishments from his benefactors.

If the military and strategic implications of the Spanish Civil War were often overstated, the psychological implications would be very hard to overstate; for it gave great impetus to a process which had been developing for some time: the tendency for people to see international disputes in ideological terms. In the literature of the time, including diplomatic papers as well as popular writings, Franco's adherents came to be called 'fascists' or even 'whites', and the government supporters 'communists', 'bolsheviks' or 'reds'. All of these terms were loose and inaccurate, but it became exceedingly easy to fall into using them, and of course it much suited the interests of real fascists and communists that people should do so. Large numbers of young people departed for Spain to fight in the International Brigade, convinced that they were waging war against 'fascism' both in Spain and elsewhere. 'Popular Front' governments, and those who sympathised with the much weaker Popular Front movement in Britain and other countries, were convinced that all 'fascists' – Italian, German or Spanish – were essentially the same. Fascist and near-fascist sympathisers encouraged a similar view from the opposite angle. Thus increasing numbers of people became convinced that, should general war occur, the line-up would be on ideological grounds rather than on grounds of perceived 'national interest' in the old sense of the term. This created great difficulties for governments in the democratic countries, who might otherwise have been disposed to drive wedges between 'fascist' states in a manner which might have given them pause on the road to war. Germany and Italy had undeniable conflicts of interest, on which diplomats of the old school would have sought to play: but opinion at all levels within the democracies had become highly emotional on such matters, and would have repudiated any statesman who was disposed to offer inducements to one to break its links with the other.

Not only was it becoming axiomatic that 'fascism' was indivisible; it was also implied by many people that 'anti-fascism' was indivisible. The idea was spread that the differences between communists and democratic socialists – or even liberals – were insignificant. That opinion was naturally viewed with considerable suspicion by leaders and many followers in the Labour and Liberal Parties; but it was attractive to unsophisticated enthusiasts. It was applied to governments as well as individuals. The Soviet Union was considered *ex hypothesi* anti-fascist. So were Popular Front governments in western Europe; so was Roosevelt's Democratic administration in the United States. The acid test of sincere anti-fascism in governments like the National Government of Britain and the Popular Front's successors in France was whether they too were prepared to oppose in all matters the known or suspected designs of all fascists everywhere. Thus governments in the democracies came under increasing pressure to adopt international stances which ordinary considerations of interest, and even perhaps of national survival, would seem to prohibit. Such problems run through a large part of our present story, and many factors played a part in their development; but among those factors the Spanish Civil War was of particular importance. Similar difficulties were not encountered by totalitarian governments, who had the immense advantages of almost complete control over 'public opinion'.

On 28 May 1937 Neville Chamberlain succeeded Stanley Baldwin as British Prime Minister. In one sense, the change did not appear dramatic. Chamberlain belonged to the same political party as his predecessor, and for most of their past careers the two men had co-operated closely on both domestic and international issues. There was, however, a large difference of temperament. With a few rather spectacular exceptions, Baldwin's political approach had been largely empirical, and in his last Ministry, age had noticeably reduced whatever dynamism he had once possessed. Chamberlain, though only a couple of years younger, took a much more positive approach to affairs. The word now indissolubly linked to Chamberlain's name is 'appeasement'. That word has various meanings and nuances; but in general the way in which it was understood by Chamberlain seems clear. It was evident to him, as to everybody else, that there would soon be great changes in the relative influence of various powers within Europe, and perhaps elsewhere as well, whatever Chamberlain or any other British Minister might do about it. The operative question was whether these changes could be effected without war and, if so, what role Britain could play in bringing them about peacefully. Nobody who reads Chamberlain's private correspondence, let alone his public speeches, can have the slightest doubt that he loathed war with every fibre of his being.

Chamberlain was a business man, and he thought as a business man. If international circumstances had changed, then surely the natural thing for people to do was to make new arrangements taking cognisance of these changes. Was it not possible to bring European statesmen together to devise new contracts which they would thereafter make a fair effort to observe? If this could be done, then new machinery must be devised. Whatever value the League of Nations had once possessed as an international mediator had long departed. Current signs suggested that a system of alliances was developing, characterised by differences of ideology as well as differences of interest. France and Russia had drawn together; there were indications that Germany and Italy were doing the same. If that process continued, then disaster was certain. The one remaining possibility appeared to be active mediation by Britain.

There was only one country with which Britain herself was currently on bad terms, and that was Italy. To add to the absurdity of the situation, Britain and Italy were not primarily arguing over some issue of current disagreement (although such issues certainly existed) but over a matter already dead – the control of Abyssinia. Nobody proposed to drive out the Italians, whether by war or by economic means; and yet Britain and most other League countries refused to recognise the Italian conquest. This created financial difficulties for Italy, involved some cost to other countries – and did no good whatever to the Abyssinians. At the time of the invasion, and the sanctions which accompanied it, Italy had retaliated by beaming propaganda embarrassing to Britain at Arab countries under British control or influence, and that propaganda was still being issued. Surely it was monstrous to allow these present injuries to persist, and future dangers to accumulate, over a defunct issue? Was not the time ripe, and more than ripe, for a serious effort to snap both Britain and Italy out of the pointless and escalating hostility which had developed between them?

So thought Chamberlain. One of the first initiatives the new Prime Minister took after settling into office was to write a personal letter to Mussolini, composed in the presence of the Italian Ambassador, Count Grandi, on 27 July 1937, urging that the two countries should make a serious effort to resolve their differences. Mussolini replied with alacrity, warmly accepting the invitation.

Timing was important, and there was a measure of urgency. One feature of any Anglo-Italian *détente* would certainly be *de jure* recognition of Italy's position in Abyssinia. Britain could hardly take such a step in isolation, for the League of Nations, though powerless as a peace-keeping body, was not dead, and Britain had obligations to other League countries who had followed her lead a year and a half earlier. If Italy's conquest was to be recognised by the League countries, then the first step had to be a declaration by the League that Abyssinia no longer existed as an independent state: a declaration, one might say, which would be difficult to confute as a statement of fact. Once such a declaration was made, it would be open to Britain and the other League powers to recognise the new Italian position in Abyssinia. The appropriate moment for this declaration would be in September, when the League of Nations was scheduled to meet.

Although there had been much general discussion about the possibility of *rapprochement* with Italy long before Chamberlain's letter was written, that critical letter was impulsive, and the Foreign Secretary, Eden, could justly complain that an important initiative had been taken over his head. Had he done so, and perhaps even forced the issue to resignation of either Chamberlain or himself, then he would have merited and secured wide approbation. Unfortunately the matter was not brought before the Cabinet at this stage. Eden and the Foreign Office neither repudiated nor sincerely endorsed Chamberlain's initiative; but instead the tactics of delay were brought into full operation. It requires little imagination to appreciate how this delay must have looked from Rome, or how easily the Italians might fall into the error of suspecting all Britons, Chamberlain included, of deep duplicity.

Gratuitous acts of folly on Mussolini's part also played an important part in the course of events. Attacks on British shipping in connection with the Spanish Civil War did not cease. Late in August the Spanish insurgents captured Santander, and the Duce boasted publicly about the part Italians had played in the victory. This derogated still further from the credibility of 'non-intervention', infuriated the French Government for mixed reasons of political ideology and national security, and enraged that large body of opinion in both democracies which detested Franco. It soon became clear that the original idea of the League taking action over the status of Abyssinia at its September meeting had receded from the realms of possibility.

So Mussolini took the option natural for a man of his temperament. If he could not get what he wanted from the democracies within a foreseeable time, he could not afford perennial isolation and must come to terms with Hitler. Late in September the two dictators met. The occasion was spectacular, and Hitler as host did all that lay in his power to impress his guest and boost Mussolini's considerable sense of self-importance.

At this point alignment within the British organs of government changed. Senior Foreign Office officials became appalled at the prospect of a full-scale *rapprochement* between Hitler and Mussolini, and began to swing round to the view that Britain must quickly come to terms with Mussolini, and grant the *de jure* recognition he required, in order to discourage even closer association with Germany. Perhaps it was already too late; but whether this was so or not, further time was lost by arguments within the Foreign Office itself; for Eden and his political second-in-command Viscount Cranborne continued to resist what their officials were now urging upon them.[12]

For some time no dramatic change took place in Anglo-Italian relations; but there were important new developments in relation to Germany. Viscount Halifax was a senior and very experienced Minister, but without heavy Departmental duties. During October he received a somewhat odd invitation, ostensibly in his capacity as a well-known huntsman, to attend a hunting exhibition in Berlin. Eden and Chamberlain both encouraged acceptance, taking the view that it would afford an excellent opportunity to meet leading Nazis, and discover what ideas they had for the future. No doubt the Germans were equally eager to discover what the British Government was thinking. So Halifax proceeded to Berlin during November, and was there able to meet Hitler, Goering and various other prominent members of the German Government.

Halifax reported to the Cabinet on his return. The one issue which lay directly between the two countries was whether those pre-1914 German colonies which had become British mandated territories after the First World War should be returned: a matter on which there had been considerable discussion over a number of years. The Germans certainly did not seem very pressing. Goering, with Hitler's approval, had declared that 'even with the colonial question in the field he could see no circumstances in which the two countries would fight'.[13] There had also been discussions about central Europe. Hitler appeared satisfied with the arrangements which had recently been concluded between Germany and Austria. As for Czechoslovakia, he declared that 'she only needed to treat the Germans living within her borders well and they would be entirely happy'. Lord Halifax concluded that 'the Germans had no policy of immediate adventure'.

The principle that Britain should 'make every effort to come to terms with Germany' – Eden's words –[14] was not in dispute among members of the government. What became increasingly an issue between Prime Minister and Foreign Secretary was whether a major effort should be made to secure reconciliation with Italy. Eden contrasted Mussolini with Hitler to the advantage of the latter: agreement with Germany, he declared, 'might have a chance of a reasonable life, especially if Hitler's own position were engaged . . . Mussolini is, I fear, the complete gangster, and his pledged word means nothing'.

At the beginning of February 1938 a great many things began to happen in quick and bewildering succession. The Prime Minister's sister-in-law, widow of Sir Austen Chamberlain, was resident in Rome, and had long been on friendly terms with Mussolini. She was summoned urgently to meet the Duce, whom she was able to reassure about her brother-in-law's continuing concern to get the Anglo-Italian talks started quickly. Mussolini again eagerly reciprocated this interest. A day or two later the Austrian Chancellor, Kurt von Schuschnigg, was called to Hitler, and was required to accept two Nazis in his Cabinet. The Austrian sought Mussolini's advice; but the Duce was incommunicado. Schuschnigg had no choice but to capitaulate to the German demands.

Just what had happened? Did all this imply that some agreement had been reached between Hitler and Mussolini, to the effect that Austria would pass from the Italian to the German sphere of influence? Was the Duce making a last, desperate, attempt to come to terms with Britain before accepting the only alternative? Were there, perhaps, contending forces at work within the Italian Fascist hierarchy itself? The one point on which there was no doubt was that the Italian Government was deeply and urgently concerned to get the talks with Britain started. Count Grandi put the matter bluntly:

> Signor Mussolini did not know where he stood or whether he was to regard the United Kingdom as a potential enemy and consequently he could not take a firm line with Herr Hitler. Until he was satisfied on the point he had no alternative but to continue in agreement with Hitler, which would eventually make agreement with us impossible.[15]

On 18 February 1938 Grandi met Chamberlain and Eden together. When Grandi's points were discussed immediately afterwards, it became clear that the Prime Minister and Foreign Secretary were in fundamental disagreement about inaugurating the proposed discussions. So, at long last, the issue came before the Cabinet. On 19–20 February there were three Cabinet meetings and various less formal gatherings. At the end Eden resigned, and Chamberlain was able to tell Grandi that discussions could begin.

This was soon followed by even greater events. On 9 March Chancellor Schuschnigg suddenly announced that a plebiscite would be held in Austria four days later. The object was presumably to demonstrate solidarity behind his own somewhat vaguely stated policy, thereby cutting the ground from under the feet of the Nazis. There is an old saying, however, that it is unwise to play little tricks on great powers. One of the Nazis in Schuschnigg's Government travelled to Berlin, where he found Hitler in a sulphurous mood. Schuschnigg was very soon forced to abandon his proposed plebiscite, and then to resign in favour of the Nazi Seyss-Inquart. During the night of 11–12 March German troops crossed into Austria; and a day or so later the country was formally incorporated into the German Reich.

Many important facts about the Austrian *Anschluss* were long misunderstood, and much is still obscure. No doubt the Germans hoped to see a Nazi Government in Austria, and effective unification of the two countries; but it does not look as if Hitler had intended, even a week before the event, to bring it about at that particular moment or in that particular manner, and events were largely precipitated by Schuschnigg's plebiscite decision. The call for German troops in Austria appears to have originated from Seyss-Inquart, the Nazi who briefly succeeded Schuschnigg as Austrian Chancellor; and Seyss-Inquart himself apparently changed his mind on the matter when it was already too late.[16] What part – if any– Eden's resignation played is still a matter for speculation. Perhaps it had no direct influence at all; but if there was a link it might be seen in two very different lights. On one view, the putatively 'anti-appeasement' Foreign Secretary had been sacrificed, and Hitler took this as the green light for his first clear act of international aggression. On another view, the Führer perceived the risk that Italy and Britain would soon come to terms, which would probably include a revived 'Stresa Front', which would block him for ever from seizing Austria. It was now or never; and when the opportunity unexpectedly presented itself, he seized it with both hands.

What did the Austrians themselves think about all this? Soon after the *Anschluss* a 'plebiscite' was organised both in Austria and in the old Reich, and recorded in each case majorities far in excess of 99 per cent for union. Of course, such figures are wholly incredible. Great numbers of people had been disfranchised, and the whole campaign was conducted in an atmosphere which would require a very brave man indeed to cast a vote in a direction different from that expected of him. Indeed, there is a substantial chance that the figures was falsified. If there had been a secret ballot on a universal franchise, without the exclusive flow of propaganda from the Nazi direction, such figures would doubtless have been reduced enormously. Nevertheless, it is quite probable that substantial majorities would still have supported the *Anschluss.*

The most disturbing feature was not that the *Anschluss* happened, but how it happened. For the first time since the early 1920s a European frontier had been violated by force of arms. If one frontier could be changed in such a manner, then why not others? There was hardly a mile of frontier in central and Eastern Europe which was fully and unreservedly accepted by the people on both sides of the line, and quite a lot of frontier was not really liked by either. The Nazi excuse for the *Anschluss* was that large numbers of people of German speech living in Austria desired it. Similar populations of German-speaking people lived in other places adjacent to the Reich: in Czechoslovakia; in Poland; in Danzig; in Lithuania; in Switzerland; in France – and also in Italy. There were substantial German-speaking communities scattered through a far wider area. Nor were Germans the only complainants. Hungarians, Poles, Lithuanians, Ukrainians, Italians, Yugoslavs and Bulgarians all had grievances. Where would it all end?

6 Appeasement

The Austrian *Anschluss* immediately focused international attention on Czechoslovakia. People who had been speculating long before that event on possible frontier changes in central Europe had spoken of Austria and Czechoslovakia almost in one breath. Both countries had belonged to the Habsburg Empire twenty years earlier; and while the Austrians were overwhelmingly German-speaking, there were large numbers of people of German language and culture in Czechoslovakia as well. These people, the *Sudetendeutsch*, were mainly clustered along the frontier with the new, enlarged, Germany.

The ethnic composition of Czechoslovakia was astonishing. In a country with rather fewer than 15 million inhabitants, the most numerous people were the Czechs, who roughly balanced all other groups combined. The Sudetendeutsch came next, with around 23 per cent of the total. Slovaks followed closely, with about 20 per cent; and there were smaller, but by no means negligible, communities of Hungarians, Ruthenians and Poles. Some members of all of these minority groups had voiced complaints about the government in Prague; although that government could justly reply that it treated minorities a good deal better than did any of its neighbours.

The Sudetendeutsch, whose fate is most important to this story, complained not of persecution but of adverse discrimination. There was a strong feeling, for example, that a government contract or job was more likely to go to a Czech than to a Sudetener; that a school in a mixed area was more likely to be Czech-speaking than German-speaking. During the Depression the mainly industrial Sudetendeutsch inevitably suffered more than the mainly agricultural Czechs. Whatever else Hitler had done in Germany, he appeared practically to have wiped out unemployment. Whether these Sudeten views were correct or false scarcely matters; the important thing is that they were believed. The Austrian *Anschluss* therefore raised the whole question of the future of the Sudetenland. A Soviet diplomat, returning from a tour of the area, confessed to the distasteful opinion that 90 per cent of the Sudeteners favoured union with the Reich.[1]

Czechoslovakia had a mutual defence treaty with France – part of the Locarno series of 1925 – by which each country was bound to go to war if Germany attacked the other. That treaty had been devised when German forces were limited by Versailles; when even Czechoslovakia, let alone France, was probably stronger than Germany, and when the French, not the Germans, occupied the Rhineland. In current conditions Czechoslovakia was not of major value to France in either economic or strategic terms; but if the 1925 treaty were activated by a German attack on Czechoslovakia, and France failed to respond, the consequence for French prestige would be catastrophic. British interests were much more indirect. There was no treaty between Britain and Czechoslovakia corresponding with the Franco-Czech treaty; and the existing treaty between Britain and France would not require Britain to go to war with Germany if France became involved through her Czech treaty. What alarmed the British was not the prospect that a German attack on Czechoslovakia might damage their own international credibility, but rather that France, their only substantial ally on the Continent, could soon be faced with the appalling choice of reneging on her treaty or going to war. If France did indeed become engaged in war with Germany, then it was difficult to see how Britain could long stay out – unless, of course, she was prepared (as diplomatic language puts it) to 'disinterest' herself in European affairs altogether. That view never appealed to either the government or its main political critics. The Opposition parties had by this time moved a very long way indeed from their semi-pacifist stance of ten years earlier. Like some of the famous critics of the government on the Conservative side of the House, they were coming more and more to see all international questions in ideological terms: as an almost Manichaean struggle between 'fascism' and its enemies, where it was impossible to achieve, and disreputable to attempt, neutrality. To people in that frame of mind, it was unthinkable that wedges could be driven between 'fascist' states. Yet there was a sort of schizophrenia evident among some of the critics; for the Labour Party, while demanding that Britain should 'stand up to' the dictators, was still unwilling to support the Defence Estimates.

When the Prime Minister Neville Chamberlain and the new Foreign Secretary Viscount Halifax learnt of the *Anschluss*, their first reaction was to consider issuing some kind of British guarantee to Czechoslovakia.[2] What stopped the Ministers in their tracks was a report prepared by the Chiefs of Staff.[3] If war occurred between Britain, France and Czechoslovakia on one side and Germany on the other, there could be little doubt that Czechoslovakia would be overwhelmed very swiftly. Britain and France would face a very serious challenge in the West; and victory would only be won – if indeed it was won at all – at the end of a long and exhausting war. The intervention of various likely minor allies on one side or the other would not greatly alter the prospect. If major powers became engaged on Germany's side, however, the outlook was appalling. The Chiefs of Staff confessed to 'the deepest misgivings' over the outcome of a conflict in which Italy and Japan were also enemies. There was no immediate cause for Germany's associates to enter such a war, and perhaps the Chiefs of Staff were considering a worst-case possibility in order to deter the government from strong action in support of the Czechs; but there was good reason for thinking that a war, once started, would soon spread to others not directly involved. With such baleful information before it, the British Cabinet concluded that a very different approach was necessary. They should attempt to bring about an 'internal solution' in Czechoslovakia: that is, they should seek to achieve reconciliation between the government of President Beneš and the Sudetendeutsch.[4] If the parties directly involved were satisfied – so ran the thinking of the time – Hitler would have neither cause nor excuse to intervene. In any event, Britain should undertake no fresh commitment.

During the spring of 1938 a number of relevant matters previously in doubt became more clear. Konrad Henlein, acknowledged leader of the Sudetendeutsch, made an important speech, full of complaints against the Czechoslovak Government; but it did not contain any demand for *Anschluss* with Germany. Apparently Henlein would be satisfied with autonomy within the Czechoslovak state, provided that various grievances were redressed. This was consistent with what the Nazis had told Halifax a few months earlier as the German view on the matter. The Czechoslovak Government, however, was by no means eager to comply, for it feared the establishment of a Nazi state within its own: a condition which would probably lead in time to complete separation of Sudetenland, and its incorporation into Germany. The Reich Nazis launched bitter and sustained attacks against the alleged enormities of the Beneš Government: but neither the Germans, nor the Czechoslovaks, nor the Sudetendeutsch themselves, struck public attitudes which would make future reconciliation impossible. Meanwhile the British were disposed to think that France was absolutely resolute and determined to stand by the Czechs in case of need. The Americans, however, had evidence the other way: that important French statesmen were appalled at the prospect of war, and deeply conscious of their country's unreadiness to fight.[5] What disturbed all sympathetic observers was the condition of French defences. The army appeared very strong indeed, and the Maginot Line of fortifications adequate to meet any possible German attack. Far more worrying was the state of air defences. Not only had Germany far overtaken Britain and France combined, but the gap was rapidly growing wider.

A feature of the situation in one sense reassuring, yet in another profoundly disturbing, was the attitude of the Soviet Union. Under a treaty dating from 1936, Russia was required to go to war in Czechoslovakia's defence should Germany attack – but only on condition that France was also engaged in war. Foreign Minister Litvinov vigorously reaffirmed the treaty after the *Anschluss*. Yet what would happen if Russia did go to war at Czechoslovakia's side? Stalin had just carried out a most thoroughgoing purge of the Red Army, in which something like two-thirds of the High Command had perished. Parallel purges had taken place in the civil administration. The ideological element which had been injected into British political thinking was so strong that most of the more vigorous critics of 'fascism' refused even to investigate, still less to believe, the plain evidence already available on such matters: evidence which cast deep doubts on the Red Army's capacity in existing circumstances to strike at any foreign enemy. Little attention was given to the plain facts of geography that the Soviet Union in those days had no common frontier with either Czechoslovakia or Germany. The only likely route of access lay through Poland. The Poles had every reason for keeping Russians from their soil – and made it abundantly plain that they would regard any move across Polish territory as an act of war.

Late in May there was an alarming and confused crisis. Apparently the Czechs feared an immediate German attack, and they underwent partial mobilisation. Many feared that others would mobilise as well, and war arise; but this did not happen, and the crisis petered out. The long-term risks remained; and Britain persisted in her attempted mediation, despite visible lack of enthusiasm from both sides in the dispute. In the summer matters were pushed further. Viscount Runciman, a retired and ailing statesman with somewhat distant Liberal antecedents, was persuaded against his will to undertake the role of mediator, and the various parties were persuaded against their will to accept him. Runciman's task was not to propose a solution but to bring the parties together to make realistic proposals to each other.

The problem was excessively difficult from the start, not least because neither side had much will for the mediation to succeed. The Czechs were appalled at the prospect of a little autonomous Nazi state within Czechoslovakia, and were disposed to rely on France, Britain and

Russia helping them in case of real trouble; the Sudetendeutsch looked with growing wistfulness towards the Reich, so near at hand. Whether or not Henlein believed that some 'cantonal' solution was possible, at least for the time being, a growing proportion of ordinary Sudeteners were looking forward to early incorporation into the German Reich. Yet neither side cared to spurn the British initiative too obviously, and Runciman persisted. At last, on 6 September, there were signs that the Czech Government was about to make an offer which had some chance as a basis of discussion.

Next morning *The Times* carried a leading article which hinted that the best solution would be to sever not only the Sudetenland, but also the Magyar and Polish areas, from Czechoslovakia. Observers in Britain suspected, and observers overseas were convinced, that this was a 'kite', putting forward the views of the British Government, without formally committing them. There was much reason for this opinion, but in fact it was wrong.[6] Very likely the Runciman mission would have failed in any event for one reason or another; but it was *The Times* leader which removed the last real hope of an 'internal' solution. How could Hitler, or Henlein, be content with a solution which gave them less than the British Government seemed willing to offer? For a few days more final defeat was not acknowledged. What eventually wrecked any remote chance of agreement was the Sudeten riots of 12 September, during which the Czech authorities killed several Sudetendeutsch. Reconciliation was now out of the question. Czechoslovak forces in the Sudetenland were practically in the position of an occupying army in hostile territory; and the Sudetendeutsch were receiving every encouragement to resistance by propaganda from the Reich.

Although the British and French Governments had made many public statements of attitudes towards the Czech situation, they became increasingly uncertain of each other as the crisis developed. The French did not know whether the British would follow them into war, for Britain had no direct commitment to Czechoslovakia. Even if the British did declare war, they had practically no army, and it would be France who would have to bear the brunt of any land fighting for years. The British, for their part, were beginning to feel doubts about French determination to honour the 1925 treaty with Czechoslovakia. In their different ways, the British, the French and the Russians had all been bluffing – perhaps without fully realising that they were doing so – and none of them trusted either of the others. Still less was anybody really certain what Czechoslovakia would do if German troops crossed her frontier.

In mid-September, the French Foreign Minister Georges Bonnet and the British Ambassador Sir Eric Phipps exchanged indiscretions. 'We cannot sacrifice ten million Frenchmen in order to prevent $3\frac{1}{2}$ million Sudetens joining the Reich', confessed Bonnet. Phipps, in return, admitted the existence of two sharply-opposed views within the Foreign Office on matters of peace and war.[7] What complicated matters a good deal more was an appalling fact on which both men agreed. Public opinion in both Britain and France was convinced that the democracies were much stronger than Germany. Neither government dare to tell the people how far that was from the truth; for the effect would be to destroy internal morale and foreign policy simultaneously.

This was not all. It was very far from clear how the ordinary people in various countries would react if war came. Many noisy demands were made for resistance to Hitler, particularly from people with strong ideological objections to 'fascism'; but nobody was certain how far 'silent majorities' were willing to follow, if need be, to the point of war. Very likely the Nazi leaders had corresponding doubts. There was also deep uncertainty about the likely behaviour of Germany's international associates. A year earlier there had been signs that Germany, Italy and Japan were disposed to co-operate closely, and the 'Anti-Comintern Pact' was reached between them – ostensibly designed against international communism, but widely seen to possess more general implications. More recently it had begun to look as if the three countries were less closely linked than had formerly seemed the case. Japan was embroiled in renewed war with China. The Anglo-Italian *rapprochement* which began in the late winter had already proceeded a considerable way, for agreement had already been reached in principle that Britain would recognise the Italian conquest of Abyssinia. It was generally agreed that Italy was in no position to fight a long war, and it could be anticipated that Mussolini's influence would be on the side of peace. The list of imponderables in the tense international situation seemed endless. Nobody on either side could feel even moderate certainty who would enter the conflict if it started, still less what course it was likely to take. In such circumstances bluff and strong nerves could play a dominant part; but the parties might very easily find themselves manoeuvred into a war which they did not intend, where the cost and the risks were completely incommensurate with the issues at stake.

Another feature of the situation was even more astonishing. Nobody was yet clear just what Germany desired of Czechoslovakia. Perhaps Hitler required no more than that the Sudetenland should be brought within the Reich. There was even an argument for the view that Nazi doctrine itself precluded any wish on the Führer's part to rule over non-

Germans. Yet it was also possible that Hitler sought the total destruction of Czechoslovakia, and perhaps much more besides. Today we know the answers to such questions, and many people gave the correct answers at the time; but those answers were by no means self-evident either to the governments or to the man-in-the-street. So Chamberlain resolved to make contact with the Führer, to try to find out. He proposed to fly to Germany: quite a hazardous adventure in the current condition of aeronautics. The decision to go was greeted with universal acclaim and admiration, not least by the government's opponents. 'Good luck, Chamberlain', was the headline of Labour's *Daily Herald*.

The two men met at Berchtesgaden, in Bavaria. Hitler launched into histrionics against the Czechs, but was brought firmly down to earth by Chamberlain. Eventually the Prime Minister discovered that the immediate demand was no more than cession of the Sudetenland. He returned home, and than set about persuading various parties concerned that the concession should be made. The British Cabinet and the French were won over with comparative ease; but the real decision lay with the Czechs, to whom the territory belonged. The Czechs probably had doubts of their own about the French. Beneš then tried to find what the Russians would do if the Czechs went to war but the French did not. He was assured that Russia would declare war. When the Czech President went on to seek information about the scale of assistance, the Soviet Ambassador confessed that he had no instructions on the matter.[8] The inference was plain, and not encouraging.

A positive inducement was offered to the Czechs to persuade them to cede the Sudetenland. The British Government was prepared to offer a guarantee to the remainder of Czechoslovakia if they would do so. Various kinds of 'guarantee' are known to international law, and the obligations they impose on the guarantor are very different. Nobody in the British Cabinet seemed very clear what was intended, and there was a rather confused discussion on the matter.[9] We may surmise that the Czechs were equally confused; but 'guarantee' surely meant, at the lowest estimate, that Britain proposed to concern herself henceforth with the country's future. That was about the best they could hope to get, and on 21 September they signalled that they were prepared on principle to cede the Sudetenland, if Britain would guarantee Czechoslovakia.

At this critical moment the general terms of the proposed bargain were leaked to the Press. There followed a sharp reaction among the more vociferous elements of 'public opinion' both in London and in Paris against the proposed solution. How far the protestors were

The Czechoslovak Crisis, 1938
The 'honest broker' from London urges Czechoslovakia not to allow himself to be shot by
the brutal German with the machine-gun, advising him instead to put his head into the
noose marked 'capitulation'.
Izvestiya, Moscow, 16 September 1938

representative of the British and French peoples as a whole was
doubtful. But Chamberlain had received the assurances he needed from
the governments of his own country, of France and of Czechoslovakia,

and departed again to meet Hitler – this time at Godesberg, in the Rhineland.

Hitler tried to screw up his demands; but Chamberlain turned at bay. He told Hitler with some asperity that he had brought the various governments to accept highly unpalatable proposals. The British public, which had warmly applauded his earlier visit to Germany, this time gave evidence of considerable hostility. It was impossible to go any further. After long argument, the only point of substance which emerged was that Hitler was prepared to hold up matters, if he could, for a few days longer. Enough information emerged from that meeting to persuade most people that war was likely in the very near future.

By this time attitudes were becoming defined. At one extreme were people whose overriding concern was that in no circumstances should Britain become involved in war for Czechoslovakia. These people were of very mixed political sympathies. They included 'natural conservatives' of an extreme kind, like Lord Rothermere, proprietor of the *Daily Mail* and Sir Nevile Henderson, Ambassador to Berlin; but they also included a substantial number of pacifists and semi-pacifists in the Labour Party and Independent Labour Party (ILP), plus a sprinkling of Liberals in the Cobdenite tradition, like Francis Hirst. On the other side stood vociferous groups demanding that Britain should 'stand by the Czechs'. There were 'rebel' Conservatives like Winston Churchill, and most spokesmen for the two opposition parties. Some of these people knew the military situation. They had probably decided that war was more or less inevitable sooner or later, but that delay would reduce the prospect of victory. Others plainly did not appreciate the military risks. When a delgation from the National Council of Labour met Chamberlain and Halifax they received a very frank exposition of the situation as then known – including the attitudes of France and Russia. The delegates gave every sign of being shocked and astonished at what they learnt about those two countries.[10] It is difficult to know what the man-in-the-street thought about it all; probably he vacillated between opinions, becoming a little more bellicose when the prospects of peace seemed to rise, and a little more pacifistic when war appeared likely.

The government sought military advice. The drift of this was that the prospects of success in an immediate war were less than they would be if the war were delayed by six or twelve months.[11] Yet that kind of thinking, important as it was, does not appear to have been the consideration uppermost in the mind of the Prime Minister. Chamberlain had hoped not merely to steer through the current crisis without disaster, but also to take a long step towards 'appeasement' in the positive sense of the term: to establish new international agreements which had a fair chance of proving durable. But it was now coming to look as if his efforts, and particularly Britain's recent diplomatic involvement with Czechoslovakia, would prove profoundly counter-productive. Beneš, and domestic supporters of a 'tough line', could legitimately point out that enormous concessions had already been offered by Czechoslovakia at Britain's behest. If these concessions did not buy off Hitler's wrath, then Britain was morally bound to go to Czechoslovakia's aid. Britain, who had no special obligations to the Czechs earlier in the year, had acquired such obligations as a result of her own officious eagerness to avert war.

On 28 September, while Chamberlain was addressing the House of Commons, a message was passed to him, reporting a new offer from the Führer. Chamberlain, Daladier of France and Mussolini were invited to a Conference at Munich. For five minutes the House went wild with joy. The leaders of the opposition parties, who knew perfectly well that any peaceful solution would involve cession of the Sudetenland – to which the Czechoslovak Government had already agreed – spoke in strong and eager support. 'Rebels' on the government side – celebrities like Churchill and Eden – did not speak at all. The only voice raised in protest was that of the sole Communist MP. Chamberlain was fully entitled to believe that any solution which kept Czechoslovakia in existence as a sovereign state would receive the fullest support of everybody who counted for anything in politics.

The atmosphere of the Munich Conference, so far from being one of tense and crucial debate, was almost one of anticlimax. The Führer fell back on proposals very similar to those which had emerged from Berchtesgaden. The most important innovations were a timetable for German occupation of the Sudetenland; an agreement to meet again in three months if the outstanding claims of Hungary and Poland against Czechoslovakia had not been met by then; and a somewhat vague agreement that all the Four Powers would eventually guarantee Czechoslovakia: Britain and France immediately, Germany and Italy at a later date. When the main Conference was over Hitler and Chamberlain had a brief meeting, and signed a document the Prime Minister had drawn up, proclaiming the intention of their countries never again to go to war. Chamberlain and Daladier both returned to wildly enthusiastic crowds in their respective capitals. Within a short time the occupation of the Sudetenland was completed with few incidents; the Czech Government agreed with Hungary and Poland about the required concessions, and Beneš resigned Presidency of his country. A little later he was succeeded by Emil Hacha, an elderly lawyer; and the country was for administrative purposes divided into three more or less autonomous regions: the Czechs lands of Bohemia and Moravia to the west; Slovakia in the middle; and the tiny, backward, area of Ruthenia, or Carpatho-Ukraine, to the east.

In Britain there was an inevitable political inquest a few days after Munich. Cabinet Minutes suggest that many Ministers were un-convinced about the durability of Hitler's word; but – with the single exception of the First Lord of the Admiralty, Duff Cooper, who resigned – they felt that Chamberlain had handled the situation about as well as it could be handled.[12] A Parliamentary debate soon followed, and is now famous as the occasion on which a number of Conservatives including both Churchill and Eden, pointedly abstained from voting for the government. It is less vividly remembered that a similar proportion of Labour MPs equally pointedly abstained from voting for their own part's motion of censure, including James Barr of Coatbridge, who told the House that he had sent the Prime Minster a two-word telegram: 'Heartiest congratulations'. Among the Liberals there was similar division of opinion. Most of the MPs were critical; but Viscount Samuel, former leader in the Commons and now a member of the Lords, gave strong support to the actions of Chamberlain. As Samuel was a Jew, this stance was particularly interesting. Careful study of statements made at the time by various critics of the government does not suggest that many of them were really contending that Britain should have gone to war rather than accept the Munich settlement. Perhaps their concern was to a degree political: to placate their own more bellicose followers; but they were also concerned to alert opinion in good time for disputes which they confidently anticipated for the future. In France it is significant to note that enthusiasm was, if anything, even more general than in Britain. When Daladier sought a vote of confidence in the Chamber, almost the only opposition came from the communists.

As many people have pointed out, 'might-have-beens' are not history. Nevertheless, it is useful to ponder what British statesmen might reason-ably have anticipated in the last fortnight of September as the likely alter-native to the policy which they were pursuring. By the middle of the month tension was so high that Germany could only relax pressure on Czechoslovakia at the price of profound anticlimax, which would irretriev-ably undermine the authority of Hitler both at home and abroad. Hitler, whatever his doubts as to the outcome of a 'forward' policy, was not the man to risk the alternative. Civil order was already collapsing in the Sudetenland, and no doubt the Germans could, at some convenient moment, have crossed the frontier with the ostensible object of 'restoring order'. This would have provided Hungarians with a pretext for the invasion of Slovakia and Ruthenia, and the Poles with a pretext for taking Teschen. In such circumstances the peoples living in the eastern half of the country would have been far too preoccupied with the fate of their own homelands to pay much attention to the west. No officer in the Czechoslovak army could have relied on the loyalty of non-Czechs if ordered to fight Germans. One may doubt whether Czechoslovakia would even have gone through the motion of declaring war; if she had done so, it is difficult to see how France, the Soviet Union or Britain could have rendered substantial aid before the country was obliterated. From Hitler's point of view, a Czech collapse in such circumstances would have been a far more satisfactory outcome than Munich; for it would doubtless have had great influence on the future policy of other countries, most particularly Poland, against which he would later have claims to make.

There were displays of official joy in Germany after Munich, but there were internal as well as external aspects of the crisis which must have been displeasing to the Nazi leadership, for there were plenty of signs that ordinary Germans were at least as appalled by the prospect of war as were their counterparts in the democracies. They were grateful indeed to Hitler: but their gratitude was mainly because he had brought the country through without war, not because he had annexed the Sudetenland. Perhaps Nazi indoctrination had been less successful than the propagandists had hoped? In Italy, the situation was not dissimilar. Cries of 'Duce!' blurred into cries of 'Pace!' The Italian people were deeply appreciative of Mussolini as the man who seemed to them to have played a large part in preserving peace, not as the man who had cut a great figure on the world stage.

Even if we could believe that Hitler honestly intended to keep his word over Czechoslovakia, there were many forces at work both in his own country and elsewhere which would have made it difficult or impossible for Munich to serve as a great step towards the 'appeasement' of Europe, as Chamberlain understood the term. Critics of the British Government went out of their way to deny the value and durability of the agreement. 'We have sustained a total and unmitigated defeat and . . . France has suffered even more than we have', was the public judgement of Winston Churchill. Others reproached the Führer as a liar whose word no man could trust. No doubt the 'hawks' in Germany were able to report such statements, thereby disposing him to the view that the British never honestly intended to reach amicable settlement with Germany, but grudgingly accepted Munich under threat of immediate war for which they were unprepared. This suspicion was doubtless confirmed when the British Government, appalled at the military weakness revealed during the crisis, almost immediately set to work to rectify the situation by extending the programme of rearmament which had begun several years earlier. In 1933–34 defence spending had stood at around £108 millions; the estimates for 1938–39 were for more than three times that sum, and the government now contemplated spending a good deal more. Conscious of the likely German reaction, they sought to ensure that the weapons constructed should be 'defensive' in the narrowest sense: anti-aircraft guns, for example; and fighter rather than bomber aircraft. Fighters were not only less provocative than bombers, they were also a great deal cheaper. At first there was a rather curious reaction in Germany, suggesting that contending influences were at work. The Press there did not all speak the same language; some argued that Britain had the right to choose the character of her own defences, while others saw the development as provocative and anti-German.[13] Those who sought to make mischief had plenty of opportunity.

What finally wrecked any remaining goodwill for Germany in Britain was *Kristallnacht* – events of the early morning of 10 November 1938. On a prearranged signal, Jewish shops throughout the Reich were wrecked, and synagogues set on fire. It was predictable that this would generate a storm of rage in the democracies; and the whole episode looks in retrospect very much like a deliberate effort on the part of so-called 'radical Nazis' like Ribbentrop to sabotage any chance of durable understanding with the West: a move really directed against the moderate members of their own party even more than the ostensible objects of this savage and violent occasion. Halifax reacted in the manner no doubt intended: deciding that 'no useful purpose' would be served by Anglo-German negotiations for a long time after such an event.[14]

By the first month of 1939 relations had deteriorated a good deal further. Chamberlain personally authorised a message to British missions abroad, warning them of the likelihood that 'Hitler was planning further adventures for the spring of 1939'[15] Reports reaching various capitals gave wildly conflicting suggestions about possible German designs. Some speculated on action in the west – perhaps against the Netherlands, perhaps against Switzerland. Others anticipated a move towards the Ukraine, perhaps in conjunction with Poland. Others again debated the possibility of an agreement between

Germany and the Soviet Union, with the almost boundless implications that might hold. It was impossible for the West to take adequate measures, either diplomatic or military, against all these varied possibilities. Relatively little attention was given to the prospect that Germany might make a further move against the helpless remains of Czechoslovakia.

One thing was now clear, which had been by no means clear a year earlier: that Britain was almost certain to be involved closely, whatever might happen in central Europe. She stood poised on the edge of war from which at best she could gain nothing, and from which at worst she might lose all. The government had many vociferous critics; but the burden of their complaint was usually that Britain had undertaken too little, not that she had undertaken too much. Nor did those enthusiasts evince much gratitude when efforts were made to reduce the number of likely enemies. In November 1938 the agreement with Italy finally came into force, and carried with it tacit recognition of the conquest of Abyssinia. This certainly reduced the chance that Mussolini would go to war as Hitler's ally; but it was widely criticised. Nor was there strong pressure for extended rearmament. Many of the government's critics seemed far more concerned that bold diplomatic attitudes should be struck than that Britain should set herself in a position to reduce or resist the German menace.

Those who had been speculating about Hitler's next move would soon receive the answer they sought. Early in March 1939 a serious dispute broke out between the Czechoslovak Government and the Ministers responsible for Slovakia. Soon the Germans intervened, 'advising' the Slovaks to declare independence, with the veiled threat that the Germans would otherwise authorise the Hungarians to invade. On 14 March the Slovaks reluctantly complied. The same day, President Hacha and his Foreign Minister Chvalkovsky were summoned to Berlin, and required to sign a document constituting the Czech lands to the west as a Protectorate of the Reich, under threat of imminent bombardment of Prague. So intense was the pressure that Hacha had at least one heart attack in the Germans' presence; but in the end he complied with the demand. On the morning of 15 March German troops entered Bohemia and Moravia, and soon took over the whole area. That left Ruthenia. The provincial government made a brief effort to establish an independent Republic; but Hungarians entering from the south occupied the area as quickly as appalling weather conditions would allow. So complete was the process of dismemberment in Czechoslovakia that scarcely anybody, even among the British

Government's most bitter critics, complained that the problematical 'guarantees' agreed during the September crisis had been activated, and that Britain was under obligation to go to war.

7   Into War

The destruction of Czechoslovakia in March 1939 represented the end of the appeasement of Germany, however 'appeasement' might be defined. German assurances given at the time of Munich were torn up less than six months later. There was no point whatever in seeking further assurances. Chamberlain saw the force of that as quickly as anybody. Just two days after the fateful 'Ides of March', he delivered a speech in Birmingham which may be regarded as the funeral oration of appeasement; and next day the Cabinet endorsed his conclusions.

By then Europe was alive with rumours of the most fantastic kind. The one thing on which all agreed was that Czechoslovakia would not be the last victim. Indeed, the move against Czechoslovakia made no sense in either economic or military terms unless it was seen as part of a much broader plan of aggression. The Czech economy was already completely at Germany's mercy; the army was being rapidly disbanded. So why should Hitler incur the problem of governing seven million reluctant new subjects, and also serve notice to the world that his treaties were worthless, unless he had further aims in mind? There was considerable military equipment available for the taking, and the country could be of strategic value in an attack on Poland.

Britain, we might say today, had a choice between disinteresting herself in the fate of Europe east of the Rhine, or of attempting to organise armed resistance to Hitler's next major move. During the 'appeasement' period, the idea of a 'grand alliance' against Germany had frequently come under consideration by the government, and had been rejected – not only because appeasement was considered preferable, but because the grand alliance idea was considered inherently bad. In the new atmosphere after the destruction of Czechoslovakia it was more or less taken for granted that this was the only possible course to adopt.

The first clear break with appeasement was made in truly astonishing circumstances. Like so many events of the period, this must be seen against its background. Czechoslovakia, Romania and Yugoslavia had had close economic links, within what came to be known as the 'Little

Entente'. In consequence of these arrangements, Romania received its armaments from the great Škoda works in Czechoslovakia. Almost immediately after the seizure of Prague Germany threatened to cut off those supplies unless Romania reached a far-ranging commercial agreement with her.[1] Just how oppressive or otherwise the German demands were, nobody in Britain knew; and the Foreign Office received flatly contradictory information from senior Romanian officials. On 18 March, just three days after the destruction of Czechoslovakia, the British Cabinet was suddenly summoned to consider the problem. Out of the discussion emerged a much broader decision. Britain would contact a substantial number of countries apparently menaced by Germany and attempt to organise a common plan of resistance. Two days later the Cabinet decided to modify its original plan somewhat, and confine its attention to the large countries affected – France, Poland and the Soviet Union.[2]

Almost immediately the gravest difficulties were discovered. Russia could hardly enter the alliance unless she had access to Germany through Poland in event of war; but the Poles had no intention of authorising such access. They had two very good reasons for this refusal. In the first place they considered that open alliance with Russia would invite attack by Germany. In the second place, they had every reason to fear that if the Russians entered their country for any reason whatever, there would be little chance of getting them out again. Thus there was a considerable hiatus, while diplomats in the various countries concerned tried to think of ways of squaring the circle.

While they were busily engaged in this operation there came a further rumour, even more dramatic than the earlier information about Romania. A young journalist who had recently been expelled from Berlin, secured interviews with Halifax and Chamberlain, to whom he imparted information indicating that a massive German move against Poland was imminent. Corroboratory – though certainly not conclusive – evidence was obtained from elsewhere. By this stage nobody was in much of a mood to sift these reports very carefully. The British Government, often accused of extreme sloth, took what would prove its most crucial decision in a matter of hours. On 31 March Chamberlain announced to the House of Commons the British Government's decision to issue a guarantee to Poland.

This guarantee was of profound significance for France as well as for Britain. The French mutual assistance pact with Poland, concluded in 1925 and similar to the agreement with Czechoslovakia, had been wearing very thin ever since 1934, and their Foreign Office had been considering the idea of terminating it;[3] but this could scarcely be done in the light of the British guarantee. To complicate matters further, the French War Office, which had considerable authority over fields which in Britain would be the province of the Foreign Office, was eager to make Franco-Polish commitments closer rather than weaker than they had been in the past, and had had some success in that direction.

The British guarantee was designed as a stop-gap measure to halt a German move anticipated in the near future, not as a long-term arrangement. With the notable exception of Lloyd George, opponents of the government did not enquire closely into its implications, or by what possible means it could be made effective if need arose; enough for them that a stake had been thrust through the corpse of appeasement, lest its ghost should walk, and a clear *casus belli* against Germany had been established. In so far as people thought of the military implications at all, they probably took it for granted that three continental countries which Britain was seeking to inveigle into her plans would all perceive a common interest in containing Germany if this were still possible, and defeating her in war if it were not.

These astonishing developments overlapped a number of others which in ordinary times would have been considered of first-rate importance, but which during the spring of 1939 seemed almost peripheral. On 23 March, even before the Polish guarantee question had been resolved, Lithuania was compelled under threat of force to return the German-speaking port of Memel, which had belonged to the Reich before 1918. Five days later Madrid surrendered to Franco, and for practical purposes the Spanish Civil War came to an end, although some time elapsed before that fact was universally acknowledged. On 7 April – Good Friday – the Italians began their almost bloodless seizure of Albania, which was completed in a few days. The country had been for many years more or less an Italian protectorate, acknowledged as such by all the powers; and so they had little incentive to intervene. Chamberlain was very angry. 'Mussolini has behaved to me like a sneak and a cad',[4] he wrote petulantly to his sister. Yet plainly there was nothing much he could do.

In the wake of these events two more international guarantees were issued. The Italian move against Albania posed a threat to Greece – a country which Britain could realistically hope to support in event of trouble. At the same time Romania, where France had considerable interests, was menaced by German economic pressure, and by the territorial aspirations of her various neighbours. The British Government did not like the idea of guaranteeing Romania, which they had no means of defending and where they had few interests; and for corresponding reasons the French were far from keen about guaranteeing Greece. In the atmosphere of the time, however, initiative and solidarity on the part of Britain and France appeared more necessary than any realistic assessment of what was feasible; and so the western democracies composed their differences by both issuing guarantees on 13 April to both threatened countries.

Meanwhile, the even bigger problem of how to defend Poland continued to lumber on. The Polish question would have been difficult enough if it had been a straightforward confrontation between two nation-states with conflicting aims. In fact it was a great deal more complicated than that, and makes little sense unless perceived in a broad context. Like Czechoslovakia, Poland was ethnically mixed. There were many German-speaking people in the west, and many of Lithuanian, Byelorussian or Ukranian speech in the east, to say nothing of Jews who in some parts lived as practically a separate community. There was the further complication that considerable numbers of people who considered themselves Poles resided in Germany and in the Soviet Union. Even the southern limits of Poland were not clearly defined ethnically: Teschen, which the Poles took shortly after Munich, had been a bone of contention between Poland and Czechoslovakia ever since the two states were established in 1918. If the ethnic composition of Poland gave little clear guidance as to its proper geographical limits, the country's history exacerbated the difficulty. At one period Poland had included most of the Ukraine, Byelorussia and Lithuania; and throughout most of that vast area there still existed substantial communities of people regading themselves as Poles. In the late eighteenth century Poland ceased to exist, and was divided between Russia, Prussia and Austria. The reconstruction of the country after the First World War created a variety of grievances and counter-grievances. To the east many Poles considered that the country's frontier with the Soviet Union had been drawn too far in one direction, and many Russians considered that it had been drawn too far in the other. There were grounds of mutual complaint between Poland and Lithuania. Of immediate relevance in the summer of 1939 was Germany's complaint over the 'Polish Corridor', that wedge of Poland, with a profoundly mixed population, which had been thrust in 1919 between the main body of the Reich and the detached fragment known as East Prussia. To compound the problem, the undeniably German city of Danzig (Gdansk) had been constituted a Free City under the League of Nations, in order to provide Poland with a port economically linked to herself, while the new town of Gydnia was being built. Perhaps, if people had been allowed time to adapt themselves to these arrangements, the many anomalies would have become tolerable; but the various grievances were exacerbated by the combined effect of international trade barriers and the nationalist ideologies so much in vogue in the 1930s.

In the spring and summer of 1939 German complaints against Poland were rapidly revived, and there could be little doubt that Poland was indeed designed as Germany's next victim. Thus the problem of organising an effective defence, and particularly of bringing the Soviet Union into the arrangements, became one of urgency. There were very considerable differences of opinion within both Britain and France as to Russia's military value in event of war, but there was little doubt that the prospect of establishing an alliance which included the Soviet Union exerted a substantial restraining influence on Germany. When it came to the point of discussing just what form such an alliance might take, however, great difficulties began to appear. Each time either side made proposals, the other seemed to baulk at what one might call the 'small print'. The Russians and the westerners both hoped – the cynic might say – that the burden of any fighting which might ensue should fall on the other. There was the even more difficult problem already mentioned: if the Soviet Union was to engage its forces effectively against Germany, it would require access in time of war to eastern Poland, and perhaps to other countries as well. It might well be necessary for the Soviet Union to have some kind of access or control in peacetime. Every one of Russia's neighbours, however, had either belonged to the Russian Empire before 1917 or had taken substantial tracts of territory which once formed part of that empire, and all were profoundly fearful that if Soviet troops entered their country, for whatever reason, it would be difficult or impossible to evict them once the immediate emergency had abated. In this matter Poland was most important of all; and Britain having guaranteed the Poles against Germany, could scarcely authorise the Soviet Union to take action which would be regarded as in Warsaw as aggression. It is very likely true that at the beginning of discussions between them, both the Soviet Union and the western democracies hoped and believed that true agreement was possible; but as those discussions progressed both sides gradually came to appreciate the insuperable nature of the difficulties. As far as Russia was concerned, an important indication of changing views came in May, when the essentially pro-western Foreign Minister Litvinov was replaced by Molotov. Thereafter, the discussions became increasingly distant and unfriendly.

Nor were the British and French wholly united. The French were deeply conscious that the first impact of any war in the West would fall on themselves and not on the British. Britain's land forces were ludicrously small by continental standards, and it would probably take well over a year before there was anything remotely comparable with 'equality of sacrifice' in any common engagement against Germany. The old joke about the British fighting to the last French soldier had considerable validity. Even in the summer of 1939 the situation did not show signs of radical improvement. When the British Government decided to introduce military conscription there was considerable political criticism; and many of the critics were people who eagerly demanded that the government should 'stand up to Hitler'. The potential yield of conscripts was not impressive and there was something to be said for the view that conscription was introduced more with the idea of stiffening the French than of frightening the Germans.

Although it was plain to the world that Britain, France and Poland might very soon be allies in war, they knew little of each other's intentions and did little to co-ordinate plans. In May the British received a hint that France was unlikely to launch an immediate and major attack on Germany in event of war;[5] but it was only a hint, and nothing authoritative was known. Perhaps the problem here was more than France's secrecy towards Britain. The French military understood very well that almost anything known to one or two French politicians would infalliably leak to the Press and to foreign agents, and probably told their own government relatively little. So France's military preparations and her diplomacy were kept more or less in watertight compartments. The French Government, well aware that Britain's early contributions to war would be slight, were not disposed to tell the British even the military information which they possessed. Meanwhile the British Government nagged the French about the appallingly slow aircraft production. What morals the Poles drew from all this is more difficult to determine; but there is a story that, long before, a senior Polish officer had been taken over the Maginot Line. The French doubtless intended to impress him with its strength, and they succeeded; but the general conclusion which he drew was not the one they wished to give. A country with such powerful defences, he decided, was not likely to venture outside them.

France was vexed by much more serious political divisions than Britain. The Popular Front Government had perished rather ignominiously in 1938; but the Chamber which had once sustained that government was still in existence. The Communists, with over seventy deputies, would doubtless remain 'loyal' so long as Russia advised them in that sense; but nobody really doubted that in event of any schism between French policy and Russian, they would strongly favour the latter. The true strength of the more or less fascist groups on the 'right' was more difficult to assess. Much more important than these fringe groups were the many French politicians, scattered at various places in the spectrum, whose overriding concern was to avert conflict with Germany at practically any cost.

It would be wrong to see French attitudes in the course of 1939 as a simple cleavage between 'right' and 'left'. Nowhere was this fact more evident than in the matter of negotiations with Russia. If a military agreement with Russia presupposed that she should be given French authority to coerce various neighbours – then should Russia receive that authority? Frenchmen of very disparate politics were to a considerable extent united in suggesting an affirmative answer. A people who had suffered such appalling losses in the 1914 war could be excused for feeling an overwhelming desire that the heat should be taken off their own country in event of conflict. Many Frenchmen doubtless found the idea of giving Russia a free hand in the east to be distasteful; but it was a price most of them were prepared to pay. The British – partly through a deeper sense of their own security, but partly through moral scruples, were noticeably less disposed to countenance Russian aggression as a counter to German aggression; but on that matter shades of opinion could be discerned, even within the Cabinet.

As the summer wore on, hopes of achieving any impressive agreement between Russian and the western democracies gradually became weaker. Both sides came to behave in an offhand manner towards the other. Molotov was almost gratuitously offensive towards the western ambassadors.[6] When a British delegation was eventually despatched to Russia, charged to work out plans, neither the composition of that delegation nor the way in which it was sent suggested that the government was sanguine about its prospects. Yet all this did not mean that the talks were pointless. So long as conversations continued, the Germans could appreciate that any major act of aggression, particularly against Poland, was likely to bring the various parties together in an *ad hoc* agreement with profound consequences. It was one thing to note that potential enemies found extreme difficulty in reaching a long-term agreement which would cover a wide range of possible contingencies; but there was still a substantial chance that they would reach agreement if some particular event occurred which threatened them all. After the frenzied events of March and April, there was a noticeable lull. Even Danzig was unmolested.

Yet what if Germany and Russia should compose their differences, and perhaps join in a new partition of Poland? Those who insisted on seeing all issues in terms of ideology refused to contemplate such a possibility; those who had a sense of history and perceived the compelling logic of the current situation were less disposed to reject it out of hand. The possibility was set before the British Cabinet even before the fall of Litvinov.[7] In the first few days of August Ribbentrop and Molotov each indicated their interest in 'normalisation' of German-Russian relations.[8] Then, on 15 August the German Ambassador in Moscow was assured by Molotov that the Soviet Government was 'convinced of the seriousness of Germany's desire to improve . . . relations'.[9] Five days later a trade agreement between the two countries was reported. Then, on 22 August, came the shattering announcement that Germany and the Soviet Union proposed to conclude a Non-aggression Pact. Despite the recent hints few people in the West seem to have taken that possibility seriously. It just did not fit in with the current obsession over ideology. Political and military talks between Russia and the democracies were still in progress; indeed, the French had recently disclosed to the Russians confidential information about their own military intentions.[10]

On the following day, 23 August, the Non-aggression Pact was signed in Moscow by Ribbentrop and Molotov, in the presence of a beaming Stalin. The two countries agreed not to attack each other directly or indirectly, and not to associate with each other's enemies. That was common form; but the clause commonly found in non-aggression treaties to the effect that they were automatically abrogated if either attacked a third party was conspicuously absent. There was, however, a sinister term by which they agreed to 'consult . . . on questions of mutual interest'. It is now known that the Non-aggression Pact also included a secret protocol dividing spheres of influence over a large area of eastern Europe.

At this moment the official German requirements seemed to be the annexation of Danzig, plus some sort of right over the Polish Corridor – possibly, though not necessarily, annexation. Could such demands really form a *casus belli*? From the German angle it must have seemed that there was a good chance that the answer to that question would be negative. The British and French had plainly been building their hopes on a four-power alliance which would threaten Germany with a full-scale two-front war. Such an alliance was now out of the question. If the Poles could be made to see the hopelessness of their military position and if the French could be persuaded that their own security would be preserved more effectively if they turn a blind eye to Poland than if they defended it – then might not Germany be able to realise her requirements without war?

There were several flaws in the argument. The recent experience of Czechoslovakia had bitten deeply into everybody's mind. One concession to Germany would lead to more later; and it was useless to place the least reliance on Hitler's word. There was also a large element of what we might call the heroic – or the irrational – particularly in Britain and in Poland. The British Government, despite many suspicions to the contrary, had no intention of defaulting on its obligations. The Polish Government, recalling the history of past partitions, had no intention of ceding an acre of land or an iota of its independence. If either government had thought otherwise, then, in the prevailing mood among politically active people of all parties, that government would have been thrust aside by its own compatriots. To emphasise their continuing determination, the British and Polish Governments replaced the old guarantee system by a formal treaty of mutual assistance, signed just a few days after the Soviet-German Non-aggression pact. Whatever the French Government – and above all Foreign Minister Georges Bonnet – may have thought on the matter, the British and the Poles were determined that there should be no possibility of anybody flinching from the test.

Frantic discussions took place within, and between, many countries in the week which followed announcement of the Russo-German Non-aggression Pact. Not all features of the situation ran in Germany's favour. The 'Anti-Comintern Pact', between Germany, Italy and Japan, whose ostensible purpose was to contain world communism, fell apart now that Germany had made her peace with the Soviet Union. The Japanese were at no pains to conceal their anger, and within a few days their 'special relationsip' with Germany was at an end. Italy was in a more dubious position, and for a time Mussolini vacillated violently between radically different ideas.[11] Among other things, he was well aware that Italy had no means for fighting what might prove a long war, and he feared an attack from France. Whatever the French may have thought about Germany, they had no reservations about their capacity to deal with the weaker partner of the Axis. In the end Mussolini sought release from his obligations towards Germany, indicating that he was willing to do what lay in his power to secure reconciliation between potential or actual contestants. Hitler was probably quite happy that his partner – now very much his junior partner – should adopt this unheroic, but perhaps very useful, line.

In the early morning of Friday 1 September 1939 the German attack on Poland began. Confusion reigned for some hours as to whether this was a frontier skirmish, or whether war had begun in earnest. Soon such doubts were laid to rest. The long-awaited Danzig *Anschluss* was announced; then followed a formal German statement that hostilities had commenced.

That morning the British Cabinet met. They were willing enough, just so soon as reports were confirmed, to issue their own ultimatum to Germany, and to follow the almost certain rejection with a declaration of war. The Chiefs of Staff – so the Cabinet was told – considered that if action was to be taken, it should be taken without avoidable delay. The real problem, however, lay with the French, who expressed concern that Britain should not declare war before they did.[12] There was also some discussion about whether Germany should be given a specific time-limit within which to reply. The eventual conclusion was to the effect that everything should be co-ordinated with the French; but action should, if possible, be taken in time for a Parliamentary announcement in the early evening.

The French, however, were far from keen to declare war immediately, whether in company with the British or not. Arguments, though not very convincing ones, were advanced about the need to evacuate civilians from forward zones. There may have been another consideration disposing both countries to delay: the lingering hope that some miracle might stop the war without the need to abandon Poland. One of the many myths which had grown up in the past year or so was the idea that Hitler was really bluffing all the time. If he could be convinced that Britain and France were determined to go to war in Poland's defence – might he even now pull out of the conflict? In the previous day or two Mussolini had been making urgent efforts to engineer a conference; and those efforts might not be at an end.

When Parliament met on 1 September such matters could hardly be explained by the Government – least of all the difficulties they were having with the French. It is easy to understand the apprehensions which critics – whether on Government or Opposition benches – were coming to feel. Was not Britain under the most solemn obligation to go to war immediately in defence of Poland? MPs who had assembled expecting to be told that Britain and France were already at war, or at least that ultimata had been issued, felt grave doubts about the nerve, or even the moral integrity, of the government. Chamberlain's enemies began to speculate whether he was planning a sort of 'super-Munich' over Poland.

On the next day, 2 September, these apprehensions were still not resolved, and it became increasingly evident that powerful forces in France – not least the Foreign Minister – were doing all that lay in their power to avoid entering the war. At a critical moment in the afternoon, when a British Government spokesman was about to address the Commons, a frantic telephone call came from Italy to the effect that Mussolini was offering again to call a conference. It later became clear that the Duce had no means of getting Hitler out of Poland, and everybody agreed that a conference while the invasion was still in progress was out of the question; but it took some vital time to check the prospect of tangible results emanating from Mussolini's new intervention. The same evening Chamberlain himself faced a major revolt in the Commons. Again it was impossible to explain the true reason for delay; but by this time fears had become much sharper than twenty-four hours earlier. The Prime Minister faced criticism more furious than he had ever experienced in his career – and signs of revolt within his own government to boot. Visibly shaken, he summoned a midnight meeting of the Cabinet. Whatever the French might do, it was impossible to hold the Parliamentary position any longer. There was nothing for it but to issue an ultimatum early the following morning, with a short time limit. At 11.15 a.m. on Sunday 3 September 1939, Chamberlain broadcast to the nation that Britain was at war with Germany. Six hours later the French followed. As earnest of his determination to wage war to the best of his ability, Chamberlain reconstituted his government, incorporating erstwhile rebels from his own party. At the centre was a small Cabinet, in which Winston Churchill would serve as First Lord of the Admiralty. Anthony Eden was not included in the War Cabinet, but became Dominions Secretary.

It is one thing to declare war, another thing to make war. The French, vividly recalling the appalling casualty lists of the earlier First World War, had no intention of launching a serious offensive against German frontier fortifications, at least until a substantial proportion of the troops involved were British. The British Government, obsessed by innumerable diplomatic reports assuring them that the German people were as appalled by the prospect of war as they were themselves, solemnly resolved to bombard Germany with propaganda leaflets night by night, in the apparent hope that the country would rise in revolt against the author of its troubles. It is easy to appreciate how the behaviour of both western allies might have looked to the beleaguered Poles. Meanwhile the Germans cut through Poland at great speed: and appalling tales were told of the incompetence of the Polish Government and High Command, contrasting with the reckless courage of the Polish troops.

Then, on 17 September, the Russians invaded Poland from the east. By the end of the month resistance had practically ceased. On 28 September a new agreement between the two aggressors was announced. The territorial changes 'regularised' by the treaty divided Poland along the 'Ribbentrop–Molotov Line', which ran roughly between the ethnically Polish areas to the west, and the mixed population of what the Poles called the *kresy* to the east. The town of Vilna (Vilnius), full of remnants from the Polish army, was handed to Lithuania. In fact the new agreement had introduced considerable changes into the arrangements set out in the secret protocol to the Non-aggression Pact of the previous month. Lithuania, originally designed for the German sphere of influence, passed to the Russian sphere, save for a small area not far from Memel, which became the topic of considerable argument thereafter. In compensation, the German zone of Poland would extend considerably further to the east than had originally been proposed.[13] The Germans divided their own moiety of Poland into two parts: an extended 'Corridor', which was incorporated in the Reich, and the 'General Government' area, which became a sort of colony.

So what was to be done next? The eastern front was extinct; there was practically no fighting on the western front. The French plainly had no intention of attacking Germany in strength for a very long time to come, if ever. Months or years would elapse before Britain could raise armies and weapons on a scale which would substantially alter the balance of forces. Even if, by some miracle, Germany could be compelled to evacuate that part of Poland which she had seized, there was no way of evicting Russia from the remainder. Would it not be wise for the belligerents to admit that they could only hope to make an impression on each other after a very long time, and at the most enormous cost in blood and treasure; that the likely effect of continued conflict would be to exhaust them all to the profit of countries who had contrived to remain neutral?

On 6 October Hitler launched his 'peace offensive' against the western democracies, arguing in favour of an early settlement. Whether the Führer really expected an interested response is a matter of conjecture; he certainly did not receive one. No influential newspaper gave any encouragement. The only politician of note who evinced the slightest sympathy was Lloyd George. There were certainly many individuals – by no means all of them on the 'right' of politics – who thought otherwise. Groups were set up to promote pacifist opinions, and the Prime Minister received many letters calling for a negotiated peace.[14]

By far the most active pressure for a sympthetic interest in peace negotiations came from a quarter where it would have been unthinkable until two-thirds of the way through August: the Communist Party. In Britain there was but one Communist MP and a newspaper, the *Daily Worker*, whose circulation was small. Even among the communist leaders there were several who had obvious difficulty in adapting themselves to the changeabout demanded of them. The activities of communist (and, for that matter, of fascist) organisations were not seriously curtailed at this stage of the war. Both groups even advanced candidates at by-elections, and secured uniformly atrocious performances. The state of affairs in France, however, was radically different; for there the communists had great influence in trade unions. On 27 August, even before war began, the leading communist newspapers, *L'Humanité*' and *Ce Soir*, were closed down and communist meetings forbidden. On 26 September the Communist Party was proscribed, and an attempt to revive it under a new name was vigorously suppressed a few days later. Early in 1940 communist deputies were deprived of Parliamentary immunity, and many were soon tried and committed to prison.

There was a general atmosphere of anticlimax. Cities in Britain, France and Germany were not bombed. Casualty lists – by land at any rate – were slight. Physical privations of war, apart from the ubiquitous 'blackout', scarcely touched the ordinary citizen. This was the 'phoney war', or 'sitzkrieg'. If the opponents of war were making little headway, not much head of steam was being generated by people who sought to wage war with greater vigour. Until some major initiative was taken, the general climate of opinion was unlikely to change dramatically either way.

8   Annus Mirabilis

An international event usually admits of at least two radically different explanations, and Soviet behaviour in the last five months of 1939 is no exception to that rule. The country's defenders argued that Russia had been compelled, though the ineptitude – or worse – of the West, to come to terms with Nazi Germany in her own defence. Most people in the democracies during this period were disposed to regard the arrangements as a cynical agreement between dictators to partition inoffensive Poland, and thereafter to seize other advantages at the expense of neighbouring countries. A few months earlier some of Russia's angrier apologists had suggested that the West was hoping to embroil Germany and the Soviet Union in war, in the hope that both would be destroyed. Now that argument had been stood on its head. Was Russia's real object in current conditions to encourage Germany and the democracies to engage in a war of mutual destruction?

Almost as soon as the campaign in Poland ended, however, Russia began to move into the other spheres of influence allocated to her under the Ribbentrop-Molotov agreement, as modified at the end of September. In October 1939 the three Baltic States – Estonia, Latvia and Lithuania – were compelled to accept large Soviet garrisons. Then the heat was beamed on Finland, who was required not only to grant bases to Russia, but also to cede territory on the Karelian isthmus, south of Lake Ladoga: territory which contained Finland's great defensive fortifications, the 'Mannerheim Line'. In return, Finland was offered a large but less useful area of the Soviet Union further north. The Finns resisted the pressure, and on 30 November 1939 the Russians attacked.

The Soviet leaders, like so many other people at the time, were evidently bemused by their own propaganda, for on the second day of the fighting they set up a 'Finnish Democratic Republic' with a group of communist émigrés in nominal charge – in the apparent belief that great numbers of Finnish workers would welcome the new administration offered to them. Nothing of the kind happened. Not only was the new 'Republic' completely ineffectual in subverting the loyalty of the Finns, but the country turned at bay and defended herself with incredible skill and bravery against the invader.

The new contest posed grave problems in many places. The Germans gave somewhat lukewarm moral support to Russia, and the Chinese – who perceived Russia as a good hope for defence against Japan – were disposed to do the same. Nearly everybody else – including the Japanese and the Italians, as well as the western democracies – gave greater or lesser support to the Finns. That support, however, was moral rather than practical. Some volunteers, and some military assistance, did indeed find their way to Finland; but the scale was not sufficient to influence substantially the course of the conflict.

As the 'Winter War' between Russia and Finland proceeded, a new line of thought began to enter the strategic calculations of the western democracies. In the far north of Sweden there existed great deposits of iron ore, from which Germany was drawing her main supplies. The British Ministry of Economic Warfare, and some of the French, convinced themselves that if this source of supply could be denied to Germany, her war machine would be brought to a standstill in about a year.[1] The Russo-Finnish War appeared to offer an ingenious way of blocking the German supplies. Suppose the western democracies were to offer assistance to Finland on a substantial scale? Their only possible route into Finland lay across the North Sea into the Norwegian port of Narvik and thence through the north of Sweden. On their way, allied soldiers or 'volunteers' would necessarily come close to the orefields, which they would then be able to control without much difficulty. Thus the Russo-Finnish War entered the military calculations of the western democracies, not – as some people later came to suggest – in order to 'switch the war' from Germany to Russia, but in order to use the new contest as a pretext to pursue their objectives in the old one.

Not surprisingly, the three countries most directly affected all felt the gravest apprehensions about such ideas. Norway and Sweden were keenly aware that the passage of allied troops would increase the threat that Russia would eventually attack them as well as Finland; but they were also aware that it would invite attack from Germany. The putative beneficiaries had different reasons for concern. If Britain and France engaged troops on one side in Finland, then there was a large chance that Germany would soon become engaged on the other. The German army was a very different proposition from the largely demoralised Russians. Thus the Finns were unwilling to invite active military assistance from the democracies.

The argument ran on in a leisurely way for a number of weeks during early 1940; while the Scandinavians found themselves in the unnerving position that military invasion could easily occur from any of three directions: Russia, Germany or the western democracies. Then, rather abruptly, the Russo-Finnish war came to an end on 13 March 1940. The Finns could no doubt see that Russia would be in a much stronger position when spring came; while Russia could see that the cost of total victory was not worth paying. The Russians had to achieve the semblance of victory, and took from Finland the Karelian isthmus, plus bases elsewhere.

Astonishingly, the idea of somehow blocking German supplies of ore did not vanish from British and French strategic thinking once the nominal justification had disappeared. If the allies could not control the ore directly, perhaps they could stop it reaching Germany? Most of the mineral was carried by sea. In the summer it went to Lulea in Sweden, and thence down the Gulf of Bothnia. In winter that route was impossible because of ice, but there was an alternative sea route through Narvik, and thence down the Norwegian coast, which was warmed by the Gulf Stream.

At the beginning of April the allies decided to block the western route, by laying mines in Norwegian territorial waters. The timing could hardly have been worse. Spring was begining, and the Gulf of Bothnia would soon be used in preference. The British Government was well aware of such considerations, and would doubtless have abandoned the whole plan if they had been free to do so. What made them agree to this astonishing idea was a curious matter of international politics, bearing strongly on the precarious situation inside France. The British Government had for some time been keen on a plan known as Royal Marine Operation, by which mines would be floated down French tributaries of the Rhine, in order to block traffic on the German reaches of the river. The most intransigent French opponent of this plan was Daladier, until recently the Premier. In March, however, there had been a strangely ambiguous vote in the French Chamber, as a result of which Daladier had resigned and was succeeded by Paul Reynaud, whom the British much preferred. Daladier remained in the government, and the British were much afraid of a total rupture between the two men, which might cause the tables to be turned once more. If the British wanted Royal Marine Operation, and they aso wanted to keep Reynaud, concessions must be made to Daladier, who was known to favour the Norwegian strategy at issue.[2] As it happens, Royal Marine Operation was never set into effect; but that is another story, and peripheral to the present account.

In the early morning of 8 April 1940 the mining of Norwegian territorial waters began. Scandinavian reactions were immediate and furious; but next day these were stilled in an even deeper indignation. On April 9 the Germans occupied Denmark and the principal ports of Norway. The Danes offered no resistance to the invader. Norway had practically no army, but she dutifully declared war and accepted the assistance which Britain and France eagerly proffered.

The next episode in the Scandinavian saga was as involved as the earlier ones. The allies were in no position to attack German forces all along the coast of Norway, and it was important to decide where they could intervene effectively. Two points came under active discussion: Narvik in the north, Trondheim in the centre. From a strategic point of view, the argument lay strongly in favour of Narvik. The argument for Trondheim was political. It had once been the capital of Norway, and had strong emotional significance for both Norwegians and Swedes. Furthermore, the French – who had long been pressing for action at Narvik – now also decided that Trondheim was the more important place. Compromise was reached to the effect that operations were inaugurated in both areas. Interest, however, was concentrated on the operation near Trondheim. A projected pincer movement was ineffectual, and at the end of April the allies reached the reluctant conclusion that evacuation was necessary.

When the Norwegian campaign came to be debated in the House of Commons on 7–8 May 1940, the argument began as a more or less routine confrontation between an opposition wishing to make what points it could, but never anticipating victory, and a government defending a difficult case, whose debating position was rendered particularly onerous through considerations of inter-allied solidarity. As the argument proceeded, a great volume of anger was injected into the controversy. The target, however, was not Churchill, who had been more or less in charge of the operation, but Chamberlain, who made no claim to be a strategist but was disposed to defer to the judgements of those who were. The object became not so much to conduct an inquest on the Norwegian campaign in order to derive useful lessons for the future, but rather to turn out the Prime Minister. Churchill, much to his credit, refused to lend himself to such tactics, but spoke eloquently in the government's defence, making no effort to hide behind Chamberlain. The House divided. The government survived with what in all ordinary circumstances would be the very satisfactory majority of 81. The nominal majority was well over 200, and on this occasion about 40 government MPs had voted with the opposition, and about 60 abstained. Plainly, the government was losing the confidence of the House, and probably of the nation as well.

While people were still trying to sort out the political crisis at home, Germany invaded the Low Countries as a preliminary to her attack on France. Anxious discussions took place as to how the government might be reconstituted as a true coalition. It soon became plain that the Labour Party would not serve under Chamberlain, and in the circumstances he must necessarily resign. What was far more doubtful was who should be his successor. Many names were mentioned; but two stood out: Halifax and Churchill. In all probability either could have formed a viable Ministry. Halifax, however, was conscious of the difficulty which would be presented by a Premier in the Lords, and was not eager for the job. Churchill had no inhibitions on that matter, and on 10 May, by agreement with Chamberlain and Halifax, was recommended to the King.

Within a short time Churchill was able to announce his Ministry. At the centre was a War Cabinet of only five members, although several other Ministers were regularly invited to its deliberations. Most of the senior politicians from all parties were included in the government in some capacity or other. The strength of such a Ministry, however, was political rather than military or administrative. No one can have believed that the new members were likely to bring out important new ideas crucial for winning the war. What Churchill managed with considerable success, however, was to ensure that there was no available nucleus of revolt outside the government. In the next few months nearly all of the remaining figures of political significance were given some sort of job to do. The one exception was Lloyd George – already seventy-seven, but by no means senile – and on at least two ocassions Churchill made serious efforts to provide him with important public duties.

The first weeks of the new government coincided with an almost unrelieved series of military disasters. Within days the Germans had occupied most of the Low Countries, and were far into France. They broke through the French line near Sedan, and soon succeeded in driving a great wedge between the northern and southern allied armies in France. Most of the British were deployed to the north of the German thrust, along with the Belgians and some French. Efforts to restore contact across the 'bulge' failed. When the Belgians ceased fire on 28 May there was no doubt that the only alternative to precipitate evacuation was annihilation, and the Dunkirk operation proceeded. In a little over a week at the end of May and the beginning of June, around a quarter of a million British and a hundred thousand allied troops were brought across the Channel through an astonishing operation, for which great numbers of non-naval vessels were pressed into commission. The numbers of men brought home vastly exceeded the most sanguine expectations which were held at the beginning: but nearly all weapons and equipment were lost.

In the aftermath the French position became increasingly desperate. Efforts were still made to give support by British troops and by home-based aircraft; but, as France's condition deteriorated, so also did Britain's eagerness to commit herself fully to her ally begin to falter. The dilemma was acute. Whether France would succeed in repelling the invader might depend on the scale of British assistance, particularly in the air; yet if France was doomed to collapse despite this assistance, then not only would men and material have been cast away in vain, but the sacrifice made on France's behalf could prove of crucial importance in encompassing Britain's own ruin in the next phase of the war. Cabinet records suggest that the general disposition of Churchill's Government was to err on France's side rather than the other, even against British military advice.[3]

By the beginning of June it was becoming increasingly clear that Italy proposed soon to enter the war on Germany's side, and on 10 June Italy declared war on Britain and France. The French, in their extremity, were nevertheless able to fight effectively on the Italian front. By this time, however, the Battle of France was more or less lost. If fighting continued, nothing could prevent the whole country being overrun by the Germans. The French Government was in a condition of panic. They had been prepared to offer extensive bribes to keep Mussolini at bay just before Italy entered the war. Now Reynaud sent a frantic plea to President Roosevelt to bring America into the conflict: a plea which could not possibly be fulfilled, for constitutional as well as political reasons, whatever the President's personal disposition might be. The British Government, appalled at the looming prospect of French surrender, made the astonishing offer of duel citizenship for the two countries – even though some Ministers were very far from clear just what the proposal entailed.[4]

The real choice before the French Government was whether to withdraw to the French Empire in North Africa and continue the fight from there, or whether to seek an armistice. After long and anguished debate, they chose the latter. On 16 June Reynaud was replaced by the octogenarian Marshal Pétain. The following day the French ceased fire, and on 22 June armistice terms were formally accepted. The north and west of France were set under German military occupation; the remainder kept its own Government, now sited at Vichy. Even the occupied zone was in theory under Vichy civil administration. The French fleet was not to be forefeited, but must be disarmed at its various home ports, under enemy control. The French Empire was not disturbed.

Britain and Vichy France were in a most anomalous relationship, and this was of practical as well as theoretical importance. Just before the French armistice, the British Ambassador departed, and neither he nor a successor returned. The French Ambassador in London withdrew a few days later; yet there was no formal rupture of diplomatic relations. Consulates remained open, and there was contact between Ambassadors in foreign capitals, notably Madrid. During the concluding phases of the 'Battle of France', the recently-promoted General de Gaulle escaped to Britain, and under eager British sponsorship set up the 'Free French' organisation. Yet de Gaulle's position was also anomalous. No effort was made to constitute a French 'Government in Exile' whom Britain might eventually recognise – rather as she recognised 'Governments in Exile' from Poland or Norway, or even Czechoslovakia. Later, when the United States entered the war, the diplomatic position would become even more confused; but to that story it will be necessary to return.

The fate of the French fleet was of absolutely crucial importance for if it should ever pass more or less intact into enemy hands the whole balance at sea might tilt against Britain with decisive effect. The French Government gave repeated assurance to Britain that this would not happen. One need not impugn the sincerity of the men who profferd such assurances; but all of them were mortal, and nobody could be sure that successors would necessarily honour the undertakings. Nor, indeed, could anyone be certain that the enemy would not find ways of seizing that fleet if it suited his purpose. The possibility of France actually going to war against Britain could not be excluded. Thus in the immediate aftermath of the French armistice the British Government resolved to take what action it could to avert the risk of French vessels coming under enemy control. Ships in British ports were captured without difficulty; while at the other extreme some were so well defended in French ports that seizure was out of the question. At Oran in North Africa, and at Dakar in Senegal, however, the balance of forces was more even, and naval actions took place. Much damage was done and many French lives were lost. From a strategic point of view the actions proved on balance a considerable success; but a fearful price was paid in both human and moral terms.

The whole run of events from the initial German attack in the West on 10 May down to the Oran action just under two months later, started a long series of recriminations which continue to this day. The British, who had long pressed France to rearm more actively in the air, were appalled by the weakness revealed in the Battle of France; the French complained that Britain was pulling her punches in order to conserve aircraft for her own later requirements. The British were not convinced that the French army fought with all its might, or that strategic planning was sound; the French protested that the British had not exerted themselves to the full to restore contact across the 'bulge', and had evacuated a disproportionate number of their own soldiers from Dunkirk. Both countries recriminated against the Belgians; the French against the Belgian decision of 1936 in favour of neutrality rather than alliance with France, the British against King Leopold's decision to cease fire. The Belgian Government in exile protested against the King; the Belgian King in turn had cause of complaint against his Ministers. As the military situation deteriorated further, fresh points of mutual grievance arose. The British deplored the French decision to seek an armistice rather than retire to North Africa to continue the war from there. Finally, the deep tragedy of Oran set a river of blood between people who had been allies just a very few weeks earlier. International diplomacy often involves sentiment as well as interest; and there is much argument for the view that the rather uneasy relations between Britain and France since the war – in both dipolomatic and economic fields – have been to a considerable extent founded on the different viewpoints from which the two countries saw events in the early summer of 1940.

It is proper, and very pertinent to our study, to ask why Britain did not join with France in seeking an armistice in June 1940, or evince a modicum of interest in the so-called 'Peace Offensive' which Hitler launched in the following month. Within the Cabinet there had been signs of doubt and apprehension towards the end of May;[5] but after Dunkirk these doubts did not recur. Those politicians and organs of the Press who carried any weight appeared unanimous in the view that the war must continue. Communists and their associates campaigned for a 'people's peace' – a delightfully vague term, which appeared in practice to mean negotiations with Germany; but their influence was negligible.

A negotiated peace, one might argue, would have been disengagement rather than surrender. The Germans were known to be preparing for the invasion of Britain. Britain's Chiefs of Staff left Ministers in no doubt that there was a good chance of resisting such an invasion so long as the navy and air force were not gravely weakened, and supplies continued to pour in from the United States. It was impossible to tell whether these conditions would continue to be fulfilled; but even if Germany succeeded in her invasion the cost for the invader would be tremendous and the victory pyrrhic in character; for she would be in no position to seize any substantial part of the British Empire, while others would be the beneficiaries. Yet Britain had not entered the war in order to protect herself from invasion, or to defend her Empire: she had done so in order to prevent Germany dominating the Continent. In this she had failed; and nobody, not even Churchill at his most sanguine, could look forward to a date when British forces would land again on the Continent and, by their own unaided effort, defeat the Germans. The prospect of victory through the blockades had vanished when Germany secured control of all resources west of the Soviet Union. No other technique, like strategic bombing, was likely to give Britain the overwhelming superiority necessary to achieve the original objective. So if neither belligerent could defeat the other, save perhaps at unacceptable cost, why should the war continue?

This question must be examined at different levels. When Hitler was convinced that his 'Peace Offensive' would be unproductive, he sought to win control of the airspace over Britain as preliminary to invasion. In the 'Battle of Britain' which ensued, there were spectacular air combats over south-eastern England. People could readily identify the combatant planes, and it soon became apparent to most observers that the British were faring a good deal better than their opponents. It now appears that the margin was not as great as most Britons – including Churchill – originally believed; but it was ample, and the prospect of Germany winning command of the skies as a necessary prelude to invasion receded rapidly.

In this phase of the war there was a massive surge of determination among ordinary British citizens to fight the war at all costs: a feeling completely different from anything which had prevailed earlier. Censors of correspondence sent abroad recorded 'complete confidence in ultimate victory' as 'the keynote in almost all letters' during August.[6] A Public Opinion Poll taken at about this time recorded a massive 88 per cent approving Churchill as Prime Minister.[7] The term 'Dunkirk spirit', terribly hackneyed ever since, has been used to describe that frame of mind; but it is not really accurate. There certainly had been a surge of enthusiasm in the aftermath of Dunkirk – despite the Prime Minister's sage warning that wars are not won by evacuations – but feelings at the time of the Battle of Britain were much stronger: a universal confidence, which we may today describe as either sublime or foolhardy, that Britain was not as other nations.

Just before the autumn equinox German invasion plans were called off, and the main attention turned to night bombardment of cities, particularly London. In retrospect, this may be seen as an act of almost incredible folly. The Germans did not possess enough bombers to have any chance of shattering either military defences or civilian morale by such means; yet by that bombing campaign they infuriated the British people beyond measure. The 'Dunkirk spirit', perhaps even the 'Battle of Britain spirit', was by its nature evanescent; the anger generated by the 'Blitz' was much more durable, and would prove of great importance in conditioning public attitudes during the years which followed.

Psychological factors among ordinary Britons were of immense importance in conditioning rejection of any kind of 'Peace Offensive' from Germany in 1940, and today we may ponder whether Hitler's decisions first to prepare invasion and later to bombard British cities were of crucial importance for the whole future of the war. At the highest level, considerations of a different kind were at work. Whether by calculation or by wishful thinking, Churchill at any rate became convinced that the logic of events would eventually cause the United States and the Soviet Union to become engaged on Britain's side; and that the new 'Grand Alliance' would prove irresistible.

During the first year or so of war, the American Government was doing what lay in its power to assist Britain. In the latter part of 1939 President Roosevelt had prevailed upon Congress to amend the Neutrality Act in a manner very favourable to the allies. Arms might be sold to belligerents; but only on condition that they collected those arms in their own vessels. As the allies alone were able to send merchant ships across the Atlantic, this could only benefit one side. In the late summer of 1940, after somewhat confused debates in both Britain and America, arrangements were made to transfer a large number of over-age destroyers to Britain in return for the right to establish bases in British possessions in or near the Americas. Even the required reciprocity was, in the circumstances, at least as beneficial to Britain as to the United States. Public Opinion Polls in the United States consistently revealed almost unanimous sympathy for the British cause; but there were also vast majorities opposed to active belligerency. The real question was whether, sooner or later, the country would be pushed over the brink into war.

The Soviet Union by contrast, gave the allies no sympathy at all. Not long before the fall of France, rather strong pressure from several quarters led to the appointment of Sir Stafford Cripps as British Ambassador to Moscow. Cripps had a reputation as a Soviet sympathiser; but the messages he sent back soon after his arrival were bleak indeed. If the Russians had to choose between the two sides, wrote

Cripps on 2 August 1940, 'there is no doubt whatever they would choose Germany'.[8]

Although the Soviet Union was unwilling to provide any sort of assistance to the beleagured allies in the summer of 1940, their discomfiture provided convenient opportunity for action on Russia's own behalf. The concluding phase of the Battle of France, and its immediate aftermath, witnessed several important territorial advances. The three Baltic States, which had been compelled to accept Soviet garrisons in the previous year, were required to change their governments and then to hold 'elections', at which only communist-approved candidates were permitted to stand. The resulting 'Parliaments' then performed the function required of them: they proclaimed their countries Soviet Republics, and petitioned for admission to the Soviet Union: a favour which was granted shortly afterwards. Attention was also turned on Romania. The country had close links with France – cultural and emotional as well as diplomatic and economic. When France collapsed Romania was faced with peremptory Soviet demands to cede Bessarabia and the northern part of Bukovina: demands with which it was compelled to comply.

What was the rationale behind these territorial changes? The Baltic States and Bessarabia had been Russian for many years before 1917, although Bukovina had formed part of the Austro-Hungarian empire. The Baltic States and Bessarabia had been allocated to Soviet influence under the Ribbentrop-Molotov agreement, and German documents leave no doubt that Germany had 'disinterested' herself in those places, save for the fate of the *Volksdeutsch* who lived there.[9] What Russia had taken was largely what was allocated to her under the deal; but why did she bother? No doubt historical, ethnic and political arguments were advanced as appropriate, but it would be naïve in the extreme to suggest that such considerations were of importance in promoting the Soviet Union action; as it would also be naïve to suppose that any but small minorities in the territories affected welcomed the changes brought about. The move in the Baltic area may be seen as action to protect Leningrad from a German attack should co-operation break down at a later date. The moves against Romania are more ambiguous. There may have been an element of defence – protection against German designs towards the Ukraine – but they also may be seen as part of a design against the Balkans, aimed at the ancient objectives of control of the Bosporus and access to the Mediterranean. The German Government certainly believed that Russian ambitions in the Balkans were being actively encouraged by the British.[10] This view may well have been correct, for it fits in well with the Churchillian design to embroil Germany and Russia.

In some ways the most remarkable, and the most important, of the Soviet moves in the high summer of 1940 was also the most obscure and – from Russia's angle – the least significant. This was the acquisition of northern Bukovina. Unlike the other territories, it had never been Russian, but had belonged to the Austro-Hungarian Empire before 1918. What was more pertinent, it had not been allocated to the Soviet sphere of influence under the Ribbentrop-Molotov agreement. The Soviet claim apparently rested on the fact that Bukovina's population was largely Ukrainian; but it is clear that the Germans had been taken by surprise.[11]

Romanians probably feared that their whole country could soon suffer the fate of these lost provinces, and had little choice but to throw themselves on Germany's mercy, as the only possible protector. The country's problems were complicated by the fact that – on ethnic and historical grounds – Hungary lay claim to Transylvania, and Bulgaria to the Dobruja, (Dobrogea) at the mouth of the Danube. At the end of August these matters were resolved by the 'Vienna award'. Some, but not all, of the Hungarian and Bulgarian claims against Romania were sustained; in return, the country received German and Italian gurarantees, which were plainly directed against the Soviet Union as well as smaller neighbours. A further strain was set upon German-Soviet relations. Just as Germany had evinced a sense of mild aggrievement over Bukovina, so did the Soviet Union register gentle complaint that the Vienna award violated provisions of the 1939 Non-aggression Pact providing for 'consultation' in such circumstances.[12] Small clouds, still no larger than a man's hand, were beginning to drift across the sunny sky of German-Soviet relations.

Plans for an eventual German attack on the Soviet Union were conceived during the late summer of 1940; but the existence of such plans must not be taken to imply that a definite decision had yet been taken to set them in operation. The Germans had various diplomatic problems to resolve. The collapse of France, and the anticipated collapse of Britain as well, might pose difficult problems between various claimants. In September Japan decided that her current campaign against China required establishment of bases in French Indo-China. Vichy was compelled to comply; but such transactions might carry implications for others as well. After all, it was Germany, not Japan, who had defeated France. In the same month Italy invaded Egypt from her own colony of Libya. Egypt was already largely in

British military occupation, and after initial successes the attack was followed by reverses and a counter-invasion of Libya. Either advances or reverses experienced by one aggressor could well carry unpleasant implications for others. So towards the end of September, the 'Tripartite Pact' was drawn up between Germany, Italy and Japan, allocating spheres of influence. Later in the year minor European countries acceded as well; but the Soviet Union was omitted. To that point it will be necessary to return.

On 28 October 1940, a month after the Tripartite Pact, Italy invaded Greece from bases in Albania. British political and military experts were not at first very sanguine about the Greek's chances of success. Within a short time, however, the Greeks turned at bay, and before the year was out had cleared their own country, and were a long way into Albania. The allied successes against Italy in Albania and Libya were to prove far more than morale-boosters in a desperate phase of the war. They posed in different ways a profound threat to the whole grand strategy of Germany.

The North African problem bore closely on the exceedingly complex politics of Vichy France. A very large majority of the National Assembly, and probably of the French people as well, gave clear support to Pétain; but among his associates very disparate currents of opinion could be discerned. Some had sadly accepted defeat in June 1940, but continued to wish – if scarcely to hope – for a British victory. Others decided that France's interests – or at all events their own – lay in full-scale co-operation with Germany, and eventually 'switching the war', so that France could actually fight against her former ally. Vichy attitudes on such matters were bound to be influenced by the general course of military events.

An important practical example of the likely Vichy dilemma soon came to hand. As matters were developing towards the end of 1940 there was a serious possibility that the Italians would be driven from Libya, and British forces would make contact with the French in their North African possessions. The French commander in North Africa was General Weygand, who, of all the leading Vichyites, was most sympathetic to the allied cause. This opened up the prospect that the whole North African littoral might go over to the allies; which might profoundly affect the future attitude of the French fleet, the French Empire – and, indeed, of France itself.

The British had been seriously deliberating the idea of putting enough forces into North Africa to drive out the Italians. Two considerations held them back: the continuing risk of invasion at home, and the conflicting demands of support for Greece. In another sense, however, Italian involvement in the Balkans was to prove of even more vital importance to the whole future of the war, and much which would follow thereafter. The Germans must have regarded with foreboding the prospect that the allies might establish a permanent foothold in south-eastern Europe, insulated from their own much stronger forces by a band of neutrals. As Italy was incapable of defeating the Greeks, much less the British, it became vital that Germany should intervene. With Romania already a client, the most natural route was through Bulgaria.

This linked closely with the existing Tripartite pact, and its potential future developments. In November conversations took place between Hitler and Molotov. The Führer made no secret that he 'did not like Italy's war against Greece, as it diverted forces to the periphery instead of concentrating them against England'.[13] He contended that Germany, Italy, France, Japan and the Soviet Union shared a common interest 'to stop all controversies among themselves and concern themselves exclusively with apportioning the British Empire'. Molotov evinced considerable sympathy with the idea, expressing apprehensions over Britain's new foothold in Greece which set her near the Bosporus – 'England's historic gateway for attack on the Soviet Union' as he called it. Russia therefore sought to give 'guarantees' to Bulgaria, similar to those which Germany had already granted to Romania.

Here was the rub; for this cut across Germany's own interest in Bulgaria, as Italy's position in the Balkans became increasingly desperate. In the first month of 1941 both parties began to perceive the seriousness of this disagreement. The Soviet Union protested that German troops in Bulgaria 'would be regarded as a violation of Soviet security interests'; the Germans retorted that they proposed nevertheless to pass through Bulgaria in order to expel the British.[14]

Thus by the turn of her year of victories, Germany was already finding herself at loggerheads with both of her great European associates. Many observers have been so preoccupied with 'ideological' issues that they have missed the striking similarities between the positions of Italy and the Soviet Union over a very long period. When Hitler took office in 1933 both countries were in an ambivalent position. Each had serious complaints over the post-1918 settlement. Russia had lost much; Italy had not gained all that was required by the 'sacro egoismo' for which she had entered the war. Yet each had much to fear from German disturbance of that settlement. Italy feared designs against Austria and German ambitions towards the Adriatic; Russia feared Hitler's dreams of eastern *Lebensraum*. In both countries fear was at first the stronger sentiment. Each turned to Britain and France as countries who shared the interest of containing Germany. Each found the western democracies unwilling to make concessions demanded of them, and thereafter turned towards Germany. This implied more than just switching sides; it also implied a fundamental change of orientation from the preservation to the destruction of the status quo. Yet the paths of aggression of Italy and the Soviet Union were both in a striking way different from that of Germany. The Germans, vanquished in 1918, had nothing to lose but everything to gain. The Italians and the Russians were moved by fear as well as avarice. The territorial gains which they made when opportunity presented itself were partly, no doubt, the satisfaction of old ambitions; but each was to a large degree still fearful of Germany, and anxious to protect herself by establishing a position of strength. Both countries, in so doing, ran counter to German wishes in the closing months of 1940 – but in ways which would lead to radically different German responses. In North Africa and the southern Balkans, Germany was as reluctant to accept Italy's *hereditas damnosa* as the Italians were to admit their own total failure; in the eastern Balkans Germany and the Soviet Union were contending over something which both sought to acquire. Hitler was already deciding that a fundamental clash of interests existed, which must eventually be resolved by force of arms.

9 Grand Alliance

Churchill's view that Germany could be defeated in the end turned on the premise that the United States and the Soviet Union would both be brought into the war on Britain's side. Although there were faint Russo-German rumblings over Romania in the summer of 1940, and rather more serious contentions over Bulgaria during the ensuing winter, it was still very far from certain that either party would regard such disputes as of vital importance, or as incapable of resolution. In January 1941 a Russo-German Trade Agreement was concluded, which suggests that in economic fields at any rate co-operaton between the two countries was still close. In the spring of that year, however, points of difference became increasingly noticeable.

Once the Germans had secured right of passage through Bulgaria, massive pressure was set upon Greece to submit to humiliating terms from the Axis countries. There were considerable doubts in Britain as to the attitude which the Greeks should be advised to adopt. Eden, who had recently returned to his old post of Foreign Secretary, wished them to resist, and after some initial hesitation the military authorities agreed with him. Churchill, with a deeper sense of responsibility, perceived the dangers this would bring to the unfortunate Greeks, and was much more hesitant.[1] The final decision was left to the Greeks themselves, and they decided to resist.

Germany also mounted pressure on Yugoslavia. Again Eden did what lay in his power to encourage resistance, with little reference to the likely fate of the victim. The Yugoslav Government was not convinced by these blandishments, and in late March senior Ministers departed from Belgrade with the object of coming to terms with the Germans. A *coup d'état* with strong British encouragement was staged in their absence, and a new government set up which favoured resistance.

What was particularly remarkable during these developments was the Soviet attitude. The Moscow Press openly condemned the presence of German troops in Bulgaria and, when the Germans appeared poised to attack Yugoslavia, took the occasion to conclude a pact of friendship and non-aggression with that country. Such unambiguous gestures of

114

disapproval did not avail, and on 6 April the Germans attacked both Greece and Yugoslavia. By the end of the month there was little serious resistance remaining on the mainland of either country, save for guerilla fighting by General Mihajlović's Ćetniks in the remoter areas of Yugoslavia.

Just a few days before the attack on Greece and Yugoslavia Churchill secured information which strongly suggested that German strategic dispositions were related to a plan for attacking the Soviet Union; but that these plans had been set in temporary abeyance while the Germans prepared to attack in the Balkans. The Prime Minister tried to get a message through to Stalin to that effect; but Cripps, who was charged to deliver it, argued over his instructions, and Eden was disposed to support him. A good deal of valuable time was lost before Churchill firmly overruled the objections; and there remain considerable doubts whether the message reached its intended destination until long after its point had been lost.[2] If Stalin received the message at all, he probably saw it as a British plot to embroil him with Germany, and ignored it.

While these developments were occurring in the Balkans, no less important events elsewhere were leading – although much more indirectly and slowly – towards the eventual involvement of the United States. In March 1941 Foreign Minister Matsuoka of Japan journeyed by rail through the Soviet Union, en route for Germany. The possibility of a Russo-Japanese Treaty was considered, but the Russians made demands which the Japanese found unacceptable. On Matsuoka's return in the following month the Russians dropped their original requirements, and a Non-aggression Pact was quickly negotiated. The reason for the change in Soviet attitudes is not clear, and admitted of several possible interpretations. Perhaps – although this was by no means certain – the Russians had decided, between the dates of Matsuoka's two visits, that a German attack was likely in the near future, and they were anxious to secure their eastern provinces by buying off Japan. Whatever may be the explanation, this Russo-Japanese accommodation would soon prove of vast direct importance to the countries immediately concerned, and of great indirect importance to everybody else.

Events on the other side of the world were leading inexorably towards the fulfilment of Churchill's anticipations about the United States. German naval activity, particularly by submarines, threatened Britain at her most vulnerable spot in the 'Battle of the Atlantic'; and that maritime contest was gradually bringing the United States closer and closer towards full participation. Roosevelt managed to convince most of his compatriots that the fate of the United States was intimately bound up with an eventual allied victory. There was no way yet of overcoming the political and constitutional difficulties in the way of an American declaration of war – indeed, there is much to be said for the view that such a declaration, even if possible, would have been counter-productive at that stage of the conflict. What the United States could do, however, was to render material assistance. On 11 March the President signed the Lend-Lease Bill, which made enormous quantities of American resources available to the Allies: a matter whose eventual implications it will later be necessary to examine more closely. Suffice for the moment to say that Lend-Lease would provide the financial underpinning for Britain, and to a large extent for the Soviet Union as well, throughout the remainder of the war. The United States had moved a long way from strict neutrality in either spirit or action.

At the beginning of June the British Foreign Office received further indications of an impending German attack on the Soviet Union, and attempted without success to warn the Russians.[3] Then, in the early morning of 22 June 1941, the attack came. Yet it was not until 3 July, nine days after the invasion began, that Stalin told his own people what part they were expected to play. Diplomats in Moscow, who had been expecting the attack, thought that the Germans would be in Moscow, Leningrad and Kiev within a month.[4] Cripps did not appear to have dissented from the views of his colleagues.

The British Cabinet had prepared its own response some time before the invasion. On the first evening Churchill broadcast his promise that 'we shall give whatever help we can to Russia and to the Russian people'. A very few weeks later an agreement was concluded for mutual assistance between Britain and Russia. Roosevelt made it clear that the United States were also prepared to extend what help they could to the Soviet Union.

There was some diplomatic argument as to whether Britain and the Soviet Union were technically 'allies' at this point, although the argument soon ceased. There was no doubt that they were fighting the same enemy, and relations between them were moving in the direction of full alliance; while the United States made no secret of its support for their cause. The position of several other countries, however, was a good deal more problematical, and would prove of great importance later on. The Polish Government, currently in exile in London, was legally at war with both Germany and the Soviet Union. Yet they knew that their own citizens in the Soviet Union were virtually hostages; and their country's prospects in the future would be likely to depend largely on Russian sympathy. The Russians for their part needed active support from the many Poles, prisoners-of-war and others, who were still inside the Soviet Union, and who might be mobilised against the common enemy. The Russians were well aware that there were many people of influence in others parts of the world – notably the millions of Poles in the United States and the far greater numbers of Catholics in Europe – who had much sympathy for Poland, but very little for Russia. Yet the two countries were still in deep disagreement over many matters, not least whether what had been eastern Poland before 1939 should be Polish or Soviet after the war. The overriding concern of the British Government in the matter was to secure at least a façade of agreement between Russians and Poles, on whatever terms they might both accept. After much argument, and strong British pressure on the Poles, a treaty was concluded at the end of July, which carefully avoided any attempt to define the eastern frontier of Poland. All Polish prisoners within the Soviet Union were to be released. A Polish army was to be recruited within the Soviet Union, under its own officers, but subject to operational control of the Red Army. There was considerable criticism of the arrangement among Poles in Britain; but Poles in the Soviet Union, who in many cases had been in great fear of their lives at Russia's hands, rejoiced in the arrangement.

No less ambivalent was the position of Japan. Japanese fear and hostility towards Russia, whether Tsarist or Bolshevik, was of very long standing. Yet, about ten weeks before the German attack, Japan and Russia had concluded their Non-aggression Pact. Which would prevail: the new treaty, or the old enmity, reinforced by the Tripartite Pact? Matsuoka's agreement had been by no means universally welcomed in Japan, and the German attack on the Soviet Union led to further recriminations against him. A few days later, however, the Imperial Council decided firmly against intervention in the new conflict. We may conjecture what part was played by interest and what part by principle in that decision. It was certainly of massive, perhaps supreme, importance; for the Soviet Union could well have collapsed under a double attack; while the alternative course of action on which the Japanese soon resolved would prove of baleful significance to Britain and the United States.

Many soldiers, as well as diplomats, in the West had anticipated an early Russian collapse, and for some time the issue was in considerable doubt. A month after the invasion began the Germans were making rapid advances – but the Red Army was still fighting. As Churchill observed, what mattered from a military point of view was not so much where the Russian front happened to lie, but that the front was still in existence.[5]

A very wide range of problems was now posed for Britain and the United States. From a military point of view there were very difficult questions of priority. The Russians began, as early as mid-July 1941, to ask for a British attack in western Europe. Churchill remitted the matter to the Chiefs of Staff, but was compelled to report that the only result would be a 'bloody repulse', which would benefit nobody but the enemy.[6]

At this stage the idea of a 'Second Front' was very different from the massive invasion which people began to urge in 1942, and which was eventually launched in 1944. It was conceived essentially as a diversionary action to take some heat off the Russians, not as a full-scale campaign designed to crush Germany between the weight of eastern and western advances. Yet even a Second Front on that scale was out of the question until there had been a massive military build-up. The one direction in which Britain and the United States could render more or less immediate help to the Soviet Union was in the matter of supply. Yet this provided a deep dilemma for all three countries. If the Anglo-Saxon countries were to do what lay in their power to supply Russia, this could only be achieved at the price of reducing supplies to Britain – thereby delaying the eventual 'Second Front' and also abandoning the prospect of clearing the Germans from North Africa and other places in the Mediterranean for a long time. By this time Britain's military position was further weakened by the interruption of supplies through submarine activity in the North Atlantic.

No less important were new developments in the Far East. The treaty concluded by the Soviet Union with Japan in April 1941 had very much the same effect as the treaty concluded with Germany in August 1939: it deflected energies of the aggressor towards others. In this case Japan began to look southwards to the British, Dutch, French and American possessions in the Pacific.

To a very large extent all this was linked to the existing struggle against China. In order to exploit her military advantage Japan needed to block supply routes into China from the south. In 1940 the two likeliest routes had been closed. Vichy had granted bases in Indo-China, while in July 1940 Britain conceded to pressure from Japan – and perhaps from Australia as well – to close the 'Burma Road' out of her own colony. The United States, however, was deeply committed to China, and American influence evidently played a large part in constraining the British to re-open the Burma Road three months later.

In the closing months of 1940, and the early part of 1941, the United

States gradually stepped up embargoes on Japanese trade, with the object of compelling Japan to relax her grip on China. This pressure led to a protracted set of negotiations which commenced in Washington in the spring of 1941, and continued right up to an abrupt and dramatic termination in December. When the Japanese decided not to take advantage of Germany's attack on the Soviet Union in order to intervene for their own benefit, they rapidly turned in another direction. On 25 July they compelled the French to grant further bases in Indo-China. These new bases, however, were located in the south, and had no visible connection with the situation in China. They were immediately seen as a threat to the European and American possessions. To this the Americans and British retorted by freezing all Japanese assets. As the British Ambassador in Tokyo commented later, 'war could only be a question of time unless some method could be devised for bringing about a *détente*'.[7]

In August 1941 President Roosevelt and Winston Churchill met off Placentia Bay in Newfoundland. The atmosphere was exceedingly amicable, and much was decided. The principle of Anglo-American assistance to the Soviet Union was agreed. By implication rather than express agreement, the United States came to take the lead in relation to Japan, the British in relation to Germany. The two leaders wanted a month more of discussions with the Japanese – not because they expected any agreement to emerge, but in order to prepare defences.[8] Later they sought to extend the period to three months. They got what they wanted, and a little more; but the eventual reckoning would prove terrible. They also considered aspects of the post-war world which they sought to achieve, and laid this down in what later became known as the Atlantic Charter. The initiative came from Roosevelt, who doubtless had very much in mind the need to assure domestic opinion that the allied cause was worth supporting; but Churchill was obviously in total agreement with the spirit of its contents – far more so, one may add, than the Protectionists among his own Cabinet colleagues, who viewed some of the provisions with consternation.[9] The signatories desired 'no territorial changes that do not accord with the freely expressed wishes of the people concerned'; they affirmed the 'right of all peoples to choose the form of government under which they will live', and promised to endeavour 'to further enjoyment by all states . . . of access on equal terms to the trade and . . . raw materials of the world'. In the following month all the allies gave formal assent to the principles of the Charter; but with very obvious mental reservations on the part of more than one of them.

In the immediate aftermath of the 'Atlantic Charter' meeting, events began to move swiftly in many directions. The Soviet Union had indeed withstood the first impact a good deal better than many observers had anticipated; but early in September Churchill and Eden had a distressing interview with the Soviet Ambassador Maisky, and the Prime Minister hinted strongly to the Cabinet that the possibility of Russia making a separate peace could not be excluded.[10] If that happened, then the prospect of ever achieving total defeat of Germany was small.

The Soviet Union was beginning to advance demands of a different kind. Today we may reflect that these proposals would prove of crucial significance as the 'first step that matters' in developments affecting relations between the democracies and the Soviet Union for many years to come; but at the time there was little to suggest that this would prove the case. Would Britain declare war on Germany's associates in her conflict against the Soviet Union – Romania, Hungary and Finland? From a military point of view this would make little or no difference; in most respects the diplomatic effect would be adverse. The only merit, apparently, was that it would please the Soviet Union.[11]

There was a deep rift in Cabinet. Eden and the Minister of Supply, Lord Beaverbrook, argued for acceding to the Soviet request, while Churchill and the Labour Party Ministers argued against. The views of the Dominions were sought; they were split on the matter. The United States refused to advise. Churchill interceded with Stalin; but the Prime Minister's message was somehow leaked to the Press, and there was a furious exchange between the two leaders. Secret contact was made with Marshal Mannerheim of Finland, to persuade him to halt his troops on the old frontier. All in vain. With the gloomy warning that 'An historic mistake is going to be committed all right. I take full responsibility for it', Churchill eventually capitulated, and war was declared.[12] Stalin had won an important diplomatic victory. If one important concession could be made, not in order to prosecute the war successfully, but in order to please Russia – then why not others? To that point it will be necessary to return repeatedly.

War had just been declared on the three countries, when far more spectacular events occurred. Relations between the western democracies and Japan continued to deteriorate; but there was also a large element of real confusion. The Japanese Government was very far from monolithic, and there were complex power struggles. Both the British and the American Ambassadors at Tokyo seem to have felt that they were being kept largely in the dark about the activities of their own governments. After Japanese assets were frozen in July 1941 it became increasingly clear that the alternative to some dramatic new agreement was war. On special instructions from the Emperor the Japanese sought a 'summit' meeting with Roosevelt, and for a moment the President was disposed to agree; but he was later dissuaded. In October a new Government took office in Japan, determined to bring matters to a head one way or the other. A particularly experienced Japanese diplomat was despatched to Washington, to assist in the conversations with the United States. Late in November, the final Japanese proposals towards a peaceful solution were submitted. America offered counter-proposals, but Japan regarded these as a final rebuff. On 7 December came the Japanese attck on Pearl Harbor, with the destruction of a large part of the American Pacific Fleet.[13] Immediately afterwards Japan declared war on Britain and the United States. A very few days later, the principal British vessels in the area – the *Prince of Wales* and the *Repulse* – were sunk. By these actions the whole balance of naval forces in the Far East was tilted decisively in Japan's favour.

For a short time, there was prospect that two great wars would be waged simultaneously, with Britain as the one major connecting link. This possibility was removed on 11 December when Germany declared war on the United States. One may speculate to what extent that apparently gratuitous gesture altered the whole character and prospect of both conflicts; for it removed whatever temptation there may have been for the United States to concentrate on the Pacific at the expense of the Atlantic and Europe.

While these tremendous events were taking place, the finishing touches were being put on arrangements for two diplomatic missions which would also have immense bearing on the future of the war – and, indeed, on events long afterwards. The Prime Minister took the cue of the Japanese aggression to depart for the United States, in order that strategy might be co-ordinated with the new allies. The Foreign Secretary, in pursuit of arrangements prepared some time beforehand, left for Moscow.

Churchill was accompanied by Lord Beaverbrook and a number of Service officials. From the Prime Minister's point of view, the visit was a great success. Most important of all, it was agreed (or rather confirmed) that over-all priority should be given to the war against Germany rather than to the war against Japan. General strategy and operational control were co-ordinated. The prevailing atmosphere was of deep comradeship between countries facing a common enemy.

In all probability everybody who knew of the preparations for Eden's visit to Moscow had expected the same sort of atmosphere to prevail there as well. The decision to declare war on Finland, Romania and

Hungary appears to have been prompted largely by that anticipation and desire. Everything, however, went badly awry. Stalin's pre-occupation seemed not to be with the war, but with the Soviet Union's international position thereafter. At his first full meeting with Eden, Stalin unfolded his plan. Let Britain and Russia sign two treaties, each more or less innocuous in appearance, pledging co-operation in war and in the aftermath. Stalin proposed, however, that a secret protocol should be appended to the treaties. Britain would acknowledge Russia's acquisitions of 1939 and 1940: the three Baltic States, and her gains at the expense of Poland, Finland and Romania. The Soviet Union would support aspirations which Britain might have for bases in France, Belgium, Denmark and Norway. A number of other territorial proposals would be agreed, affecting the future limits of Italy, Bulgaria, Turkey, Czechoslovakia and others.[14]

Nobody in the British Cabinet appears to have anticipated anything remotely like these suggestions – and, of course, Eden would have been in no position to sign such a document, even if he had wished to do so. The Prime Minister, the Cabinet and the Dominions had a right to be consulted; and the United States as well. This had to be explained to Stalin, who may or may not have believed Eden's protestations. A day or so later Stalin brought forth reduced proposals for the Secret Protocol. What particularly interested the Soviet Union – so it was explained – was her own position. She required the frontiers she had had at the moment of the German attack. The furthest Stalin was prepared to go was that he was prepared to write a letter indicating that it did not entail agreement on the Polish frontiers. Again Eden had no authority to agree; but he made a very important concession. He promised that on return he would attempt to secure a favourable answer for Stalin.

Nevertheless the atmosphere cooled considerably. Stalin made it plain that Russia would not sign the treaties without the protocol. The Soviet Union would not join in the war against Japan for the time being at least. Indeed, she had few reserves left with which to do so, however matters had fared with Eden. The possibility of a joint Soviet-British attack in the vicinity of northern Finland had been broached by the Russians themselves earlier in the discussions. Now there was studied silence on the matter. Eden departed from Moscow, visibly under a cloud.

Churchill had staked everything in 1940 on the view that it would be possible to establish a 'Grand Alliance' between Britain, the United States and the Soviet Union. If that gamble had not come off, the price which Britain would have been compelled to pay would have been unspeakable. Now that it had apparently succeeded, there was still no certainty that the three allies would hold together, or that they would achieve final victory: indeed, for a long time their prospects of so doing appeared poor. Yet the meeting which Eden had with Stalin just a fortnight after the 'Grand Alliance' came into being suddenly raised problems of a different kind. Stalin evidently saw international questions not in the idealistic vision of the Atlantic Charter but in a light which would have been wholly familiar to Catherine the Great or to other old-time practitioners of 'power politics' of the very worst kind. If the allies did win through to total victory in the end, then part of the price of that victory would assuredly be some massive concessions to international ideas of that kind, and a great many people would be left at the mercy of the Soviet dictator. To say such things today is not to show wisdom after the event; it was already plain enough from what Stalin had told Eden. Yet had not Churchill also won the eager support of the United States, largely through his personal rapport with the President? The American alliance would also carry a heavy price, though a price of a very different nature.

10 Strains of Empire

Down to the last month of 1941 the Second World War had been essentially a European conflict. Other parts of the world – the overseas British Commonwealth and the United States – had given massive support to the allied cause, and without that support eventual victory would have been impossible. On the other side of the medal Britain had found it necessary to mobilise many of her scarce resources in defence of places in Africa which came under German or Italian threat. Yet Europe was still the centre of the war, in the sense that action outside Europe, and action by non-European countries, was designed essentially to produce a European result. In that sense, the Second World War was for the first two years similar in character to the First World War, or even to the Napoleonic War.

When Japan entered the war in December 1941 the whole nature of the war changed, and the British Empire – the most tangible expression of Britain's world power – came under imminent and vital threat. This threat was at first seen in simple terms: the Japanese were attacking British possessions. In truth, the threat was much deeper and more fundamental than that, and the process of Imperial disintegration which Japan played such a large part in bringing about was to continue long after Japan had gone down in utter defeat. To understand the nature of that threat it is necessary to reflect on developments which had been taking place within the Empire over a very long period.

Before 1914 many parts of the British Empire enjoyed more or less complete internal self-government. When war broke out, however, constitutional theory prescribed 'unity of the Crown' – the King could not simultaneously be at war in respect of some of his possessions and at peace in respect of others . . . For practical purposes, the Empire functioned as a unity. In some places, notably South Africa and Ireland, there were serious wartime disturbances; but in general the arrangements functioned remarkably smoothly.

Even in those days it was plain that the future of India was to a very large extent the key to the whole future of the British Empire. Most of India was ultimately controlled by Britain, although day-to-day administration was in the hands of a specifically Indian Government. Preponderent influence, however, lay with people of British origin. Large tracts of India fell within 'Native States' under the authority of autonomous princes with whom the British had treaties. Throughout all India the problems of acute poverty and ignorance were immense. As late as 1941 only 12 per cent of Indians over the age of five were literate. A further problem, which was to become increasingly important as time went on, was the division of Indians into Hindus and Moslems, as well as smaller communities of Christians and Sikhs.

It had long been widely acknowledged that Indians – or at least educated Indians – were entitled to join to a greater extent in the administration of their own country. There had been repeated attempts at the highest levels of government to work towards true racial equality. Few people, if any, contended that India was ready for 'democracy' in the British sense of the term, but it was generally felt that no Indian should be disentitled by reason of his ethnic origin from rising to the highest levels of government within his country. Indeed, this notional equality cut two ways, and there had been one or two cases of Indians being elected to the British Parliament. How far the theory conformed with practice is another matter; and Viceroys with outlooks as different as Lord Ripon and Lord Curzon found their endeavours in that direction more or less frustrated by bitter resistance from Europeans living in the sub-continent. In 1917 the new Secretary of State for India, Edwin Montagu, made a public announcement deeply critical of the 'indefensible' and 'antediluvian' character of the Indian Government. He came down strongly in favour of future developments towards responsible government for India, which should nevertheless remain an integral part of the British Empire. As an important step in that direction the Government of India Act of 1919 set up a bicameral legislature, most of whose members were elected. The franchise was exceedingly limited, and the authority of the legislature very incomplete; yet the Act provided a foundation upon which development in a democratic direction, within the fabric of the British Empire, might proceed in the future. Yet the year which witnessed this piece of enlightened statesmanship also saw the Amritsar massacre, where troops fired into a vast unarmed crowd, killing 400 and injuring 1200 more. The officer responsible was removed; but admirers contrived an elaborate presentation on his return to Britain. Truly, British rule in India wore two very different faces.

Although the Dominions were for most practical purposes sovereign and independent countries, that independence was established by custom rather than by formal definition, and in the 1920s there was considerable pressure in some places for an unambiguous statement of Dominion rights. South Africa, where politics were largely related to a dichotomy between British and Boers, was a front runner here. The Boers were much the more anxious to assert national independence, and in 1926 a predominantly Boer Government was in office. The Prime Minister, General James Hertzog, called for a formal proclamation of equality between the Dominions and the United Kingdom. Later in the year, an Imperial Conference was held in London. Conceding the wishes of South Africa – eagerly seconded by the Irish Free State – Earl Balfour, sometime Prime Minister, attempted a definition of imperial relationships. Britain and the Dominions, Balfour proclaimed:

> are autonomous Communities within the British Empire, equal in status, in no way subordinate one to another in any respect of their domestic or external affairs, though united by a common allegiance to the crown, and freely associated as members of the British Commonwealth of Nations.

That definition won general approval from the Imperial Conference, and five years later was enshrined in the Statute of Westminster passed by the British Parliament. The Statute went further than Balfour's statement, asserting that Britain would not legislate for a Dominion unless requested by the Government of that Dominion to do so. Furthermore, so the Statute declared, any Dominion which so desired was at liberty to withdraw from the Commonwealth.

For the time being, nobody made any attempt to take advantage of that right of secession. Membership of the Commonwealth conferred practical advantages. The British navy provided defence for all; while people and goods could pass with relative ease from one part of the Empire to another. But there were also powerful ties of sentiment, and it would be quite wrong to disparage their importance. Most British families had relatives and friends in the Dominions, and those recent émigrés continued to speak and think of Britain as the 'mother country'. King George V, a man with a punctilious sense of duty, was much more than a formal and legal symbol of unity.

In addition to India and the Dominions, there were, of course, the Colonies and the new Mandated Territories, over which Britain exerted direct rule, and a number of Protectorates which were under strong British influence. Many people looked forward to the day when all those lands, too, should be fully self-governing within the Empire or

Commonwealth. A few, such as Southern Rhodesia (Zimbabwe) seemed already well advanced on that road. In many of the others this development seemed to belong to a date in the very remote future. How far people anticipated the establishment of full racial equality was another matter; and different parts of the Commonwealth were developing in very different directions.

Within a few months of passage of the Statute of Westminster, the Commonwealth came to experience strains of a new kind. Until 1932 Britain was a Free Trade country – although from 1915 onwards exceptions and qualifications to her Free Trade position had begun to appear – the McKenna Duties, the Key Industries Duties, and so on. But these had made little difference to imperial trade. Fiscal policies of the Dominions and India – often strongly protectionist and directed against Britain as well as foreign countries – were more serious barriers in that respect. The Abnormal Importations Act passed by Britain in November 1931 interfered with imperial as well as foreign trade, but was acknowledged to be temporary only. The Import Duties Act which passed through the British Parliament in the early part of 1932 posed, by implication, a much more general threat to imperial trade. The *ad valorem* tariff of 10 per cent was subject to a number of exceptions, notably on goods from the Dominions, but there was no guarantee that these exceptions would be permanent, particularly if the Dominions and India maintained discriminatory policies against British goods. There was a very considerable risk that goodwill between the Commonwealth countries would soon be destroyed in the atmosphere of trade war.

The Imperial Economic Conference held at Ottawa during the late summer of 1932 sought an answer to this problem. J. H. Thomas, the Dominions Secretary, declared that the object of the Conference was to break down barriers between different parts of the Commonwealth, and in a sense that was true. The arrangements which emerged from Ottawa, however, were by no means entirely in the direction of trade liberalisation. Broadly, the overseas Commonwealth countries agreed to give British goods preferential entry to their markets, and Britain undertook reciprocity. The nature of these agreements, however, required Britain to retain, or even to impose, tariffs against goods from non-imperial sources. It was this element of the Ottawa agreements which proved the cause, or at least the occasion, for the departure of the Free Trade Ministers (the Liberals, and Viscount Snowden) from the National Government, at the end of September 1932.

Nor did Ottawa resolve all the trade disputes within the Commonwealth. By a remarkable chance the intense debates which occurred in Britain, first over Protection and then over the Ottawa agreements, coincided closely with important developments in Ireland, which were to have a direct effect on Anglo-Irish relations and a considerable indirect effect on the stability of the Commonwealth as a whole. After a long and bloody stuggle, southern Ireland broke from the United Kingdom in 1922. A treaty was concluded between the Irish and British Governments under which the country was constituted the Irish Free State. The Free State was to have internal self-government, but the British retained certain entrenched rights, notably in matters of defence. Some Irishmen accepted this compromise more or less willingly; others made no secret of their continuing resentment. The Irish Free State was acknowledged as a Dominion by the Statute of Westminster.

For a decade after the 1922 settlement, the government of the Irish Free State had been disposed to co-operate with Britain in the spirit of the treaty concluded between them. Under impact of the world depression the Free State Government applied economic policies which incurred considerable domestic unpopularity, and it appears that these policies rather than any change of attitudes on Anglo-Irish questions were of dominant importance in producing a large swing at the Irish General Election of February 1932. Fianna Fáil, the party of de Valera, which contained many intransigent republicans, became for the first time the largest party in the Dáil. With some support from Labour Fianna Fáil secured a small, but sufficient, over-all majority, which it was destined to retain until after the Second World War. De Valera made little secret of the fact that his overriding objective was to establish the whole of Ireland – north and south alike – as a sovereign Republic. Almost immediately a series of issues, both constitutional and economic, was raised. These ranged from the nature of the oath required of members of the Dáil, to financial claims and counter-claims between Britain and Ireland which had arisen during over a century of union, and were still not resolved. By the latter part of 1932 the two countries were locked in a 'trade war', and the concluding stages of passage of the Ottawa Agreements Bill through Parliament coincided with the issue of Treasury Orders imposing or increasing duties against goods from the Irish Free State. The 'trade war' was eventually resolved more or less amicably; but it served as a sharp reminder of the tensions which policies of economic discrimination inevitably produce.

These problems affecting the Dominions overlapped with a long chain of events relating to the political structure of India. In 1927 Baldwin's Government set up an all-party Statutory Commission on India, headed by Sir John Simon – a Liberal in those days. The Simon

Commission was still sitting when the Labour Government took office in 1929, and a new twist was suddenly given to Indian affairs. After consultation with the British Government, the Viceroy, Lord Irwin – the future Viscount, then Earl, Halifax – announced the intention 'that India should in the fullness of time take her place in the Empire in equal partnership with the Dominions'. Apparently Baldwin, leader of the Conservative Opposition, had assented to this announcement on condition that the Simon Commission approved; but the Commission had not been consulted.

It was arguable that Irwin's announcement was no more than a restatement of earlier declarations, including the preamble to the 1919 Act. Be that as it may, a huge political furore developed in Britain, and continued intermittently throughout the remaining life of the second Labour Government. Deepest feeling lay within the Conservative Party, where a 'cave' of intransigents, headed by Winston Churchill, fought bitterly against the relatively liberal approach of their leader. By the time the National Government was formed in August 1931 Churchill was so deeply estranged from the leading men of his Party that he had no credible claim to be included in the new administration. Thus the original reason for Churchill's omission from government during most of the 1930s had nothing to do with his attitude to European politics.

The Simon Commission eventually reported in 1930. That report, however, had little effect on India itself, and during the autumn a new body, the so-called 'Round Table Conference', was called into being, with Indian as well as British members. Of crucial importance here was the attitude of Congress, the most influential Indian body pressing for independence. Congress at first declared a policy of 'non-violent' resistance to British authority, and refused to participate in the Round Table Conference. Eventually a deal was done with Irwin, by which Congress called off its campaign against the British, in return for an amnesty of political prisoners. Shortly afterwards Congress members joined the Conference; but, like its predecessor, this Conference failed to come up with a credible long-term solution which might form the basis for major legislation.

In 1933 a new initiative was made, with establishment of a Joint Select Committee. This ran into the immediate difficulty that Churchill and some of his associates refused to serve. Late in 1934, however, a report was produced, though with much less than unanimity. 'Diehard' members of the Committee thought that it was going too far in the direction of Indian independence, Labour members that it was not going far enough. Despite these difficulties, the government decided to attempt legislation. The gigantic majority of the National Government did not assure the Bill an easy passage, and throughout its course through Parliament it was beset from both sides. In the end it received Royal assent as the Government of India Act 1935.

The Act separated Burma and Aden from the Indian Empire, and devised a complicated structure for the remainder of the country. Much of the difficulty sprang from attempts to protect the interests both of the Moslems and of the princes towards whom Britain had treaty obligations. British India would be divided into eleven autonomous Provinces, each with a much wider electorate than hitherto, but falling far short of universal franchise. The Act prescribed that – if rulers representing half the population of 'princely India' agreed – both British India and the native states would eventually constitute a united Federation, whose government would control those matters which affected the whole country. Application of the Act, however, proved very difficult. Congress did not like it, and was only with difficulty persuaded to participate in the provincial elections which were held at the beginning of 1937. Meanwhile, prolonged and complex negotiations for the establishment of an Indian Federation continued; but at the outbreak of war in 1939 they were far from complete, and were promptly suspended.

Passage of the Government of India Act in 1935 coincided rather closely with the emergence of a new series of constitutional questions between Britain and Ireland, which had wide implications elsewhere. The Irish Free State, like other parts of the Commonwealth, allowed appeals against decisions of its own courts to be heard before the Judicial Committee of the Privy Council in London. One such decision, in 1935, turned on whether the 1921 Treaty which set up the Free State was void to the extent of repugnancy with the 1931 Statute of Westminster. The Judicial Committee decided affirmatively. The 1921 Treaty had denied the Irish Free State the right to secede from the British Commonwealth; the 1931 Statute had explicity affirmed the right of any Dominion to do so. The matter came under close attention in the course of 1936; and the crisis surrounding the Abdication of Edward VIII at the end of the year served as a sharp reminder that the Free State was still formally linked to the Crown. The Dublin Government had first wished to treat the abdication issue as one of indifference to themselves; but they were eventually reminded that unless the Dáil passed an Abdication Act of its own, Edward VIII would remain King of Ireland. Reluctantly they pushed through an Act to the necessary effect. These events led to the adoption of the Eire constitution recommended by De Valera in 1937. References both to the Crown and to the Commonwealth were vague, although no formal attempt was made to establish a Republic. In 1938 an agreement was reached between the British and Eire Governments which dealt with various financial and commercial questions, but the most important clauses were those by which Britain abrogated her right to certain naval bases in southern Ireland: a matter which would prove of much practical significance in the Battle of the Atlantic.

In South Africa, as in India and Ireland, there were significant developments during the 1930s which gave evidence that the bonds linking the country to Britain were becoming perceptibly weaker. The world depression produced its political effects in South Africa as in most other countries, and in 1933 a Coalition Government took office, with the leaders of the two main Parties – Generals Hertzog and Smuts – serving as Premier and Vice Premier respectively. Out of this Coalition there soon grew a new 'United Party', headed by the two Generals. As usually happens with fusions of this kind, there were recalcitrant sections of both bodies who refused to participate. Hertzog's former associates were to prove the more important. Headed by the future Premier, Dr Malan, they constituted themselves an opposition party, the 'Purified Nationalists', and cursed their erstwhile leader as an apostate from Nationalist principles. For the time being their influence on South Africa's actions was small; but they could afford to await the day when the government's massive authority would decline, and the electorate would turn to themselves as the alternative. Indeed, long before war broke out there were already plenty of signs of rising Boer nationalist feeling, although it still fell well short of the ideas of Malan. There was intense discussion over the flag and National Anthem of the Union, and wild enthusiasm surrounded celebrations in commemoration of the centenary of the Great Trek. During the Czechoslovak crisis in September 1938 the South African Government made it plain to Britain that if war arose over the Sudetenland, South Africa at any rate would not take arms alongside Britain and France.

When war came in 1939 the old doctrine of 'unity of the Crown' had vanished. It was generally acknowledged that the Dominions, and India too, must make their own declarations of war. There was no doubt about Australia, New Zealand or Canada; but even the Canadian Government insisted that the decision was a matter for their own Parliament, and a week elapsed before the country was formally at war. India was brought into the war by a declaration from the Viceroy, Lord Linlithgow; but he immediately ran into great trouble with those provinces which were under Congress control, whose Ministers promptly resigned. A new campaign of 'civil disobedience' followed swiftly, and led to thousands of arrests. Eire refused to declare war at all, and was neutral throughout.

In South Africa, the question of entering the war brought on a profound internal crisis. The Cabinet was split; Hertzog favoured neutrality, Smuts participation in the conflict. The matter was set before the South African Parliament which decided by 80:67 in favour of war: no overwhelming majority indeed, but rather more than many had anticipated. The position of opponents of war within the United Party became impossible. Hertzog more or less dropped out of politics and died a year or two later. Most of his associates were eventually reconciled with Malan's 'Purified Nationalists', who thus came to assume the character of a serious challenger to the government rather than an insignificant splinter group. Smuts inevitably became Premier, and on most wartime issues he got his way, although beset by bitter and intransigent opponents. A few extremists went on to the point of supporting Nazi Germany; while the tide of neutralism ran strongly.

The new Japanese war increased immeasureably the strains of empire. Within a very few weeks Britain, like the United States, had lost much of her Pacific fleet, and in the first months of 1942 the Japanese cut like a scythe through the possessions of the various allied powers. By the late spring they had more or less completely occupied Malaya, the Dutch East Indies (Indonesia), the Philippines – then American – and a very large part of Burma. At one point there were at the gateway of India; at another, within a very short distance of Australia; at another, half way to the western seaboard of the United States and Canada. Japan controlled nearly all the Asian littoral southwards from the frontiers of the Soviet Union; half the Pacific from the latitude of Kamchatka to that of the northern tip of Australia: and a substantial part of the Indian Ocean. In May the Battle of the Coral Sea imposed a certain check on this progress; but, until the air-sea battle of Midway Island at the beginning of June, nobody could feel certain that even a brief respite had been secured.

In these desperate straits the British Government was forced to give attention to India in a new light. In those parts of Asia which had belonged to the European Powers, the Japanese behaved far more wisely than their German allies were behaving in the conquered territories of Europe. A serious appeal was made to the native peoples in order to secure active co-operation in what later came to be known as the 'New Order' or 'Co-prosperity Scheme' of eastern Asia.

Invasion of India by Japanese forces appeared by no means unlikely in 1942. What, if anything, could be done to ensure Indian co-operation with Britain, or at least to minimise the danger that Indian nationalists would assist the enemy? At the end of January 1942 the opinion of Lord Linlithgow was circulated to the Cabinet. His general conclusion was that no new constitutional initiative would improve matters; but the Viceroy went a good deal further than his brief demanded. India and Burma, he declared, were in the Empire 'because they are conquered countries which have been brought there by force and kept there by our control'. As for the future:

> the moment they think that we may lose the war or take a hard knock, their leaders would be much more concerned to make terms with the victor at our expense than to fight for ideals to which so much lip-service is given.[1]

Labour members of the government could scarcely let that one pass without comment. Attlee wrote a strong Memorandum criticising the Viceroy's opinions, questioning his suitability for office and demanding a new initiative designed to end the embarrassing non-co-operation policy of Congress and to win active support for the war effort.[2] Despite the very disparate views which leading members of the Cabinet had entertained on Indian questions a few years previously, they eventually concurred with Attlee's main proposals. Sir Stafford Cripps, long an advocate of Indian nationalism, who had recently joined the Cabinet after a spell as ambassador to the Soviet Union, would undertake a special mission to India. The government would also draw up a Declaration about India's future. After discussion it was agreed that his document could not be published at once, but that Cripps woud first endeavour to 'sell' its ideas to the Indians.

The Declaration eventually devised made an unequivocal promise of Dominion status for India after the war, with safeguards for Moslems and for the princely states. Even a year or two earlier such a pronouncement would very likely have been greeted with considerable enthusiasm in India. But it came too late; for the war in the Far East was developing in a way which cast a most baleful light on British military capacity and British morale. Singapore had fallen on 15 February, and even the War Cabinet minutes record that 'our military performance in Malaya had left much to be desired'.[3] No doubt many Indians would have set this judgement in stronger terms. Several weeks earlier, the Japanese had commenced their advance into Burma, where they were receiving a substantial measure of indigenous support. Cripps reported that in most of India 'morale amongst the Indian and in many cases the European population is deplorable'; that 'anti-British feeling is running very strong and our prestige is lower than it has ever been'.[4] Congress opinion was by no means unanimous. Some, including Gandhi, were more or less strict pacifists. Others might be prepared to co-operate on certain terms; but to cede these terms would alienate the Moslems, who were providing a disproportionate number of army recruits. There was no way of squaring the circle, and the Cripps mission ended in failure.

The Japanese rapidly occupied Burma, and were sufficiently confident of local support to grant nominal independence to a sympathetic Burmese Government. For the time being they stopped short at the Indian frontier, but in the spring of 1944 invaded Assam. Later in that year the tide turned; the Japanese were driven from India, and the reconquest of Burma began. The sufferings directly occasioned by the fighting were small, however, by contrast with a disaster partly related to wartime disruptions: the appalling Bengal famine of 1943–44. The death-toll from starvation and the epidemics which followed was eventually estimated at $1\frac{1}{2}$ millions: a calamity without parallel since the early years of the century.

In the closing period of the war pressures both of battle and famine began to abate and political questions again came to the fore. A new Viceroy, Field-Marshal Viscount Wavell, was appointed in October 1943, and in the course of 1944 imprisoned Congress leaders were released. Meanwhile Moslem fears became more acute. The idea of total separation of the Moslem areas from the body of India – the notion of 'Pakistan' – gradually moved from the vision of extremists to the normal currency of Moslem League thinking. On the Hindu side Gandhi appeared to be showing some sympathy as well. Towards the end of 1944 elections for a central Assembly produced a stark confrontation on ethnic lines: Congress making a clean sweep of 'general' constituencies, the Moslem League of Moslem seats. In the spring of 1945 Wavell visited London for discussions, and then returned to India, where the possibility of establishing a new Indian Government contained the main political groups was considered. Congress and the Moslem League failed to agree, and the talks broke down.

Just as the Second World War accentuated old problems in territories which had long formed part of the British Empire, so also did it increase Britain's difficulties in places where her influence and power were of more recent date.

The origin of British interest in the Middle East had much more to do with the geographical location of the area than with the anticipated value of its trade or products. The Middle East stood on the route to India; it could prove of crucial importance either to support or to coerce the Ottoman Empire; it was likely to be of value in the future development of East Africa. With such considerations in mind Britain acquired Aden in 1839, the Protectorate over Cyprus in 1878, and a large measure of control over Egypt from the 1880s onwards. The first major sign of interest in Middle Eastern oil appeared early in the twentieth century, when a private undertaking secured concessions from the government of Persia. In 1914, however, the British Government acquired controlling interest in the Anglo-Persian Oil Company, which operated those concessions.

The First World War greatly extended the British interest, and also gave France an important position in the Middle East. With the primary aim of subverting Arab loyalties to the Turkish enemy, the British High Commissioner in Egypt made an offer of independence to Arabs under Ottoman rule in event of an allied victory. The document in which the promise was made – the 'McMahon Letter' to the sherif of Mecca, written in October 1915, made ambiguous reference to Palestine; a matter which would later acquire much importance. In 1917 Arthur Balfour – sometime Prime Minister, but currently Foreign Secretary – made a different offer, the 'Balfour Declaration', promising the Jews a 'national home' in Palestine. Nobody really knew what 'national home' meant, but Jews assumed that it meant that Palestine would eventually become Jewish, while Arabs, laying stress on the McMahon Letter, assumed that the country would be theirs. Whether the two documents are capable of logical reconciliation or not, there can be no doubt that the British Government hoped to attract both groups by the offers, and probably cared little whether they were compatible or not. Like most governments engaged in major warfare, they were prepared to promise anything to anybody if they judged that the promises might contribute significantly to victory.

Shortly before the Bolshevik revolution in Russia, there were discussions between the British, French and Russians about future partition of the Ottoman lands. When Russia dropped out of the war, the British and French settled matters between themselves. The Arabs were duly stirred up, the Jews enthused. At the end of the First World War lands lying between the Mediterranean and the frontiers of Persia were divided into British and French spheres of influence. France secured League of Nations Mandates over Syria and the Lebanon – 'the Levant States', Britain secured a Mandate over Palestine. Transjordan and Iraq also came under strong British influence.

During the inter-war period British policy towards most of the Middle Eastern countries was, by international standards of the time, conspicuously liberal. Iraq and Transjordan became self-governing, although British influence remained. A serious dispute with Persia led to a radical revision of the oil royalties arrangements in that country's favour. The British Protectorate over Egypt was abandoned in 1922. In 1936 – at a time when Mussolini was on the rampage in East Africa and British military support was important for the Egyptian Government – the two countries signed a new treaty, which was so generally welcomed by Egyptians that all political parties in the country insisted on participating in its signature.[5] This happy beginning to a new relationship between the two countries was not an accurate augury for the future; and to the later fate of that treaty it will be necessary to return repeatedly.

Britain's deepest difficulties in the Middle East at that time turned on troubles in Palestine, and repercussions of those troubles in nearby Arab countries. When the mandate was granted, Palestine's population was not much over half a million. It was composed overwhelmingly of Moslem Arabs, although there were a number of Jewish settlements. The Arabs were mainly peasants with a very low standard of living, with a small feudal aristocracy and a rising middle class. There were also some Bedouin nomads.

Whatever 'national home' meant, it certainly included the right of Jews to settle in Palestine if they wished. Soon there was a large influx. Many immigrants had Zionist sympathies, and there was a high proportion of educated young people. By 1925 the Jewish population of Palestine had almost doubled. Predictably there was tension, frequently resulting in violence, between the Arab population and the incomers. In the 1930s the arrival of Nazism in Germany, and a great deal of anti-Jewish activity in other places as well, led to further Jewish immigration into Palestine. Just as this immigration was getting under way British relations with Italy deteriorated sharply, and the Italians sought to exploit their nuisance-value by beaming radio propaganda at the Palestinian Arabs, thereby increasing the difficulties of the British authorities who sought to maintain order. By 1936 disturbances had reached a very serious level. Meanwhile the population of Palestine was increasingly rapidly – partly as a result of Jewish immigration, but largely as a result of natural increase both of Jews and of Arabs.

In the late 1930s British official ideas vacillated between two possible solutions for Palestine. One suggestion was that the country should be divided into Jewish and Arab states, the latter being perhaps annexed to the adjacent Arab Kingdom of Transjordan. There might also be a sort of buffer zone, including the Holy Places of the Christian, Jewish and Moslem relgions. The main difficulty was the usual one attending geographical partitions: that any line of division would leave large numbers of people on the side to which they did not wish to belong. The alternative policy considered was to preserve the unity of Palestine, but control Jewish immigration. This was the line eventually accepted by the British Government, and it was set out in the famous 'White Paper' issued in May 1939. Jewish immigration would continue for a further five years, to an annual maximum of 15 000. When 75 000 had been admitted immigration would cease, unless the Arabs agreed to the contrary. This would preserve an Arab majority in Palestine of more than two to one for the foreseeable future. There is something to be said for the view that Britain and the Middle Eastern countries were set on a path of peaceful evolution towards a durable settlement when the Second World War broke out. Thereafter all kinds of new problems arose, and old ones became vastly more acute.

Some of these problems concerned inter-allied wartime co-operation. When the Soviet Union was attacked by Germany, the only serious assistance which the West could immediately render was supply of goods; and there were few possible routes through which supplies could enter. Iran – formerly Persia – afforded one of these routes. In August 1941 British and Soviet troops occupied different parts of Iran, meeting little resistance. In the aftermath of war, the continuance, or memory, of those two wartime occupations would lead to considerable international discord.

Other wartime problems relating to the Middle East were also to have intense and lasting reprecussions on Britain. The 1936 Treaty with Egypt authorised the presence of 10 000 British troops in the Suez Canal Zone, until the two parties were agreed that 'the Egyptian army is in a position to ensure by its own resources the liberty and entire security of navigation of the Canal'. The treaty, however, also authorised the return of British troops in unlimited numbers in times of emergency, and this provision was followed from 1939 onwards. Attempts were also made, though without success, to induce Egypt to declare war on the Axis Powers. In the autumn of 1940 Italian troops entered Egypt from Libya, and for practical purposes the defence of Egypt was taken over by troops from the British Commonwealth. As the ding-dong campaign in the North African desert proceeded, and Germans became increasingly involved alongside the Italians, efforts were made by some Egyptian politicians to establish friendly contact with the Axis Powers. In

February 1942 the British compelled King Farouk to dismiss his Prime Minister and appoint a more amenable successor: an incident widely resented in Egypt. By the middle of the war the considerable goodwill towards Britain which had existed in 1936 had largely evaporated; and there was not much doubt that Egypt would take a much more baleful view of her relationship with Britain as soon as the war ended.

Thus the Second World War involved Britain in increasing difficulties in her eastern possessions and in areas of British influence: difficulties arising partly from the actions of her acknowledged enemies, and partly from the desire of large elements of the indigenous populations to free themselves from British control. It will later be necessary to consider difficulties of a different kind, deriving from the character of the wartime alliance itself. Before the war, and in the first phases of the war, the Anglo-French association represented co-operation between countries which – however sharp their differences of interest – were both 'great' mainly by reason of their overseas possessions. Thus they were to a considerable degree conscious of a kind of common interest, and in that sense they were natural allies both in war and in peace. The great new allies who had appeared in 1941 had made their historic expansion across continents, absorbing or destroying native populations, and neither had much interest in overseas possessions. For reasons rooted in their very different ideologies, neither the United States nor the Soviet Union anticipated or desired that the British Empire should persist into the indefinite future.

11   The Course of War

Most of 1942 was a grim time for the western allies. Not only did they experience appalling defeats at the hands of the Japanese, but the war closer to home was profoundly discouraging. The Battle of the Atlantic went extremely badly. Nearly every month the U-boat toll of merchant shipping rose: from close on 300 thousand tons in January to well over twice that figure in June. The Arctic Convoys, by which supplies were sent to northern Russia, suffered such severe depradations that they were suspended. True, the course of war in North Africa and the Mediterranean was less catastrophic; but even in those places it was hard to say that the tide was yet running in favour of the allies.

By contrast the Soviet Union appeared to be faring remarkably well. At the turn of the year the Germans were cleared from Rostov and from the vicinity of Moscow. In the south considerable gains were made from the invaders. Morally the British Government was beleaguered. Although the government was a three-party coalition, loyally supported by the leaders and organisations of all parties, no fewer than four seats were lost to Independents in the second quarter of 1942. The victorious candidates were in no sense communists, or anything like it; but their impressive triumphs coincided with a powerful swing of British opinion in Russia's favour. The Press and the BBC, naturally concerned to sustain public morale at a time of defeat and disaster, had been focusing attention on the Soviet victories, and perhaps even magnifying their importance. The public swung violently from the deeply anti-Russian sentiments entertained at the beginning of the war to the opposite extreme. The tremendous courage and suffering of the Soviet people in face of a ruthless and barbarous enemy, was reflected to the glory of Stalin and the political system over which he presided. It is a striking paradox that, within the Soviet Union itself, communist ideology was being deliberately played down in favour of unity in the 'patriotic war'; yet, at the same moment, many people in the West were regarding the military successes of the Red Army as evidence of merit in the communist system.

The background of public enthusiasm and sympathy for the Soviet

Union and its government was of vital importance in the astonishing developments of British foreign policy which began very early in 1942. As Eden explained to Stalin during the ill-fated Moscow visit, his own good offices were available in support of Russia's claims to the frontiers which existed at the moment of the German attack – at least in respect of the Baltic States and Finland. The idea was submitted to the Prime Minister, still away in the United States. Churchill's reaction was sharp. He was 'surprised' at Eden's view. The Baltic States, declared the Prime Minister, 'were acquired by acts of aggression in shameful collusion with Hitler'. The transfer of their peoples against their will would be 'contrary to all the principles for which we are fighting this war and would dishonour our Cause'. Any British Government which Churchill headed must adhere 'to those principles of freedom and democracy set forth in the Atlantic Charter, and . . . these principles must become especially active whenever any question of transferring territory is raised'.[1]

When it became possible to assemble a full Cabinet, early in February, there was a deep schism. Eden, backed strongly by Lord Beaverbrook and with some support from others, favoured concession to the Russian demands. Churchill, and even more strongly the Labour leaders Attlee and Bevin, argued against. On Churchill's insistence the matter was remitted to the Americans for their observations. Roosevelt and his advisers reacted very much as Churchill had done, emphasising in particular the total incompatibility of these proposals with the principles set out in the Atlantic Charter.

Then some sort of change, whose nature is still obscure, took place in Britain. For whatever reason, Churchill, of all people, was found interceding with Roosevelt early in March, proposing that the President should turn a blind eye to the whole business.[2] This Roosevelt proceeded to do. The British Cabinet then agreed in principle to the signature of a treaty with Russia which would acknowledge the Soviet position in the Baltic States.

At this point there was a leakage, and a considerable number of influential MPs recorded furious protests to Eden.[3] The animus behind these protests appears to have persuaded the government that it was impossible to proceed further without a massive furore; and so they turned to another gambit. The original idea of two treaties with a secret protocol was abandoned; instead, a completely different instrument – the 'Twenty Year Treaty' between Britain and the Soviet Union – was successfully negotiated. That treaty made no mention of the Baltic States; but the Foreign Secretary contrived to placate the Russians in a manner which would circumvent domestic criticism. In the course of discussion with the Soviet delegates Eden made it plain that Britain acknowledged their position in the Baltic area.[4] This acknowledgment, of course, was not published. Thus the essential Soviet requirements were satisfied, and the opponents of the concession were not alerted.

These obscure transactions represented in truth a most massive shift of foreign policy by both Britain and the United States. They had abandoned the solid and defensible ground that no decisions over frontiers should be reached until the end of the war; while the Atlantic Charter had lost all meaning. It required no deep insight into political processes inside the democracies for Stalin to discern that there had been a long and involved struggle within Britain and the United States, at the end of which he would be getting his own way on what really mattered to him. The British Government could be squeezed if the pressure was sufficient; the American Government would not make public any reservations which it might feel on the matter. The thin end of a very thick wedge had been inserted.

During the summer and autumn of 1942 the military situation underwent considerable changes, which were strongly reflected in diplomatic behaviour. After Midway, the tide of war in the Far East fluctuated; but the run of sensational and easy Japanese victories was over. In the Soviet Union, on the other hand, the German advance was resumed, although at a somewhat slower pace than in the previous year. By autumn the enemy had reached Stalingrad on the Volga. The course of war in North Africa continued to fluctuate, and Atlantic shipping losses were substantially reduced. Thus the war became a much more even affair, both between the two contending sides and among the allies themselves.

By this time Russia was pressing imperiously for a 'Second Front', and a massive campaign was mounted in Britain in support. The idea of a Second Front had shifted considerably, for it was now understood to mean a full-scale Anglo-American invasion of Western Europe. Omens for the success of such a venture were not good. A substantial but brief raid on Dieppe involved casualties quite disproportionate to any military achievements.

In the eyes of British and American war leaders a much more realistic target at this stage of the war was French North Africa; for, if that could be secured, the whole southern littoral of the Mediterranean might soon pass into allied hands. But any substantial allied action against French territory, whether occupied by the Vichy Government or by the enemy, was almost certain to stir up a hornets' nest of diplomatic and political problems of immense importance not only to the immediate matter in hand but also to all future relations with France – and, indirectly, to Britain's future world role as well. These problems derived in part from the confusions which accompanied the fall of France in 1940, but in part to attitudes with much deeper origins.

The rupture, or rather the attenuation, of diplomatic relations between Britain and Vichy France which took place in the summer of 1940 was not paralleled in the United States. Nor did relations between Washington and Vichy alter dramatically when the United States entered the war. To some extent the difference of attitude between the Anglo-Saxon powers was founded on historical accident. The British had received de Gaulle in 1940 as in some way representative of the 'real France', to whom they were under moral obligations for his part in organising the Free French – even though they refused to recognise the Free French as a 'Government-in-Exile', and relations between Churchill and de Gaulle were often stormy. The Americans were under no corresponding obligations. The situation became increasingly complicated when various parts of the French Empire declared for de Gaulle. The deeper problem was that the British – and Churchill in particular – believed that France could, and should, be restored to his historic greatness after the war. The Americans had no such idea. They had no liking for the French Empire, and at times even discussed whether France herself should be restored to her full pre-1940 frontiers.

As war proceeded the Vichy French were compelled by their military weakness to submit to various pressures from the enemy. As far back as the early summer of 1941 the Germans had compelled Vichy to permit military material to pass through Syria, which was under French control. The Free French backed the British in capturing Syria for the allies; but it soon became apparent that British and French ideas for the country's future were very different. In the Far East, too, Vichy was incapable of resisting external pressures. In 1940 the Japanese had required them to grant bases in French Indo-China, which were needed for the campaign against China; in 1941 Vichy was compelled to grant further bases in Indo-China to assist the Japanese designs against allied possessions in south-east Asia.

But it was not only enemy action and pressure which was undermining France's position as a world power. Neither the Americans not the Russians felt any interest in pretending that French authority counted for much while the war lasted. Yet French world power, annoying and embarrassing as it often was to the British Government, was also a vital buttress to British world power. To what extent this point was realised during the war is a matter of some conjecture; but the sort of problem involved was illustrated by the complex dispute involving the British, French and Americans in North Africa from late 1942 onwards. Much turned on the accident that the western allies felt themselves strong enough to invade French North Africa, but by no means strong enough to invade western Europe.

The Battle of Alamein in Egypt, on 4 November 1942, was of critical importance to the story. It represented the ruin of Axis hopes for reaching the Suez Canal; and it was also the point from which forces of the German Commander, Rommel, passed into general retreat. While the allies were advancing westwards through Libya in pursuit of the defeated Axis forces, Anglo-American landings took place in North Africa, under command of General Eisenhower. For a variety of reasons, among which security was a major consideration, de Gaulle was not informed until the last moment, and the principal French officer associated with the operation was a certain General Giraud. De Gaulle was predictably furious; but almost immediately events took an astonishing turn. At the very start there was substantial French resistance to the invasion; but at Algiers the Anglo-Americans made contact with Admiral Darlan, Vichy Minister of Marine, who was in the town in order to visit his sick son. In a sudden turmoil of events Darlan successfully negotiated a cease-fire leaving the allies in control; Pétain repudiated the Admiral; the Germans – evidently deciding that Vichyites were both unreliable and ineffectual – occupied the remainder of France; the French fleet at Toulon was scuttled; and diplomatic relations between the United States and Vichy were broken.

The allies now found themselves dealing with a sort of duarchy of Darlan and Giraud, with an enraged de Gaulle hovering in the background and a growing body of civilian opinion, especially in Britain, evincing considerable concern about the credentials of the Admiral. Drama followed upon drama. On 24 December Darlan was assassinated, apparently by a young French royalist. A couple of days later it was announced that the assassin had been court-martialled and shot. Perhaps we shall never know the true circumstances of Darlan's death. The historian may reflect that for very disparate reasons the British, the Americans, the Free French, the Vichy French and the Germans must have viewed the event with some relief; while the astonishing speed with which the putative culprit was removed from the scene made it difficult to learn much from the person who presumably knew most about the matter.

For some time there was renewed confusion about where French authority was vested. In the second half of January, however, Roosevelt and Churchill met at the recently-occupied Moroccan town of Casablanca, and contrived a sort of compromise. A body known as the French National Committee had already been in existence for over a year, in order to give a kind of legitimacy to de Gaulle's 'Free French'. In January 1943 it was broadened to incorporate both de Gaulle and Giraud, and later in the year it metamorphosed into the 'French Committee of National Liberation'. Within the new system de Gaulle and his associates proceeded gradually to squeeze Giraud from effective authority.

The net effect of all this was to create the nucleus of a new France, which for different reasons would prove embarrassing to the two Anglo-Saxon allies. The Americans were saddled with the charismatic figure of de Gaulle, a very able politician, whose loyalties were first, foremost and all the time to the French State and his own sense of Messianic mission – and who was quite prepared to make or break any international alliance in the perceived interest of France. The British discovered that their erstwhile *protégé* was deeply alienated from, and resentful of, their own country, and was no more willing than the Vichyites to restore the old Anglo-Fench *entente*. Both the British and the Americans would have much reason to regret de Gaulle, both during the war and in the aftermath. Churchill probably only exaggerated a little when he declared that the heaviest cross he had to bear was the Cross of Lorraine – the Free French symbol.

All these events in North Africa were in most eyes quite eclipsed by the Battle of Stalingrad, which was being fought at the turn of 1942–43. The very name of the city gave it importance in the minds of both sides. By the time the German resistance ended something like three-quarters of a million people had died on each side, and not far short of half a million Germans had been taken prisoner – of whom vast numbers would never return. Many commentators have claimed that Stalingrad was *the* decisive battle of the war. Be that as it may, the whole epic gave the Soviet Union immense moral prestige in the Anglo-Saxon countries. Stalingrad was followed by other spectacular Soviet victories, notably the battle of Kursk in the summer of 1943, which destroyed enormous numbers of German tanks. The scale of human and material destuction elsewhere bore little comparison with events on the Eastern Front, and in the course of 1943 it became apparent that the war would eventually end with the Soviet Union in physical control of great areas of eastern Europe.

The fields of conflict in which the western allies were engaged were also developing favourably. The process of clearing German and Italian troops from North Africa developed apace. By mid-May all that remained of those armies were vast numbers of prisoners of war. At the same time, the Battle of the Atlantic was turning dramatically in favour of the allies, and great numbers of U-boats were sunk. Just over a week after the fighting in North Africa ended Grand Admiral Dönitz called off submarine attacks on the North Atlantic convoys. The Japanese war was also developing in the allies' favour.

News of their own victories cheered the British and American people; but to most they were regarded as little more than side-shows by comparison with the struggle in the Soviet Union. The campaign for a Second Front developed apace. The military argument as to whether a Second Front could, and should, have been set in operation during 1943 continues to our own day. Meanwhile the Soviet Government missed no opportunity of exploiting any military successes against the enemy in order to advance its own diplomatic position in relation to the other allies. The Second Front campaign was useful to the Soviet Government, not because of any effect it exerted on military strategy, but because it rendered both the peoples and the governments of other allies willing to make diplomatic concessions to atone, as it were, for lack of military support.

Poland was, and would long remain, the centre of diplomatic attention. As the Red Army advanced westwards it became increasingly difficult to postpone some kind of decision as to who should administer territory which had been Polish before the war, once the Germans had been driven out; and everybody appreciated that temporary wartime expedients were likely to become permanent in the aftermath. There was no kind of agreement as to where the frontiers of Poland should lie, either in the east or in the west; and still less was there any general understanding as to what sort of government should administer the country, or how far post-war Poland would be truly independent in either domestic or external affairs. Although the 1941 treaty seemed to have established a new amity between the Polish Government-in-Exile and the Soviet Union, that spirit did not last. In the course of 1942 relations deteriorated, and eventually Polish forces were removed from the Soviet Union, to serve with the British in the Middle East. In March 1943 the situation became critical when more or less formal claims were made by the Soviet Union that the future eastern frontier of Poland should follow roughly the 'Curzon Line'.

The Curzon Line was rather similar to the dividing line between German and Soviet occupation which had been agreed between

Wer zuletzt · raubt, raubt am besten ·

A German Wartime Forecast, 1943
The smallest fish – Britain – is being swallowed by the United States, which in turn is being
engulfed by the Soviet Union.
Das Reich, Berlin, 2 May 1943

Molotov and Ribbentrop in September 1939, but it had more
respectable credentials. It had been drawn up by the allies in 1919 as a
division between overwhelmingly Polish areas to the west and areas of
mixed population – Polish, Ukrainian, Byelorussian, Lithuanian and
Jewish – further east. The Curzon Line had never been a political
frontier in the past, and in the aftermath of the Firt World War nobody
was definitely proposing that it should become one. In 1920 the British
Foreign, Lord Curzon, suggested it as a cease-fire line between Polish
and Russian armies; but neither side accepted the proposal. By the
Treaty of Riga in 1921 a line well to the east of the Curzon Line was
accepted by both sides as the frontier, and remained so until the invasion
of September 1939. Between the Curzon Line and the Riga Line lay a
considerable number of important towns with overwhelmingly Polish
populations, of which the most important was Lwów – or Lvov, as the
Russians called it.

The argument about the future of eastern Poland which the Russians
had reopened in March 1943 became general. On 12 April Foreign
Secretary Eden told the British Cabinet that 'differences between the
Russians and the Poles were now acute'.[5] They were much more acute
than he realised; for on that very day the German news agency had

released news of the discovery of a mass-grave of Polish officers – the number was eventually stated at 8000 or 10 000 – in Katyn forest,near Smolensk, within the German-occupied area of the Soviet Union. These officers, the Germans declared, had been murdered by the Soviet authorities in the spring of 1940. The Russians retorted furiously, declaring that the Germans themselves were responsible for the atrocity. They could hardly do otherwise, whatever the facts of the case.

In the next few days Churchill and the other British leaders learnt a great deal about the background to Katyn. There was little doubt that the Russians were the culprits, although the numbers of dead whom the Germans claimed to have found at Katyn is now known to have been exaggerated considerably. There were, however, two other camps where great numbers of Polish officers disappeared about the same time as those at Katyn, and where the fate of the inmates is not known to this day. The Polish Government's reaction to the charges and counter-charges was to propose that the International Red Cross should investigate the matter. The Germans – most embarrassingly – eagerly took up the suggestion. The Soviet Government retorted by breaking diplomatic relations with the Poles. Thereafter the British and American Governments did all that lay in their power to persuade the Russians to relent, but in vain. Evidently the Soviet Government found it convenient that they should have a free hand in Polish affairs, without any sort of commitment to the London Polish Government; and the Katyn question had provided a useful pretext.

Despite the continuing argument over Poland, relations between the Russians and the western allies were generally good, and all of the 'Big Three' appeared determined to thrust aside any political differences in order to win the war, and in the cause of amity thereafter. This spirit appeared to prevail at the first meeting of Churchill, Roosevelt and Stalin at Tehran towards the end of the year.

The Tehran Conference witnessed exceedingly important military agreements: the approximate date for launching a 'Second Front' in western Europe, and plans for the Soviet Union to attack Japan after the end of the German war. It was also the occasion where Stalin revealed his own ideas for Poland's future geography. The eastern frontier should be the Curzon Line, with perhaps minor variations. The western frontier should be the Oder. This meant incorporating into Poland a great area with an almost exclusively German population: an area extending much further to the west than anything the Poles themselves had coveted. In other words, Poland was to be bribed to acquiesce in Russia's gains to the east by the promise of German land to the west. It required little imagination to see that this arrangement would be profoundly resented by all Germans, and that the only way by which Poland could avert a future war of revenge was through military dependence on the Soviet Union. No doubt such dependence would imply economic and diplomatic hegemony and perhaps political hegemony as well, by the Soviet Union.

Churchill received Stalin's proposals with considerable enthusiasm. Roosevelt 'feigned sleep'. Privately, he warned Stalin that a Presidential election was forthcoming in 1944, and he did not propose to set at risk six or seven million American-Polish votes by committing himself on the matter.[6]

When the London Poles heard what was proposed for them they reacted sharply and aversely. They had - so they explained to their British informants - no constitutional authority to cede Polish territory to anyone. Churchill, when he learnt of the Polish reaction, at first stopped in his tracks. Then he begun to bully the Poles towards compliance. The Poles - even their Prime Minister, Stanislaw Mikolajczyk, who was usually amenable to British suggestions - stood firm. Nor did Roosevelt assist Churchill's efforts with the Poles. When Mikolajczyk visited the President he received advice to the effect that Lwów, and even places further east, could be saved for Poland.[7]

By the early summer of 1944 the Russians were far into Poland and a Polish 'Committee of National Liberation' was set up, based first on Chelm and later on Lublin. For the time being, nobody - not even the Russians - gave the 'Lublin Committee' the status of a quasi-government. Despite the breach in diplomatic relations with the London Poles, Mikolajczyk was invited to Moscow in July 1944. Both Churchill and Roosevelt encouraged the journey, and unsuccessful efforts were made to secure some kind of accommodation between the London Poles and the 'Lublin Committee'.

Meanwhile the long-promised Second Front had been launched. On 6 June 1944 the Normandy landings began, and within a short time it became apparent that the bridgehead was likely to become permanent. This now raised in an acute form the questions which had been rumbling on for years. Unless some unforeseen and unlikely catastrophe intervened, the allies might expect to close in on Hitler's Reich from all quarters. The Russians would advance from the east, the western allies from France and Italy, and eventually from other accessible points on the Mediterranean like Greece. Various guerilla forces of widely different political complexions would play a greater or lesser part in clearing the Germans from their own countries.

Two recent issues highlighted the importance and urgency of some kind of top-level understanding between the major allies. In the summer of 1944 German power in the Balkans was crumbling. Romania, which lay in Russia's path, contained many important personalities who had strong links with the West, and in pre-war days France had had substantial economic interests there. Greece, which lay in Britain's path, contained many pro-communist guerillas, and was likely to collapse into civil war as soon as the enemy was evicted: a state of affairs which would prove costly and embarrassing to the British. Both the Russians and the British Foreign Office were anxious for a deal on the basis of Russian paramountcy in Romania and British paramountcy in Greece; but they suddenly discovered that the Americans were deeply opposed to any such arrangement, on the not unreasonable grounds that this would start new 'spheres of influence' arrangements which would continue into the peace: arrangements of a kind which had done infinite damage in the past.[8]

Far more tragic and immediately dangerous was the situation in Poland. In July 1944 the advancing Russians were close to Warsaw. The Russian radio called for a rising in the city, and at the beginning of August the Poles rebelled against the occupying Germans. Within a few days, the Russians began castigating the rebels with great savagery for the alleged foolhardiness of their rebellion. They gave no help to the rebels in the city. The western allies did what they could to provision Warsaw from the air, but the Russians refused them authority to land planes on territory controlled by the Red Army. After long wrangles Soviet truculence was reduced. American planes were permitted to land, and even a few Soviet supplies were sent into Warsaw; but by that time the rising was at its last gasp, and on 4 October the insurgents capitulated. Plainly, the 'inwardness' of this extraordinary chain of events was a profound power-struggle over the future of Poland.

On the face of it there was everything to be said for a top-level Conference to resolve the urgent three-way problems which was developing between the major allies. Unfortunately there was an incurable difficulty: the American constitution. 1944 was a Presidential election year; and nothing that anybody could do would prevent American politicians preoccupying themselves with that matter until it was resolved. Nobody knew whether Roosevelt would win the fourth term of office he was currently seeking, or what kind of foreign policy a victorious rival might determine. The Americans were therefore in no position to participate in any long-term arrangements. Events, however, would not wait on the American constitution. Action was urgently required, particularly over eastern Europe. So in October 1944 Churchill and Eden voyaged to Moscow for discussions with the Soviet leaders at the so-called 'Tolstoy' Conference. The American Ambassador had a watching brief; but that was all.

Almost as soon as the British arrived, they judged the moment appropriate to 'invite' – 'order' would be a better word – Mikolajczyk to join in the discussions. With reluctance, the Polish Prime Minister acceded. Great efforts were now made to compel him to come to terms with the 'Lublin Committee' about the future composition of the Polish Government, and about Polish frontiers to east and west. Whatever Mikolajczyk may have thought of the merits of such an arrangement, he was well aware of the weakness of his own position among his London compatriots. To Churchill's visible chagrin no agreement was reached, and Mikolajczyk returned to London in order to argue with his colleagues.

In another respect, however, the 'Tolstoy' Conference was more successful. British and Soviet representatives agreed about their respective influence in the Balkans, and went so far as to set this out in percentages. In Greece, Britain should receive 90 per cent of the influence, in Yugoslavia 50 per cent, in Hungary and Bulgaria 20 per cent, in Romania 10 per cent – the balance going to Russia. Theoretically, the arrangement was for the wartime period only; in practice, it rapidly became permanent – which was exactly what the Americans had feared.

The Polish Government in London lived in the rarified, unreal atmosphere common among émigrés of all kinds. They debated the proposals brought back by Mikolajczyk at great length. At last everybody's temper gave way. Mikolajczyk resigned, and was succeeded as Polish Prime Minister by an elderly Socialist, Tomasz Arcieszewski. Then Churchill made an incredible announcement in the House of Commons, acknowledging not merely the Soviet claim to the Curzon Line in general terms, but specifically their claim to Lwów – despite the fact that Roosevelt was known to consider that he could still save that very important town for the Poles. Then, at the turn of the year, the Russians recognised the Lublin Committee as *de jure* Government of Poland. Thus there were two 'Polish Governments' in existence. Each was headed by a Socialist; each consisted in form of a broad coalition; each was recognised by some of the allies. Neither had been in any way selected or approved by the Polish people or their representatives. Neither had the faintest chance of ruling the country, save in the wake of somebody else's army. Both were ostensibly fighting the same national enemy, who still occupied a good deal of the country; but they were condemning each other in unmeasured terms – uniting only in mutual detestation of Mikolajczyk. There was no kind of agreement as to the boundaries, either in the east or in the west, of the Polish state to whose allegiance both laid claim.

In November 1944 Roosevelt was re-elected. Political and formal duties detained him for several weeks more; but at last, in February 1945, the 'Argonaut' Conferences could be held. First Churchill and Roosevelt met in Malta; then both met Stalin at Yalta, in the Crimea. By the time of the Yalta meeting a large part of the eventual agreement had already been reached; but quite a lot of issues were unresolved. There was already agreement about the principle of the future occupation of Germany; but Churchill won rather reluctant acquiescence from the other two for the proposal that a military zone for France should be carved out of the area originally proposed for Britain. The armies would advance in order to secure 'maximum surrender' from the Germans; while tacit agreement already existed as to who should eventually occupy various places in the immediate aftermath of war. In general the countries of 'liberated Europe' would be free to decide on their own political destinies; but until elections could be arranged, it was more or less tacitly accepted that most would be set under coalitions in which communists and parties in the western Parliamentary tradition would participate – everybody, in fact, who was not tainted by 'fascism', which in practice meant past collaboration with the enemy.

Yet again Poland provided the most deeply controversial issues. The eastern frontier was agreed on the lines which Stalin had proposed long before. Roosevelt made a last stand for Lwów, but after Churchill's statement two months earlier his position was hopeless. The western frontier also accorded with Soviet requirements. The principle that the lower reaches of the Oder should form the frontier had long been more or less accepted, although the western statesmen had fears that this was extending Poland too far. It was also already agreed that the Neisse, tributary to the Oder, should form the frontier further to the south. Unfortunately the Oder has two tributaries of that name, and there was doubt which was intended. Stalin made it clear that it was the more southerly river, which meant that a good deal more of Germany still would come under Polish rule. A form of words was accepted as to the character of the government which was to rule Poland in the interim before elections could be held. This looked like a most important step forward in dealing with an exceedingly difficult problem; but, as we shall see, the agreement was more apparent than real.

Even before the principal statesmen got home the 'settlement' over Poland began to break down. The London Polish Government condemned it root and branch as a new 'partition'. There was a great deal of more muted concern on the matter among British politicians with a very wide range of political outlooks. Further and deeper trouble soon appeared; for it became apparent that Churchill and Stalin had departed from Yalta with very different ideas as to what had been agreed over the character of the new government which should rule Poland. Churchill had taken it to mean that both 'Polish Governments' would be disbanded, and a new one set up by agreement between the major allies; Stalin had taken it to mean that the government which his own country recognised would be modified slightly by injection of a few individuals acceptable to the Soviet Union. Roosevelt was compelled to tell Churchill that the second interpretation probably accorded the more closely with the wording agreed between them.[9] The western statesmen, however, were in full agreement that the Soviet-dominated administation which was in practice governing Poland was not complying with what had been agreed at Yalta about the condition of civil liberties which should prevail in the country; instead there appeared to be 'wholesale deportations and liquidations'. While this state of affairs persisted then – even if Stalin's interpretation of the Yalta agreement were accepted – the western allies could not consider recognising the Soviet-sponsored government in Poland.

The dispute over Poland began to broaden out into what later became known as the 'Cold War'. Throughout February 1945 the Prime Minister had been defending Stalin's *bona fides* to all comers: to the Cabinet; to the Prime Minister of New Zealand; to British politicians who evinced doubts on the matter – and finally, at the end of the month, in a *tour de force* before the House of Commons. Yet by 8 March he was so deeply shaken by reports received from Poland and the informed criticisms of Yalta which were beginning to appear, that he wrote to Roosevelt expressing fears lest 'you and I by setting our signatures to the Crimea settlement had underwritten a fraudulent prospectus'.[10] By the middle of March he was threatening, in a gesture almost of despair, to reveal the whole story of recent events in Poland,[11] virtually admitting to the world that he had been duped.

By this time Roosevelt was a very sick man; but his death on 12 April came as a general shock to the world. Roosevelt's successor, the relatively unknown and inexperienced Harry S. Truman, had not been kept *au fait* with the deeper secrets of government by his predecessor. Truman had an established reputation for an acid tongue, and on 23

April his first full meeting with Molotov took place. This concluded with a savage exchange on the matter of Poland. 'I have never been talked to like this in my life', declared the Soviet Foreign Minister. To this Truman retorted, 'Carry out your agreements and you won't get talked to like that'.[12]

One matter about which the two men had just been arguing was the forthcoming United Nations meeting in San Francisco. The Russian demanded that the satellite Poles should attend; the American refused point-blank, pending proper agreement and establishment of an acceptable regime. At one moment it looked as if Russia herself would withdraw unless her own condition was satisfied: a threat which both Truman and Churchill contemplated with equanimity, but which was eventually withdrawn.

By this time the European war was almost at an end. On 30 April Adolf Hitler committed suicide in his Berlin bunker, and on 7 May Grand Admiral Dönitz, second and last Führer of the German Reich, surrendered unconditionally to the allies. A conflict which had cost over forty million lives, half of them from the Soviet Union, was over. The war against Japan was certainly swinging in the allies' favour, but it was very far from ended. Yet, in this moment of apparent triumph, Churchill was in no mood for rejoicing. A very few days after Germany's final collapse the Prime Minister was writing to Truman in most sombre language, warning the President that current plans included the speedy withdrawal of British and American troops from the Continent, where Russia retained two or three hundred divisions.[13] This was the occasion on which the term 'iron curtain' made its appearance, as a description of the barrier which already existed between the region of Europe occupied by the Russians and that occupied by the western allies.

So disconcerting did all this inter-allied controversy seem that Truman made his own attempt to discover what lay behind it, and what action – if any – might be taken to avert further deterioration. Roosevelt's former associate, Harry Hopkins, was sent on a special mission to Stalin, whom he already knew well. Hopkins sought to explain how deep were American apprehensions about the suppression of civil liberties, particularly in Poland. These discussions led to a new agreement over Poland, by which the Russian-supported administration was broadened to include Mikolajczyk and some other Poles from the West. This relieved the uneasy consciences of the British and American Governments to the extent that they felt able to transfer recognition from Arcieszewski to the regime which was by now established at Warsaw.

Shortly after the German surrender the Labour Ministers in Churchill's Government decided that the moment had come to withdraw from the wartime coalition. A predominantly Conservative 'Caretaker Government' took office until an election could be held and its results declared. So Britain prepared to go to the polls, for the first time in nearly ten years. The general view – certainly the view of the Labour leadership, and also of Stalin[14] – was that Labour would improve its position, but fall short of a majority. Voting took place on 5 July, but problems involved in collecting votes from the forces delayed the declaration of poll for three weeks. In the event, Labour won a large over-all majority of seats, although – as nearly always happens – no party had an over-all majority of votes.

These results would prove of quite exceptional importance. From the standpoint of British domestic politics this represented the first occasion on which Labour received an independent majority in the House of Commons. The victorious party's programme had been laid out in an unusually clear and comprehensive manner, and its application was to prove of importance to the story which is here considered. One matter attracted immediate and world-wide attention. At Yalta the 'Big Three' had been the immensely prestigious war leaders, Stalin, Roosevelt and Churchill. Soon after that Conference preparations began for another top-level Allied meeting, to be held in the Berlin suburb of Potsdam at the end of July and the beginning of August. Before the conclusion of the Potsdam Conference two of the 'Big Three' had changed. Truman stood in place of Roosevelt, Clement Attlee in place of Churchill. Neither could hope to acquire the personal prestige of his predecessor; although Attlee, unlike Truman, had been for years associated with all the major decisions of his country's government.

The Potsdam Conference, appropriately code-named 'Terminal', began with Churchill still in office in Britain. Two remarkable pieces of information emerged almost at once. The Japanese had put out peace feelers in Moscow; and Truman learnt of a successful test explosion conducted on a totally new kind of weapon, based on fission of atomic nuclei. This 'atomic bomb' was the product of years of research conducted in the United States, with active British participation. By an agreement reached between Churchill and Roosevelt in 1943, the two countries shared control over its use. Truman – who had known nothing of the project when he succeeded Roosevelt – informed his counterparts at Potsdam of the new bomb.

Discussions at Potsdam were certainly not preoccupied with the atomic bomb, which would produce such an enormous effect on the last phases of war and on everything which has happened since. Nor do they seem to have given very high priority to discussions on the visibly deteriorating relations between the major allies, and the radically different views of a post-war world which lay behind these views. The main concern was Germany, and to an extent Japan. The delegates agreed that Germany should be treated as a single economic unit. This seemed reasonable, for the agricultural east balanced the industrial west. Then an unexpected question arose: what is Germany? Hitler's acquisitions from 1938 onwards could doubtless be excluded; but the lands east of the Oder which were destined for eventual Polish occupation by the Yalta agreement were of vital importance in feeding the rest of Germany. Stalin declared that all Germans had fled ahead of the advancing Red Army: therefore, that the only way of cultivating the land at all was by treating it as part of Poland. Churchill did not believe the truth of Stalin's assertion; but whether it was true or false there was nothing which the western allies could do about it. For practial purposes they had to feed western Germany largely from its own resources, and from what they were prepared to supply from outside. To add to the difficulty, millions of Germans had poured, and were still pouring, into the western zones from other parts of Europe, including a great many from the Russian zone; while the industrial base of the country had been gravely damaged in the war. This problem would certainly pose enormous difficulties for the western allies; yet it is striking to observe that all of the 'Big Three' continued to plan on the assumption that Germany was to be restored as a political entity at a later date. The occupying allies agreed to set up a Control Commission which would administer the country, and under whose authority a German bureaucracy could grow up, which would eventually administer the country on a decentralised basis.

The Japanese question appeared rather more straightforward. A formal message was sent from the governments of Britain, the United States and China, calling for surrender; and the Japanese for their part were prepared to come to terms. The real problem was the demand that this surrender should be unconditional, which the Japanese appeared determined to resist. Nobody could doubt that Japan would be defeated in the end if war continued; but she was apparently able to compel the allies to pay the price of a very long war in order to achieve this; and in that war the British and Americans might very well sustain more casualties than in the conflict against Germany. Such a price could prove unacceptable in democratic countries, and the Japanese had a realistic prospect of compelling them to agree to a face-saving compromise. The Soviet intervention which had been promised at Yalta would doubtless reduce the casualty lists; but Russia was not proposing to intervene as an act of gratuitous kindness to her allies. She obviously sought both territory and influence in the area which Japan currently controlled. Surviving accounts of whether the Anglo-American leaders still really wanted Russia to intervene at the time of Potsdam are in conflict; perhaps in truth top-level opinion in both countries was deeply divided. In any case the question was a theoretical one. If Japan did not surrender very quickly indeed, the Russians certainly would intervene, whether this suited the British and Americans or not.

On 2 August 1945 the Potsdam Conference ended. In the next few days massive attacks by 'conventional' weapons were launched against Japanese cities, in order to encourage a speedy decision from Tokyo. Then, on 6 August, the first atomic bomb was dropped, on the Japanese town of Hiroshima. The action was American, but British consent had first been obtained, as required by the Roosevelt-Churchill agreement of 1943. Two days after the destruction of Hiroshima the Soviet Union declared war on Japan. Next day, 9 August, the second atomic bomb was dropped, this time on Nagasaki. On the following day the Japanese Government announced its willingness to surrender, with reservations about the position of the Emperor. There was a good deal of face-saving diplomacy on both sides. Eventually, on 14 August, Japan agreed to surrender. The allies insisted on the word 'unconditional', although in truth some quite important conditions were introduced into the instrument of surrender signed on 2 September in Tokyo Bay. But the war was over.

12 Uneasy Peace

The condition in which Britain had emerged from the Second World War appears more favourable than that of most European countries. Her war dead, including civilian and merchant navy casualties, were about 400 000: around half the number she had lost in the 1914 conflict, about one-fiftieth the number of dead the Soviet Union had just sustained. The scale of destruction in her cities bore no comparison with Germany. She was still acknowledged one of the 'Big Three' for all international dealings: the co-equal of the United States and the Soviet Union.

The economic burden, however, was tremendous. It is not easy to make an accurate assessment – partly because it is often uncertain which expenses were strictly due to the war, partly because of currency fluctuations. In 1944 the total British war expenditure to date was calculated at £25 thousand millions.[1] This sum must be multiplied many times to convert it into modern money values. Taxation was greatly increased, but less than half of the money had been raised in that manner. The overseas investments sold are usually set at £1118 millions, while external debts of over £3350 millions were incurred.[2] Britain's total 'invisible income'. £248 millions a year in 1938, was less than half this figure eight years later.[3] The mercantile marine was reduced by 30 per cent, while British exports were down to 40 per cent of pre-war exports at comparable money values. At the same time Britain had acquired a burden of external expenditure from military occupation and other causes which could not easily be reduced for a long time to come – that is, unless Britain was prepared drastically to alter her world role. During the war the American system of Lend-Lease had enabled Britain and the Soviet Union each to make net borrowings in the region of £9 thousand millions; but on 17 August 1945, just three days after the surrender of Japan, Lend-Lease was brought to a sudden halt.

What had changed even more profoundly was the world milieu in which Britain found herself. Before 1939 Britain and France, Germany, Italy and Japan were the powers whose activities attracted most attention in the world. Now Germany, Italy and Japan were no longer

158

THE PRICE OF FLAGS

"Whatever I pay, it will have cost me more than anything I have ever bought before."

The Cost of Victory, 1945
Just before the end of the European War John Bull ponders on the drain which the war has
imposed on British resources.
Punch, London, 25 April 1945

powers at all, and France could hardly be taken seriously as a major
force. The two great 'outsiders', the Soviet Union and the United States,
had been drawn right to the centre of events, and neither of them could
withdraw even if they wished to do so.

As we have seen, there were already profound apprehensions in Britain and the United States as to the immediate aims of the Soviet Union. No doubt there was determination to ensure that the 1941 invasions should never be repeated, and Russia wished to establish a protective zone of sympathetic states on her margins. It is possible – though a good deal less certain – that there was real fear that the western democracies were meditating military action, and some writers have argued that the Soviet leaders were deeply apprehensive that the United States was preparing to use her current monopoly of nuclear weapons as a threat against themselves.

Another more subtle consideration almost certainly played a substantial part in Soviet behaviour. The political philosophy of the Soviet leaders was avowedly Marxist. Without arguing too closely just what 'Marxism' meant, or to what extent the Soviet Union had departed from pristine Marxist teaching into various 'heresies', Marxists were undeniably people who regarded the current condition of all countries outside the Soviet Union as unstable, and bound by the inescapable dialectic of history to succumb to revolutionary changes leading to the establishment of 'socialism'. During the war the Soviet leaders had played down Marxism both inside and outside the Soviet Union – indeed, they could hardly have done otherwise, since they desperately needed help from the West, and from the many Soviet citizens who retained exeedingly bitter memories of Stalin's behaviour in the 1930s. But what role had the Soviet leaders cast for themselves in the aftermath of war? If Russia proposed to be passive, to allow events in other countries to take their own course, then governments in those countries would doubtless deplore her prognosis of their fate, but had no reason to make this a matter for mutual hostility. But perhaps Russia would not remain passive. Some, at least, of the early Bolsheviks had seen the Russian revolution as the spark which would ignite a world-wide conflagration. There was good reason for thinking that the current leaders of the Soviet Union, and not least Stalin himself, still visualised the Soviet Union playing a major part in catalysing the breakdown of other states. Indeed, it may not have mattered much whether the Soviet leaders actually desired to play that part or not. Much could be said for the view that they would not willingly expend one Soviet life or one rouble in support of anybody else's revolution; but if they believed that they were 'predestined' to act as the revolutionary spearhead of the world proletariat, then this would inevitably colour their international behaviour. They would coerce everybody they could reach; they would do everything in their power to disaffect the subjects of other states; and they would prepare for eventual war with 'capitalist' countries whose role as enemies of the Soviet Union was also cast for them by the inescapable laws of Marxist dialectic. When people perceive a conflict as 'inevitable' then, even if there are no 'vital interests' truly at stake, the conflict is very likely to occur.

At first sight, the fears which Churchill expressed in May 1945 to the effect that the Soviet Union was in a position to build up an irresistible array of 'conventional' forces, might seem exaggerated and far-fetched. The democracies had a combined population far in excess of the Soviet Union; their technology was in most respects superior, and their productivity far greater. Yet in the spring of 1945 there was no certainty that the democracies would see major international events in the same light as each other. There was a more subtle point. A democratic government is under constant barrage from a critical and vigilant public opinion. It would be politically impossible to keep vast numbers of men under arms indefinitely to meet an uncertain threat, and inter-war experience suggested that similar pressures would be exerted to curtail spending on 'defence' – partly for pacifist reasons, partly for reasons of economy. By contrast, the Soviet Government had total control over organs of public expression, and encountered no comparable difficulties.

What cut across all these calculations was the arrival of the atomic bomb in the summer of 1945. When the two atomic bombs were eventually deployed against Japan in August, there was no suggestion that any allied government, including the Soviet Union, had reservations on the matter. Yet immediately after the first bomb was used – even before Nagasaki's fate was known – there was grave anxiety at the highest national levels in Britain about the implications of the new weapon.[4]

In the period which immediately followed the destruction of the two Japanese cities, various suggestions were advanced in international circles as to *who* should be allowed to know *what* about the new technology, and how its future development and use might be controlled. For a considerable time there was no clear idea in either Britain or the United States on such matters. Informed people did not doubt from the beginning that the western monopoly would soon be broken by the Soviet Union, and eventually by others as well, if the production of atom bombs remained in the hands of nation-states; indeed, in 1945 it was anticipated that the rate of international proliferation would soon be a good deal more than has actually proved the case.[5] No doubt nuclear powers would periodically jump ahead of each other in technological development; furthermore, nobody could be certain just how far rivals had progressed at any particular moment. In that sense there might be a kind of terrible 'security', for nobody could employ an apparent temporary superiority to coerce a rival through war or the threat of war. No doubt the best plan, if it could be made to work, would be to give a monopoly to the United Nations; but this attractive suggestion foundered on three rocks. First, the 'Great Powers Veto', built into the constitution of the United Nations, made it impossible to use United Nations coercion against the Big Three: in other words, the only countries against which the United Nations might conceivably wish to use such dreadful weapons in the foreseeable future were the very ones impervious to the threat. Secondly, it was excessively unlikely that an adequate system of inspection could be devised to ensure that nobody broke the rule. Thirdly, most serious of all was the fact that the cat was already out of the bag. Hundreds of people knew a great deal about the manufacture of atomic bombs; vastly greater numbers of people understood enough of the essential physics involved to be able to 're-invent' atomic bombs, should the need arise.

As soon as people began to take measure of the power of the new weapon it was appreciated that the fears Churchill had expressed in May about Soviet military might in Europe and the incapacity of the western democracies to resist that might should Russia desire to use it against them, were no longer applicable. In strategic terms the atomic bomb was worth a great many divisions of soldiers. Whatever might happen to anybody's nuclear technology, the Soviet Union would not be in a position to use its superiority in 'conventional' forces in order to coerce a rival who had atomic bombs available.

How far the Anglo-American monopoly of the atomic bomb really affected relations with the Soviet Union thereafter is far from clear, for we have no means of knowing how either side would have behaved without it. Truman had not been particularly communicative to Stalin about the matter at Potsdam, and the western democracies showed little eagerness to tell him of its details; but this behavior was probably taken as quite reasonable by the Soviet leaders. It is unthinkable that they would have been one whit less secretive if at that stage it had been Russia who possessed the monopoly.

In 1945, and on into 1946, there was an 'iron curtain' in Europe, but there was little of what might be called 'cold war', for neither side was taking active steps to push back the effective area of control possessed by the other. The allies, in east and west alike, were currently more worried about how to handle the enormous tracts of territory which had fallen into their control than about what other allies might happen to be doing. Right at the centre was a tremendous uncertainty about the future of Germany.

No doubt, when the final settlement came, slices of German territory would be given to various neighbours; but what would happen to the remainder? In the short term, of course, the military occupation would continue, and the western countries would be compelled in practice to accept Germany as an economic dependency. Various long-term solutions had been bruited in allied circles long before the war came to an end. The 'Morganthau Plan', emanating from one of Roosevelt's senior officials, proposed the destruction of German industry and the establishment of Germany as an agricultural state. A political proposal – not necessarily inconsistent with the Morganthau Plan – recommended that Germany should be re-divided into a number of smaller states. Both suggestions would obviously be disliked by the Germans themselves, and could only be enforced by coercion maintained for the whole foreseeable future. Both suggestions really presupposed close and permanent allied co-operation; both were quietly abandoned. Any other system of treatment immediately available would seem to involve the establishment of some kind of self-governing German state – perhaps federal or even cantonal in structure, but in the last analysis corresponding with the wishes of the German people themselves. Granted the mutual suspicions, not to say hostility, existing between the Soviet Union and the western democracies by the middle of 1945, neither could afford to risk Germany siding with the other – or that Germany might seek to play them off against each other to her own advantage.

By contrast, the initial stages of an Austrian settlement proved rather simple. Everybody took it for granted that the 1938 union with Germany would be broken. A few days before the European war ended, the Russians set up a Provisional Government within their own occupation zone, and soon afterwards established a 'Democratic Republic'. During October 1945 elections were held throughout the country, in unexceptionable conditions. The 'People's Party', a Catholic group, won a small overall majority, the Social Democrats came next, while the communists won a derisory four seats.

The treatment of Germany's principal European ally was also comparatively straightforward. The main burden of the war against Italy had been shouldered by the Anglo-Americans, who occupied most of the country, while part of Venezia Giulia was held by Yugoslav partisans. In the aftermath of Italy's defeat, Russia lay claim to a share of the Italian navy, but made no special claim for direct influence in the peninsula itself. Italian communists, however, were well-organised and influential. Their main weakness was that Yugoslavia, a country under communist control, lay claim to the permanent possession of Venezia Giulia. As communism was generally assumed to be monolithic, Italian communists could hardly oppose claims made by Yugoslav communists to part of Italy – while other Italians profoundly contested those claims on patriotic grounds, and the western democracies were disposed to side with them, for tactical reasons if for no others.

Many of the problems affecting Poland have already been discussed; but in the other Slav allies, too, great issues were being decided which had important implications for the 'Big Three' as well as for themselves. Czechoslovakia had had a functioning democracy on the western model before 1938; yet she lay in the area dominated by Russia. A precarious balance was set up between communists and their associates on one side and politicians in the western tradition on the other – with the prestigious, but declining, Edvard Beneš restored to the office of President. Almost immediately, Czechoslovakia was required to cede the backward eastern province of Ruthenia to the Soviet Union. The cession of the Sudetenland seven years earlier had been a matter of major international concern; the cession of Ruthenia attracted little world interest. What the people living in the area though about it is unknown; nobody bothered to ask them. Czechoslovakia, like Poland, proceeded to deal with ethnic problems which had proved so baleful before the war by expelling non-Slav peoples. Millions of Sudetendeutsch, and hundreds of thousands of Magyars, were thrown out of the country.

In Yugoslavia the international difficulties already considered were complicated by problems of internal politics. We have seen how, on British advice, support had been transformed from the 'official' Ćetniks to Tito's partisans, while the war was still being fought. Strenuous British efforts led to a frail political compromise – the 'Tito-Subasić agreement' – between the officially-recognised Government-in-Exile and the partisans – an agreement whose legality was, to say the least, dubious. In the event, Tito was soon able to rid himself of Subasić, who departed from the government in October 1945; whereafter the Marshal and his associates were in complete control. Most people thought that Yugoslavia would henceforth act as a Soviet satellite, like other countries in eastern Europe. That judgement was reasonable, but wrong.

In other countries of south-eastern Europe the 'Tolstoy'

arrangements of October 1944 led to exactly the result which Roosevelt had feared – a permanent division of spheres of influence. In Greece, allocated to British influence, occupying forces encountered great trouble from insurgents of very different political complexions; as an all-party Parliamentary delegation later reported, 'right and left wings share responsibility for the disorders and they are not prepared to say which group is the more culpable'.[6] Bad as this situation was from the point of view of the western allies, there is something to be said for the view that the 'Tolstoy' arrangements of 1944 had at least permitted them to retain some foothold in south-eastern Europe – which might otherwise have been difficult. Within the area allocated to the Soviet Union the pattern varied considerably from country to country. In Hungary the Coalition Government decided – against Soviet advice, but without express prohibition – to hold an early General Election on the western pattern, with parties making independent appeals to the electorate and not merely setting forth a single list of Coalition candidates on a common programme. The upshot was a great over-all majority for the Smallholders' party; but, by common consent, the Coalition system was retained. For the first time in its history Hungary seemed really set on the path towards a democratic parliamentary government. Romania and Bulgaria contrasted both with Hungary and with each other. In Bulgaria the communists operated something of a reign of terror in the countryside, and yet the staunch anti-communist Nikola Petkov remained in the government. In Romania conditions were much more peaceful, and yet the one really prestigious anti-communist, Iuliu Maniu, was pointedly excluded from office. The western countries still seemed to preserve a vestige of influence in the Balkans. In August 1945 Bulgaria was poised to hold an 'election' in conditions where there could clearly not be any proper expression of popular opinion. Right at the last moment, and on his own authority alone, the American representative Maynard Barnes intervened and secured an indefinite postponement.

In the remainder of Europe – roughly speaking, the area which had had long experience of democracy – indigenous institutions developed freely. Even Finland was permitted to follow her own course, without too much interference from her great neighbour. Spain, whose experience of democracy had been brief, and which was still ruled by Franco, was in an anomalous position. On one hand, Spain had contrived to remain neutral when it would have been very embarrassing to the allies if she had intervened on Germany's side. Yet she had sent 'volunteers' to fight against Russia. In practice Spain was treated as a pariah. There was no formal rupture of diplomatic relations, still less an attempt to throw out Franco by force; but the victorious allies all found it convenient to exclude Spain from the political, military and economic arrangements which they were making.

However deep the arguments between the allies about the future of European countries, in the great majority of cases political development was determined by various wartime arrangements defining areas of military occupation. *Cuius regio, eius religio.* In eastern Asia, by contrast, there were no rough-and-ready wartime agreements about future military occupation. Russia entered the war only a matter of days before the Japanese collapse. At the moment of that collapse Japanese troops were still in occupation of vast areas of Asia. The British, the Americans, the Russians, the 'Nationalist' Chinese of Chiang Kai-shek, the 'communist' Chinese of Mao Tse-tung, the French and the Dutch all had claims to make in respect of both territory and weapons currently in enemy possession. In a good many cases those allied claims ran into conflict with each other. In practice the decision usually turned on who happened to be where at what moment. The fact that the Chinese 'communists', who had been in a state of intermittent civil war with the country's government for many years, were in a position to take over large quantities of Japanese military equipment would perhaps prove of vital importance in determining the eventual upshot of the civil war. A more or less arbitrary arrangement, patched up at the last moment between the Americans and Russians, prescribed the division of occupation zones in Korea along the parallel 38°N: an arrangement whose consequences would prove momentous a few years later. In many territories formerly belonging to European empires there was the further complication that 'nationalist' movements of various complexions disputed the claim of their former masters to resume control. In some places 'nationalist' movements themselves were in bitter conflict with each other. The 'old' Japan – the islands which had been Japanese before Japan's career of expansion got under way in the 1890s – was to be placed under joint military control. That control soon passed largely into the hands of the American General MacArthur, with more or less tacit agreement from the other allies. In some ways the remarkable thing is how smoothly all these disputes between important allies were resolved.

War inevitably produced a great many other problems besides those which have just been considered. The measure of destruction and dislocation in the Soviet Union far exceeded that of the other major allies; but Russia appeared determined to solve her own problems, and the problem of the lands which she dominated, in her own way, and made little serious effort to secure help from others. What lay behind this reticence is an interesting matter for speculation. Probably several quite different factors were at work; but among them we may guess there was anticipation that general economic collapse of the 'capitalist' states would soon follow.

Almost immediately the war ended the British Government came to the conclusion that it was vital to negotiate a large loan from the United States. The principal British negotiators were the Ambassador to Washington and former Foreign Secretary, now Earl, Halifax, and the distinguished economist Lord Keynes; but at one point the talks almost broke down. The British were persuaded – or persuaded themselves – that their American counterparts were not without sympathy for Britain's predicament, but were compelled to take a stern line in order that the eventual agreement should have some chance of passing Congress. A British Government can usually undertake international negotiations in the confident expectation that parliament will take any action which may be recommended; an American Government cannot make similar assumptions about Congress.

The agreement concluded in Washington on 6 December 1945 was in some features very generous to Britain. A total loan of $4400 millions (£1100 millions at the prevailing exchange rates) was to be granted, of which $650 millions would be used to extinguish the Lend-Lease debt. The remaining sum of $3750 millions (£937 millions) could be drawn to the end of 1951, whereafter it was repayable in up to fifty annual instalments, carrying 2 per cent interest. This credit was earmarked for specific purposes, and goods and services purchased thereunder could only be bought in the United States. Its most controversial feature, however, was the requirement that Britain should immediately ratify the Bretton Woods agreement which had been concluded between the wartime allies in July 1944. At that time Bretton Woods had been a matter of little controversy. The parties had agreed to end the competitive depreciation of currencies and the exchange restrictions which, by the received wisdom of the time, had been among the principal causes of unemployment and international tensions during the inter-war period. It was at Bretton Woods, too, that agreement was reached on the establishment of what would later become known as the International Monetary Fund (IMF).

The new agreement of December 1945 – if ratified – would require Britain to grant full and immediate convertibility of pounds into dollars, and would also require her to co-operate with the Americans in the rapid removal of restrictions on external trade. The principle that these measures were eventually desirable was widely accepted; but, as so often happens, there was great dispute over the matter of timing. The controversy was fought at many different levels, and astonishing alliances and antagonisms arose within British politics.

A week before the two governments agreed on the loan, there was much argument in the British Cabinet. Two ministers generally regarded as spokesmen of the 'left', Aneurin Bevan and Emanuel Shinwell, fought strenuously against acceptance of the terms, and others were somewhat lukewarm in support.[7] It appears, however, that the controversy within the Cabinet was not over the necessity of the loan itself. The critics seem to have believed that it would be possible to avoid the Bretton Woods requirement by accepting more onerous interest terms. In the debates which ensued in Parliament the arrangements were challenged by Socialists who contended that they were incompatible with economic planning, and by Conservatives who saw them as incompatible with Britain's imperial position. In the end the matter was resolved by Parliamentary whipping. Government tellers naturally recommended acceptance, but 23 Labour MPs went to the point of voting in the opposite lobbies; while controversy was so deep in the Conservative Party that the leaders could only preserve a measure of unity by recommending abstention. In spite of this eight of their MPs voted with the government and 71 against it. The debate in Congress was no less confused, and a good deal more protracted. When the two Houses eventually voted, in May 1946, rather slender majorities supported the loan. Both parties were deeply split; but the Republicans divided with something like 2:1 majorities against.

Although at the end of 1945 relations between the 'Big Three' – indeed, relations between Britain and the United States – were far less than idyllic, there were many signs that a kind of recovery was taking place. Broadly, this pattern continued into 1946; yet nobody got very far with the critical problem of Germany. The idea that Germany should be preserved as an economic unit had already dissolved in miasma. The Soviet zone was the main food-producing area, and Russia plainly had no intention of helping the others to overcome their problems in feeding their own parts of Germany. The French were in a special position, partly because their zone was economically profitable and partly because there was a considerable movement for the annexation of parts of that zone to France. The British and American zones were both left with regions which were economic liabilities. By the end of 1946 the two Anglo-Saxon powers had agreed on economic amalgamation of their zones; but there was at that moment little sign that the French – still less the Russians – would join in.

By contrast, the allies made considerable headway towards a peace treaty with Italy. Although the treaty was not signed until February 1947, its general provisions were clear by the autumn of 1946. Italy was to lose all her external possessions. Albania had already recovered independence. The Dodecanese passed to Greece, the Dalmatian islands to Yugoslavia, the Italian colonies would be lost – but the victors failed to reach agreement about their eventual disposition. A sliver of territory would go to France, and most – though not all – of Venezia Giulia to Yugoslavia. The town of Trieste, about which much argument raged, was constituted a 'free territory'. Italy was readmitted to the comity of nations; the problems over Trieste and the Italian colonies were for others to decide.

Throughout 1946 the precarious arrangements in Poland continued. In Czechoslovakia, elections held in the spring – at which non-Slavs were disfranchised – confirmed the strange balance between communist and non-communist forces. The coalition remained. A Communist, Klement Gottwald, became Prime Minister; but democratic politicians like President Beneš and Foreign Minister Jan Masaryk stayed. In Czechoslovakia, more than any other country, there was a real 'test case' to determine whether true co-operation was possible between communists and non-communists. Meanwhile the Soviet grip was visibly tightened in Hungary and Romania. The great triumph of the Hungarian Smallholders rapidly turned to dust and ashes. The Soviet Union required Hungary to bear the impossible burden of 600 000 occupying Russians: numbers completely indefensible on strictly military grounds. This led to a collapse of the currency, and the most extreme inflation any country has ever known; while the morale and prestige of the Smallholders was rapidly eroded in consequence. In Romania 'elections' were held amid conditions of general malpractice, and were followed by show trials, plainly designed to intimate all anti-communist elements, and to set the scene for their total elimination at no distant date. Curiously, the pattern was different in Bulgaria. Elections were held in conditions which, by Balkan standards, were almost unexceptionable, and a substantial opposition remained after those elections were over.

The countries of western Europe followed the more uncertain developments of democratic politics. Most remarkable was the experience of France. As we have seen, there was much wartime argument between the allies about whom they recognised as the country's spokesmen, and what authority they were prepared to grant to any French administration; but in the end they all acknowledged a government presided over by de Gaulle: a very broad coalition including communists. In the course of 1946 de Gaulle made a temporary withdrawal from politics. It required no deep understanding to guess that he proposed eventually to return as the 'man of destiny'. A series of elections and constitutional referenda gave no very clear results. The communists emerged, by a narrow margin, as the largest single group; but in a land of multiple parties and constant coalitions they were not remotely in view of an over-all majority.

Although in some respects international relations appeared to have stabilised in the year or eighteen months which followed the end of the war, there was a sombre and growing recognition that great issues remained unresolved. In a famous speech of March 1946, delivered at Fulton, Missouri, in the presence of President Truman, Winston Churchill warned that the Soviet Union sought the 'fruits of war', though not war itself; and the implication seemed to be that Britain and the United States should co-operate to resist. Churchill spoke as a private individual: at most, as the leader of a defeated British political party; but the Soviet leaders and a good many critics in Britain and the United States as well, saw his utterance as a major statement carrying some kind of authority with the governments both of his own country and of the one in which he was speaking. In September the United States Secretary of State, James Byrnes, made a more clearly authoritative speech at Stuttgart, which to a considerable extent reassured people who shared Churchill's apprehensions; but his most important observation was that 'as long as an occupation force is required for Germany, the army of the USA will be part of that occupation force'. The Americans had come a long way in eighteen months; for at Yalta Roosevelt had told the other allies that in his judgement Congress would not authorise American armies to remain in Europe for more than two years.

Although one may recognise forces at work which would soon commit the United States firmly to the defence of western Europe against possible communist aggression, the measure of that commitment was by no means clear in 1946. Byrnes, despite the apparent clarity of his Stuttgart speech, had an established reputation in both internal and international politics as a compromiser. A sharp controversy, turning in part on that very speech, led to the peremptory dismissal of Truman's Secretary of Commerce, Henry Wallace, who then set to work organising a new American political party with markedly pro-Soviet sympathies. At the mid-term Congressional elections in November 1946, the Republicans took control of both Houses, and the President's position was greatly weakened.

Thus, by the end of 1946, American politics seemed in a greater state of confusion than they had been for a very long time. The Democratic administration was torn by deep dissension, and now had to contend with hostile Congressional majorities. Although, for the time being, 'isolationism' seemed on the retreat, nobody could be sure that it would not return. There was also a very influential 'China lobby', who argued that the Far East was more important to American defence than was western Europe. If a major depression were to arise, then anything could happen.

If the position of the United States was uncertain, the capacity of any country in continental Europe west of the Soviet Union to stand on its own feet – whether in political, economic or military terms – was dubious in the extreme. From Britain's point of view, there was no certain long-term friend anywhere. During this period of deepening anxiety over American policy and European stability, one exceedingly important British decision was taken. The 1943 arrangements over the atomic bomb required revision, or at least restatement. In November 1945 Attlee visited Truman to discuss problems of nuclear development, both in peaceful and in military fields. They agreed that a Commission of the United Nations should be set up to make recommendations, and in early 1946 the appropriate body was established. Yet nobody could feel much confidence that any effective control of future nuclear weapons would result, and discussions developed between Britain and the United States about their own attitudes on the matter, should United Nations agreement prove impossible. The British Government seems to have thought at first that the Attlee-Truman conversations would lead to arrangements not wildly different from those of 1943; but, for a variety of reasons, no new agreement emerged. Nobody could feel certain that Britain and the United States would continue to see world affairs in essentially similar terms. In 1947 a specifically British programme for the manufacture of atomic weapons was inaugurated. Details of how the relevant decisions were taken are still not clear. Not all the Cabinet was told, and the matter was kept as a closely-guarded secret for the next five years. Plainly, the object was in one sense to deter the Soviet Union from aggression in Europe; but it also looks very much like an attempt to ensure that the United States did not resign from her interest in Europe.

Here was the uneasy, but also tolerable, 'iron curtain' condition which had developed in Europe and parts of eastern Asia about the end of 1946 and the beginning of 1947. There was little goodwill remaining between the Soviet Union and the West, and not all that much goodwill between the western democracies themselves. To all appearances, however, nobody proposed to make any really dangerous incursions into what others might regard as their vital interest for some time to come. In theory, the governments of many European countries on both sides of the 'iron curtain' were coalitions, including communist and non-communist members. In practice, in most of those countries true co-operation was breaking down. The countries of eastern Europe were coming more and more under communist control. Czechoslovakia was the only one in which some degree of true co-operation remained. At the other extreme communists and non-communists in Greece were on the verge of civil war. The wartime vision of post-war co-operation between allies might have vanished; but there was still some prospect that power could be divided in a peaceable manner, without the actuality or direct threat of physical force.

13 1947

In the early part of 1947 the British Government took a number of decisions whose importance nobody doubted at the time, but which would prove of even greater importance than most contemporaries contemplated: decisions which would determine in outline the future of Britain and of a very large part of the world from that day to this. These decisions bore on Britain's economic position; on her role as an imperial power; on her mandatory duties; and on much wider question of international relations in the developing 'cold war'. To appreciate the circumstances in which these decisions were taken, it is necessary to look at the background of events in several parts of the world.

Not long before the Congessional elections of 1946 Byrnes indicated to the President that for reasons of health he must soon resign the Secretaryship of State. Relations between the two men had not been good, and at the beginning of 1947 he was succeeded by General George C. Marshall: a soldier with Democratic proclivities, but with sufficient charisma in his wartime record to commend him to non-party opinion: a matter of substantial importance in current political conditions. Marshall was no implacable opponent of the Soviet Union for, during the war, he had been an early and enthusiastic advocate of the 'Second Front' which Russia was demanding, but he differed from Byrnes in his far greater loyalty to the President and by showing much less disposition to compromise on matters of principle. In a couple of years of office Marshall was able to establish himself as one of the most visionary statesmen of the post-war era.

As Marshall assumed office, a major crisis was developing in Britain and other parts of Europe: a crisis with many economic, political and military overtones. That crisis had various causes; but the abominable winter of 1946–47 played some part in precipitating it. Exceptional weather conditions led to a shortage of fuel in Britain so intense that street lighting was switched off at night and domestic use of electricity was banned for much of the day. The impact on industry was dramatic. The coal shortage had repercussions on many branches of production, and unemployment, which had been well below the 'frictional' level since 1940, returned briefly to inter-war dimensions. The drain on dollars from the American loan was becoming uncontrollable. In the third quarter of 1946 it had been only around $70 millions a month; by January 1947 it stood at $137 millions, while in March it had reached $323 millions, and seemed likely to remain at that sort of level for a long time to come. Meanwhile, prices of goods which Britain required were rising rapidly. Perhaps most serious of all was a desperate world shortage of dollars. Countries requiring dollars to pay for goods from the United States promptly changed any sterling they received into American currency.[1] So the British Government became increasingly eager to liquidate external commitments, and most particularly those which were economic liabilities.

One of these commitments was a quite recent one which could be shed fairly easily, although the international consequences of British withdrawal might prove serious in the extreme. As we have seen, the British had entered Greece during the war for military reasons, but in the aftermath the country moved into something close to civil war. A series of weak and unattractive Greek governments drifted in and out of office, but they all agreed that it was very important that British troops should remain. If these troops withdrew without alternative provision being made, the Russians and their Balkan allies would very soon be able to produce a decisive victory for the communist-led ELAS. The Soviet Union would then be in a strong position to exert pressure on Turkey – indeed, there had been recent indications that nineteenth century Russian interests towards control of the Bosporus were still very much alive. Should this strategy succeed then the Soviet Union would dominate a large part of the Middle East and the eastern Mediterranean, with consequences alarming in the extreme.

The only possible way in which Britain might withdraw from Greece without Russia moving in was by handing over responsibility to the United States. Yet would the Americans accept such an *hereditas damnosa*: a country where they had few economic or strategic interests and which was bound to remain a heavy burden for a long time to come? Behind the problem of Greece was the much greater question of whether the United States would gradually take over from Britain the prime responsibility for defence of Europe and adjacent countries. There were considerable forces at work in the United States which might be expected to return a negative reply. People like Wallace sought to reduce areas of possible friction with the Soviet Union. 'Isolationsists' argued that involvement outside the American continent entailed risks and costs quite incommensurate with possible benefits. The 'China lobby' still contended that the Far East, rather than Europe, should be the main external concern of the United States. The President's political position, in the face of a hostile Congress, was weak in the extreme, and the temptation for either his critics or his supporters to 'play politics' was acute.

Towards the end of 1946 Byrnes had suggested a compromise: that Britain should attend to the military requirements of Greece and also Turkey, while the United States should attend to their economic needs. Attlee and Foreign Secretary Bevin both reacted sharply against this suggestion, suspecting that the effect would be for Britain to incur the obloquy while America reaped the credit.[2] The economic crisis, however, was pressing, and at the end of Janauary 1947 the Cabinet resolved that British forces in Greece would be reduced to a single brigade, which itself should be withdrawn as soon as the Russians pulled out of Bulgaria. With Marshall now Secretary of State, the United States was willing to take on the dual responsibility, and on his subordinate's urgent prompting, Truman accepted the challenge. The immediate need was to provide a loan of $250 millions for Greece and $150 millions for Turkey. In appealing to Congress on 12 March for this grant the President did not confine himself to the immediate matter, but promulgated the much wider principle which became known as the 'Truman Doctrine': 'It must be the policy of the United States to support free peoples who are resisting attempted subjugation by armed minorities or by outside pressure'. He sought not merely money, but authority to send American soldiers and civilians if necessary. No doubt was left in anybody's mind that the immediate appeal, if granted, would be followed by further, and probably much greater, requests. The President ran into the predictable difficulties at home. Perhaps it was the very diversity of these attacks which enabled him to fend them all off, and by May he had secured convincing Congressional majorities for the grants demanded.

In the very difficult economic conditions of early 1947 a great many countries were certain to ask for financial assistance from the United States; while America, whose production was in vastly better shape than anybody else's, had excellent financial reasons for acceding to some, at least, of these requests. By 7 April programmes for loans totalling close on $2500 millions were either already in front of Congress or in active preparation. Yet even American capital was not unlimited, and it was necessary to decide – both for economic and for strategic reasons – how the available money should be allocated. On 12 May the Joint Chiefs of Staff sent forward with approval a report recommending an order of priorities on essentially strategic grounds. Western Europe, including Great Britain, took first place, followed in order by the Middle East, North-West Africa, Latin America and the Far East. Assistance – they proposed – should be given on a scale adequate to enable the recipient to maintain a sound economy and defend itself in a manner which would be of real assistance to the United States in the event of what was rather delicately called 'ideological warfare'.[3]

Britain's needs, grave as they were, were a good deal less acute than those in many countries both inside and outside Europe; but the American planners had no doubt that Britain ranked first of all in importance for American security. Despite the dramatic decline of the previous few years, she was still the third country in international importance. Thus when Marshall made an exceedingly important speech at Harvard on 5 June 1947, it was Bevin who was tipped to take it up, and who thereafter assumed the principal initiative at the European end of the transaction.

The gravamen of Marshall's concern was not very clear from his speech; but his aim was to persuade the Europeans to draw up their own lists of their respective requirements for American aid, and to provide some sort of indication as to how it would be used. Thus the so-called 'Marshall Plan' was not really Marshall's plan at all, but an invitation to others to devise their own plans. The Americans were anxious to avoid the invidious task of distinguishing between the special pleadings of the various claimants, and they were also anxious to ensure that the massive contributions which they were prepared to offer did not get frittered away through trade restrictions erected by Europeans against each other.

The Marshall initiative was set out in terms broad enough to permit any European country, including the Soviet Union, to participate. No doubt great problems, as well as great opportunities, would have arisen if Russia had chosen to do so. But Molotov made impossible stipulations – demanding that the Americans should first be asked how much money was available; whereafter the claimants should be invited to present their own separate and individual requests. This, of course, ran counter to the whole idea, and could reasonably be regarded as a rejection of the Marshall offer. Thereafter Britain and France issued invitations to all other European countries except Spain. The countries outside Russia's orbit all accepted. Poland, Czechoslovakia and Hungary thought of doing the same, but were compelled to refuse by Soviet Pressure. What became known as the European Recovery Program was devised to meet and harmonise requirements, and

THE TIDE IS COMING IN

Marshall Aid, 1947-48

Western Europe is marooned, as the tide of Communism rises. American Secretary of State Marshall calls for economic assistance. Not only is President Truman responding to the appeal, but so also is the Republican and formerly isolationist Senator Vandenburg.
Daily Herald, London, 3 March 1948

Congress eventually approved this without too much difficulty. It is interesting to ponder why the Soviet Union should have rejected the Marshall offer both for itself and for its satellites, in view of the intense need for aid in reconstruction. Whatever the idea may have been, the unfortunate side-effect of the Marshall offer and Soviet rejection was to sharpen the division of Europe into two economic groups, one looking towards the United States and the other towards the Soviet Union for leadership. Deplorable as that division now appears, the practical alternative was probably to allow western Europe to disintegrate through economic decay and human misery, and eventually to collapse into the chaos of revolution and counter-revolution, whose outcome would be anyone's guess.

Within a very short time, the vestiges of co-operation between communist and non-communist forces in Europe had largely disappeared. In the spring of 1947 communists were driven from the ruling coalitions in France, Belgium and Luxembourg, and thereafter they were kept out. About the same time the vestiges of influence from democratic parties in eastern Europe were practically extinguished. Leading political figures were dramatically victimised. Maniu of Romania was sentenced to lifelong imprisonment, Petkov of Bulgaria was executed, Ferenc Nagy, the 'Smallholder' Prime Minister of Hungary, went into exile. More spectacular still, Mikolajczyk of Poland, nominee of the Anglo-Americans, was induced to flee from his country, with the kindly assistance of a truck driver equipped with a monkey-wrench and half a million zloty, and prepared to use either. Only in Czechoslovakia did a precarious sort of co-operation between communists and non-communists persist for a little longer.

Thus did the economic crisis of early 1947 provide the occasion for Britain's final withdrawal from any claim to dominant influence in Europe. The same year also witnessed the clearest evidence of her retreat from an imperial role in Asia. Again it is necessary to see events of that crucial year in an earlier context.

The offer made by the Coalition Government in 1942, that India should receive independence when the war was over, could not be rescinded, even though in one sense it had 'lapsed'. Most serious politicians in all parties took the point, although there was some vociferous resistance by people who found it difficult to adjust to the realities of the mid-twentieth Century. In any event the Labour Party entered office in 1945 with a formal commitment to grant India independence.

At this time, most people in Britain probably assumed that 'independence' for India would mean 'Dominion status'. The country would thereafter co-operate voluntarily in a 'special relationship' with Britain and the other Dominions – rather as Canada, Australia, New Zealand and – to an extent – South Africa had been doing for several decades. Perhaps there was an unspoken assumption that all the future Dominions would continue to look to Britain – 'the mother country' – for guidance and leadership; but if they did this it would be out of free choice, not out of compulsion.

India was particularly good ground for testing the hypothesis that, granted goodwill on Britain's part, countries with non-British populations would evolve from dependencies into free Dominions. Many members of the British Government had campaigned for Indian independence long before the war, at a time when there were no political advantages and some disadvantages to be derived from so doing. The Indian leaders with whom they had associated, could have no doubt about their good faith. Yet almost immediately it took office the new government ran into the old question which had vexed the Coalition, and to some extent the National Government before it. How, and to whom, should independence be granted? In a vast and varied country where most people were desperately poor and illiterate peasants, there were also considerable numbers of highly educated and articulate men who could be regarded as the natural spokesmen. The Congress leaders could make reasonable claim to speak for the small minority who had the vote in the predominantly Hindu provinces; but did they speak for anybody else? One could not assume that a majority even of Hindus shared Congress's aspirations; while there was little doubt that most of the articulate Moslems were deeply opposed. Among the various difficulties encountered by Cripps in 1942, not least had been the fact that Congress considered that any plan guaranteeing entrenched rights to the Moslems struck at the political unity of India, while the Moslem League insisted that entrenched rights were absolutely vital for protection of their own permanent minority. Indeed, they had criticised the British proposals on the grounds that they would leave too small an area for Moslem autonomy, with many of their co-religionists coming unwillingly under Hindu rule. There was the further complication of the Indian princes. Congress – and, for that matter, the new Labour Government in Britain – might deplore princely rule on a variety of political, economic and social grounds; but, long ago, Britain had entered into treaty obligations with the Princes, which she could not forego without loss of moral authority.

Whatever difficulties might lie ahead, the next step at least was not in serious dispute. There must be new elections, first for the Provincial legislatures and later for the Constituent Assembly. The process would be protracted, the atmosphere was far from encouraging. Messages from the Viceroy warned that Congress was likely to resort to force, perhaps even before the first batch of elections.[4] These fears were not realised, and in the spring of 1946 the Provincial elections were held. The result, however, was not encouraging for those who hoped for some compromise between extreme Hindu and Moslem positions. As in the Assembly contests a couple of years earlier, Congress won almost a clean sweep of seats where there was a Hindu majority, while the Moslem League achieved a similar performance in Moslem areas.

Long before the elections the British Government was already planning the next step in the process of granting independence. Some kind of Indian body would need to prepare the country's constitution, and British advice would be required. The Cabinet resolved to send a mission of three senior Ministers which included Cripps. The mission was authorised to inform the Indians that the British Government would support any constitutional arrangements which might emerge, provided that these met certain essential conditions, including safeguards for minorities.[5]

Very soon after the Provincial elections, it became apparent that the Indians were not likely to reach agreement without outside assistance, and the Cabinet mission was authorised to set forth its own proposals. At first it seemed as if the mission's long-term recommendations, at any rate, were a resounding success, for both Congress and the Moslem League accepted them. 'For the first time,' rejoiced Cripps, 'the Indian politicians . . . seemed to accept the sincerity of our efforts on India's behalf'.[6] Soon, however, new difficulties began to appear. Everybody agreed that some kind of Coalition Government should be set up to cover the period which would elapse before the Constituent Assembly could meet, but for a long time there was deadlock as to what its composition should be. Moslem apprehensions were acute, and in August an 'Action Day' was held under the League's sponsorship. Although the original intention had apparently been that demonstrations should be peaceful, riots occurred at Calcutta where thousands of people were killed. Hindu reprisals followed, culminating in counter-massacres at Bihar, where casualties are said to have been even higher. There was much dispute about the true number of victims; but there appears general agreement that the British Government's official estimate of 6700 as the total deaths sustained in the various communal riots erred heavily on the conservative side.

In the light of after-knowledge some people had been disposed to regard these communal riots as crucial and fatal to India's future unity.[7] Perhaps that was so; but a considerable time elapsed before hope was abandoned. In October the Viceroy was at last able to set up a credible Coalition Government, to the great satisfaction of the British Cabinet. But this relief did not last long. In the following month the Moslem League decided that their representatives would not attend the meetings of the Constituent Assembly, due in December. So representatives of Congress, the Moslem League and the Sikhs were summoned to London to consult with the Viceroy and the Cabinet. Those meetings were not encouraging, and strong doubts began to be expressed in Cabinet as to whether the Indians had even the will, still less the capacity, to reach agreement. Yet there was a strong current of opinion that the various Indian groups did really hope in the end to reach a settlement, but were engaging in dangerous brinkmanship with the object of securing the best possible terms for themselves – relying on the British presence to contain the periodic outburst of disorder within manageable limits, while the haggling continued.

The Viceroy advised that Britain was very near the limit of her power to contain the situation with forces currently at her disposal. In December he told the Cabinet that civil war between Hindus and Moslems might break out 'at any time', while Britain could not maintain control beyond March 1948 – if indeed for as long as that. Wavell suggested that the position might prove different if the British Government were to declare its intention to remain in India for a further fifteen years, and to reinforce its army there by four or five extra divisions.[8] Politically, this was out of the question. Quite apart from the promises and predilections of the Ministers and the Parliamentary majority which sustained them, nobody could visualise the British public at large making the sacrifices which would be necessary. The British Government was gradually steeling itself to ask some very penetrating questions about its existing military commitments, and there was no possibility whatever of undertaking new ones of that character.

The worsening economic situation in Britain at the beginning of 1947 may have played a substantial part in encouraging the government to force the pace, and an announcement was prepared to the effect that they proposed to transfer power not later than the following year. For a moment there was a glimmer of hope that Congress and the Moslem League might reach agreement without that pistol being pointed at their respective heads, and so the announcement was held in reserve. Then, suddenly, a new cleavage appeared – this time between the Cabinet and Wavell. Perhaps the Viceroy had been bluffing, and had overstated the risks. In any event he strongly opposed the intended announcement. There was even deeper disagreement as to the manner in which British withdrawal should take place. Wavell thought that it should be 'planned on the lines of a military evacuation from hostile territory'[9] – presumably meaning that the British would do all in their power to salvage their own personnel and possessions, while leaving India to whatever chaos might supervene. The Cabinet was convinced that the consequences of such a policy would be appalling for India and Britain alike. There was still a fair chance that power could be transferred in an orderly, even a friendly, manner.

So two critical issues were handled at once. On 20 February Attlee made the announcement that power would be handed over not later than June 1948; furthermore, that Wavell would be replaced as Viceroy by Admiral Lord Mountbatten. The new Viceroy at first entertained hopes that a settlement might be achieved which would preserve Indian unity; but by May he had reached the conclusion that no such arrangement was possible.[10] In Mountbatten's view an early announcement from Britain as to the manner in which power was to be transferred was imperative in order to avert 'widespread and uncontrollable disturbances'. Paradoxically, the one encouraging aspect of the situation was that the various Indian parties had at last agreed on the necessity of partition. Thus the principle of a separate 'Pakistan' was no longer a matter of controversy at all.

On 2 June 1947 Mountbatten made a final effort to secure agreement between the various Indian groups on some solution which did not involve partition, but neither he nor anybody else believed that this had any serious prospect of success. The alternative plan for transferring power to two separate authorities was favourably received by all concerned. There was nothing to be said for further delay, and the agreed plan was pushed forward with great speed. Pakistan would include the Moslem areas in the north-west of British India, and also the Moslem part of Bengal – even though East Pakistan had little except religion in common with the major area of the new country, from which it was separated by several hundred miles. The princely states would need to make their own arrangements with the new Dominons. The Indian Independence Bill was moved on 15 July, and received Royal assent thirteen days later. On 15 August 1947 the two new Dominions formally came into existence.

Partition left considerable minorities on both sides of the line. The respective majorities saw them as alien enemies; the minorities were resentful and fearful. A great wave of massacres and counter-massacres ensued, while vast number of refugees wandered one way or the other. The future of some of the princely states would continue to vex all concerned for a long time to come. Yet, from Britain's point of view, imperial rule in India was over, and the future of the two new Dominions had passed largely from her control.

New and important constitutional questions would soon arise, and to that story it will be necessary to return. But it was clear for all to see that the gigantic precedent of India, the first non-white Commonwealth country to become independent, woud exert vital influence on the course of events in a great many other places.

In another very important area the economic crisis of 1947 also played a large part in catalysing processes which had been developing for a long time. Not long after the Labour Government took office in 1945 there had been serious discussions over the future of the Arab world. It was common ground that existing governments in the area were feudal monarchies, within which vast disparities of wealth and poverty existed: regimes both corrupt and inefficient which, from a long-term point of view, were inviable. For the time being, however, no credible alternative existed. Bevin expatiated to the Cabinet about the need to 'remedy the maldistribution of purchasing power in the Middle Eastern countries and to raise the standard of living of the masses of the people'[11] – arguing that such a policy would not only benefit those living in the area, but would also simplify the problems affecting Britain. At the time when the Foreign Secretary delivered himself of those laudable sentiments few people in the world would have questioned the underlying assumption that the initiative in such matters would naturally come from Britain.

At that time there appeared good reason for thinking that one kind of British burden would become reduced in any event. It appeared likely that amicable agreements would soon be reached with Egypt and Iraq, by which they would undertake their own defence more or less entirely, and yet continue to co-operate closely with Britain. If the burden of policing Palestine could be discharged or substantially reduced as the result of some kind of agreement between Arabs and Jews, then there was good reason for thinking that the general prospect both for Britain and for the Middle Eastern countries was bright.[12]

Unfortunately the Palestine problem had been deteriorating as the war proceeded, and would soon have disastrous consequences throughout the Middle East. The celebrated White Paper of 1939 had appeared at a time when it required no prophetic genius to foretell European war within a few months; while everybody knew that the Nazis had long been pursuing a savage and vicious poilicy of persecution against Jews in the Reich. What few people foresaw was that this policy would lead to deliberate genocide against Jews throughout a large part of Europe. Even after war began the Nazis themselves appear to have taken a considerable time to settle on that appalling plan. Once it was set in operation, however, the pressure of desperate Jews seeking to enter Palestine mounted to an enormous extent. But why did these tragic refugees seek to reach Palestine rather than other destinations? To an extent, this was a response to the growing Zionist sentiment among Jews themselves: itself a natural reaction to the sufferings of their people, and recognition that anti-Semitism was by no means confined to Nazi

Germany. In other cases, no doubt, Jews sought to reach a country where friends were already established. But there was a further important factor at work; for other countries were unwilling to accept large numbers of immigrants, anticipating social and political problems if they did so. Ugly stories were circulated, suggesting that a great many Jews who perished in the holocaust might have been saved if Britain and other allied countries had behaved more generously towards them, or exerted themselves more eagerly on the Jews' behalf. This is not the place to assess the truth or falsehood of such allegations; what matters is that they were made and often believed. Yet at the same time as Britain's moral standing among the Jews was declining through such reports, the Arab world was becoming increasingly fearful that the White Paper policy would eventually be abandoned in favour of massive Jewish immigration, and the Jews would come to swamp the Arabs in Palestine. Naturally Axis propaganda during wartime sought to fan such fears, and for that reason considerable numbers of Arabs gave more or less support to the enemy cause.

In the last phase of the war the matter of future British policy, once the White Paper quota of 75 000 was reached, came under active discussion in British Government circles. The question was still not resolved when the war in Europe ended and the Coalition left office. President Truman immediately began to set pressure on the new Labour Government to remove the limits on Jewish immigration into Palestine which had been imposed by the 1939 White Paper.[13] By September 1945, when the Cabinet had time to review the situation, immigration was within three thousand of the final quota; yet pressure from Jews seeking to enter Palestine was in no way abating. Four months after the collapse of Nazi Germany, actual persecution of Jews had not ceased in some parts of Europe, while in many places they were living in conditions of great privation.[14] By this time, Jews in other countries – notably the United States – were pressing for much more Jewish immigration into Palestine, and the figure of a further 100 000 immigrants was often proposed. In Attlee's view such immigration 'while it would lead to an explosion in the Middle East, could not solve the problems of the Jews in Europe'.

The Prime Minister sought to persuade Truman that there were other places which were capable of receiving large numbers of Jews.[15] The overriding British concern, however, was not so much how the problem should be solved, but the Britain should not be compelled to face it alone. In particular the government hoped to persuade the United States to participate in a general enquiry in which the future of Palestine and the settlement of European Jews could both be studied. The American

Government, however, was not willing to examine the two questions separately. In the view of the British Ambassador to Washington, the approaching mid-term elections of 1946 were already casting shadows forward, and considerations influencing Washington included such matters as Zionist proclivities among the large Jewish population in the crucially important state of New York, and the disposition of the likely Republican candidate for the Presidency, Thomas Dewey, to bid hard for that vote.[16] For whatever reason, the Americans were unwilling to consider the problem of Jewish settlement except in the specific context of Palestine. This was far from satisfactory for the British, but it was better than nothing, and in November 1945 a Joint Committee was established. For the time being a stop-gap policy of limited Jewish immigration was grudgingly accepted by all concerned.

The Report which emerged in April 1946 looked forward to a condition in Palestine wherein Christians, Jews and Moslems would all be protected under international guarantee. The feature of the Report which attracted most attention, however, was the proposal that 100 000 Jews should be admitted to Palestine in the near future. This naturally appalled the Arabs; but it was exceedingly embarrassing to the British who would have to contain the disorders which would inevitably follow. Worse still, President Truman promptly and unilaterally announced his personal approval of this recommendation. Attlee retorted by indicating that his government would ask the United States to share in the responsibilities of Palestine, and declared that Britain would not authorise large-scale Jewish immigration until Jewish para-military organisations had been disbanded. Less tactfully, Bevin blurted out the opinion that the Americans were helping Jews to enter Palestine because they did not want them in the United States.

The immediate effect of the Anglo-American Committee's Report had apparently been to deepen animosities all round. But what should Britain, as the Mandatory Power, do next? The old arguments about possible partition still raged in the Labour Cabinet, just as they had raged in the Coalition Government and in the National Government before that. But any particular line of partition which might appear just to Britain – or, indeed, any other kind of solution which the British might consider reasonable – would be almost certain to provoke armed violence from both sides. The government's military advisers left them in no doubt that forces in the quantity which were likely to be available would be totally inadequate to contain that sort of situation. If Britain was to remain in Palestine at all, it would be necessary for her to propose a solution which one side would be prepared to accept; whereafter she

might be able to defy the other. In the last analysis, if no acceptable
solution could be proposed, Britain might be compelled formally to
abandon the Palestine mandate. This would reflect severely on British
prestige, not only in Palestine, or even the Middle East, but throughout
the world, and could only be contemplated as a last desperate resort.[17]
The American administration faced serious difficulties of its own.
Political pressures operated in one direction, while the State
Department pushed the other way, warning the President of general
risks which would flow from massive immigration. The Joint Chiefs of
Staff took a third view. Appalled at the growing demand for American
military support in many parts of the world, they were anxious that
nothing should be some to drag American forces into that particular
vortex.

The situation continued to deteriorate. In July 1946 Jewish terrorists
blew up the prestigious King David Hotel in Jerusalem, with many
civilian casualties. There was a considerable world shock reaction; and it
became increasingly plain that Britain's capacity to contain
development in Palestine was being rapidly eroded. The problem
admitted of no satisfactory solution. The British Government's Service
advisers – apparently influenced by nineteenth century ideas about the
vital importance of all Middle Eastern strategic positions – insisted on
the need for maintaining a military presence in Palestine, and implied
that the softest available option was to back the Arabs. There were
serious difficulties of international law attending any solution,
particularly one involving partition, for Palestine was a Mandated
Territory, not a colony. Yet a mandate from whom? Not from the
United Nations, but from the defunct League of Nations. The one thing
plain for all to see was that no solution would prove acceptable to both
races. A Joint Memorandum from the two Ministers most deeply
involved encapsulated the matter:

> The essential point of principle for the Jews is the creation of a
> sovereign Jewish state. And the essential point of principle for the
> Arabs is to resist to the last the establishment of Jewish sovereignty in
> any part of Palestine . . . There is no room for compromise. There is
> therefore no hope of negotiating an agreed settlement.[18]

The date of that Memorandum is significant. It was circulated in
February 1947, at the time when economic problems at home were also
compelling the British Government to take momentous decisions about
both Greece and India. In desperation the government decided to refer
the whole Palestine question to the United Nations.

Events in Palestine could not be separated from questions of east-west relations which were already becoming acute at the turn of 1946–47. It is important to remember that the radical change in American foreign policy signalled by the departure of Byrnes and the arrival of Marshall did not take place until the beginning of 1947, and was not fully evident for some time after that. Nobody could be sure, right to the end of 1946 and even for a few weeks after that, that the United States would be prepared to underwrite those British policies, either in Europe or in the Middle East, whose primary object was to contain communist incursions. Was there any way, Britons began to ask themselves, by which their country could defend her vital interests against possible Soviet aggression if the Americans refused to co-operate?

Some remarkable debates arose between Prime Minister Attlee on one side, and Foreign Secretary Bevin on the other: debates which at one moment threatened a fundamental cleavage between them. At the risk of some over-simplification, one might say that Attlee sought a general *détente* with the Soviet Union, affecting not only the Middle East but many other places as well. Such a *détente*, if achieved, would probably have resulted in abandoning British plans for Middle Eastern development; for the area woud be likely to become a sort of neutral buffer-zone. Bevin contended that this neutrality would be short-lived and spurious. Military advisers pointed out the strategic importance of the area in event of war. These debates were not resolved;[19] for new events both in the Middle East and elsewhere swept aside the arguments of both sides. The United States came to involve itself far more actively in the defence of Europe once Marshall became Secretary of State; while the Palestine problem became increasingly critical, and profound repercussions developed elsewhere.

In the late winter of 1947 the United Nations set up a Committee to examine the Palestine question. The Committee deliberated for half a year, but eventually reached the unanimous conclusion that the Mandate should be terminated and independence granted to Palestine as soon as possible. They were deeply divided, however, as to whether the country should be partitioned or not. A majority favoured partition, although it was very plain that deep trouble would persist in the area allocated to the Jews; for the existing population in that area was divided approximately equally between the two races. Gloomily Bevin predicted 'an Arab rising in Palestine which would have the moral approval of the entire Moslem world'.[20] The British might well find themselves involved in the task of suppressing that rising, with the certainty of infinite damage to their position in all Arab states, yet with no prospect of favour from the Jews, or benefit to themselves in any other way. The Chiefs of Staff continued to argue against withdrawal, but the Cabinet, fortified by the United Nations view, tilted the other way. Bad as the outlook was if Britain abandoned Palestine, the outlook if she attempted to hold on was even worse. On 20 September the formal decision was taken to surrender the Mandate and withdraw from Palestine. Two months later the United Nations upheld its Committee's majority recommendation for partition. The British Government declared that they would do nothing to obstruct that decision, but had no intention of becoming involved in its enforcement. British civil administration would terminate on 15 May 1948, and withdrawal would be completed by 1 August.

Thus did the year 1947 signal the end of Britain's role as one of the major determinants of world events. The most populous part of the British Empire had become independent, and the example would certainly be followed – indeed, it was already being followed – by others. Britain had demonstrated not only that she was incapable of taking the lead in defending non-communist areas of Europe against Soviet incursions, but even her incapacity to enforce her own policies in the Middle East where – thus far – the issue still lay between relatively small numbers of Jews and Arabs. The decision to retreat from these commitments had certainly been accelerated by the economic crisis, but it had not been caused by that crisis. Nor, indeed, may it be attributed to deliberate policies of either the United States or the Soviet Union. Before the war many people had seen with more or less clarity that Britain's continuing international importance depended on the avoidance of general conflict, or at least on Britain herself keeping out of that conflict. British statesmen of 1947 were adjusting themselves to an inevitable decline; and we may reflect today that they deserve credit for recognising the situation in time and averting much worse disasters which might very easily have occured.

14 The Lines are Drawn

Relations between the Soviet Union and the western democracies, bad enough in 1947, continued to deteriorate in the period which followed. Although by the end of 1947 Europe was arrayed in two sharply-defined camps, there still appeared some possibility that Soviet military domination and a western-type democracy might persist indefinitely in Czechoslovakia. This was not to be. On 20 February 1948 most of the non-communist Ministers tendered their resignations to President Beneš on a matter relating to control of police. The Foreign Minister, Jan Masaryk, by far the most influential non-communist after the President himself, did not join with his colleagues in this action. There followed five days of confusion, during the course of which communists armed with rifles paraded the streets of Prague. In the end Beneš invited the communist Gottwald to form a new Ministry. Among the noted anti-communists only Masaryk was included, and Marsaryk himself was found dead in mysterious circumstances a fortnight later. In May 'elections' were held at which voters had no choice between candidates, but were given to understand that it would be 'tantamount to treason' not to support the nominees. Nobody emerges with much credit from the final phase of Czechoslovak liberty. Beneš may perhaps be exculpated, for he was already suffering from a cerebro-arterial condition which may have affected his judgement, and which contributed to his death later in the year; and Masaryk expiated for his inglorious part by suicide – or was it murder? Neither politicians, soldiers nor ordinary citizens had tested whether the communist guns were loaded. The Russians, of course, were present in the background; but they appear to have done little or nothing to intimidate anybody who might have thought of resisting the take-over. In a much less clear-cut manner, the remains of Hungarian political freedom were destroyed during 1948 and 1949.

Just as the seizure of Prague in 1939 disposed governments and peoples in other countries to resist any further Nazi advances at whatever cost, so did events in the same city nine years later engender a similar determination in respect of communism. In both cases the ground where the eventual stand would be made was far from ideal; but people stood firm where they did because the alternative seemed to be to stand nowhere. Well-informed observers in the West, who had hitherto been convinced that the Soviet Union did not want war, were becoming more doubtful on the subject.[1] A secret approach was made by the British to the Americans, proposing military co-operation against aggression in western Europe; to which the reply came that initiative in such matters must be taken by the Europeans.[2] At that moment, the defences of western Europe were fatuously small. More than one and a half million Soviet troops – or so it was believed – were stationed in Europe outside the Soviet Union itself. The British and Americans had about six divisions between them in Europe, the French roughly the same total, other countries practically nothing.[3]

Much turned on how the powers handled the great, unsolved, 'German problem'. The Foreign Ministers' Conference, which had been charged to work out a peace settlement, continued to meet at intervals, but was getting nowhere. Its discussions became occasions for angry and futile invective, designed for propaganda purposes rather than to advance the ostensible object of the meetings. In the Soviet zone Russian political influence was becoming increasingly strong. The Social Democrats had been compelled to amalgamate with the Communists, and nobody doubted whose influence was stronger in the resulting 'Socialist Unity Party'. Meanwhile the old arrangements for military occupation persisted, with the important modification that the British and American zones were to a large extent amalgamated.

France, however, was playing very much for her own hand, for Frenchmen had good reason to fear both Germany and Russia, and some hoped to annex considerable areas of Germany to their own country. With the wisdom of hindsight we may easily decide that the German threat to France was dead; but people who could recall the sight of occupying Germans on French soil only four years earlier could be excused for thinking otherwise. Was it possible to strengthen the defences of Germany, or of part of Germany, in a way which would hold back Russia without threatening France? By June 1948 the Americans came out with what appeared to be the answer, for they indicated that they were willing to remain in occupation of German territory indefinitely.[4] This seemed to kill both birds with the same stone. Whatever use, or otherwise, relatively small numbers of occupying troops might prove against a Russian attack in a strategic sense, at least their presence served the Russians with notice that a serious incursion into the western zones of Germany would constitute a *casus belli* against the United States. The other French fear was also met. A Germany which remained in foreign military occupation could not possibly be a military threat to anybody.

By 1948 the prospect of any real agreement over Germany emerging from the Foreign Ministers' Conference within the foreseeable future could be written off. The western powers must either leave the German problem in limbo for ever, while the Soviet Union proceeded to reorganise the eastern zone to suit its own requirements, or else they must make their own arrangements for the future on the assumption that division was permanent. Yet formal acknowledgement of that patent fact not only raised problems with France, but with Germany as well; for the one thing about which all Germans were agreed, whatever their past or present politics, was that Germany should eventually become again a united country.

Despite such difficulties the recent American commitment disposed the three western democracies to accept the idea that their zones of Germany should be united as a federal state. This proposal produced a real cliffhanger in France; for the French Chamber only accepted the proposal by 300:286, with Communists and Gaullists voting together in the minority. In mid-June 1948 plans for the establishment of the German Federal Republic were set afoot. Among those plans a feature which did not attract much immediate attention was the proposal to inaugurate a new currency in place of the old Reichmarks which had hitherto circulated throughout Germany.

While these proposals were under active discussion, the special problems of Berlin also attracted consideration. The capital was an island, set in the middle of the Soviet zone, and under four-power administration. Just a couple of days before the currency reform was announced, this four-power arrangement for Berlin broke down. Very soon the Russians proposed that a new currency should circulate in Berlin. The western allies retorted that they would not permit this currency to circulate in their own zones. That highly technical wrangle rapidly led to a far more serious crisis.

There is oblique evidence which suggests that the Russians hoped to resolve the anomalous position of Berlin by some sort of trade-off, through which part of the Soviet zone of Germany would be 'ceded' to the western allies in return for incorporation of the whole of Berlin in the area of Russian occupation.[5] The emotional significance of the capital, however, was too great, and no interest was shown by the other occupying powers. Then, on 24 June, the Russians established an almost complete blockade of land communications from the western zones of Germany into Berlin.

Neither the British nor the French appear to have been very sanguine at first about the chances of beating the Soviet blockade, and there was a good deal of doubt in the United States as well. Byrnes, as usual, argued for compromise, and some of the military men were dubious.[6] The lead, however, was taken by Marshall and Truman, and they decided to arrange that necessary supplies should be airlifted into the city. The prospect was daunting; for it was by no means certain that it would be technically possible to sustain an airlift on an adequate scale, particularly during the winter, when great quantities of coal would be among the requirements. For the time being, however, the airlift could be maintained, though at very high cost. The Russians no doubt hoped to force the western allies to come to terms under which they would leave Berlin, but evidently had no intention of interfering with the airlift in a manner which might bring everybody dangerously close to war. And so, throughout the remainder of 1948 the airlift continued; and as time went on the Americans and British became increasingly convinced that they could, if necessary, maintain it indefinitely.

How grave the risk of war over Berlin really was is far from clear. Quite likely it was exaggerated. Both sides certainly behaved as if they were anxious to avoid pushing the other over the brink. The Anglo-Americans preferred the cumbersome and costly airlift to a military challenge like attempting to open the land route to Berlin by force of arms. The Russians did not harass the airlift or cut off utility supplies to western areas of the city. Fear played a large part in holding both sides back; but fear also had played a large part in bringing about the confrontation. It is worth spelling out explicitly what those mutual fears were.

The Soviet Union was evidently appalled at the developing alliance between non-communist powers, and particularly at the prospect that Germany might be brought into that alliance. Perhaps they were already deeply alarmed at the rise of nuclear technology. The converse fear of the Anglo-Americans was that within a very few years a great Russian-controlled bloc might be established, enforcing a system as inimical to personal liberty as that of Nazi Germany, and threatening to engulf the remainder of the world at a later date. Whether initially realistic or not, both sets of fears were largely self-serving; and by 1948 there existed in the West a desperate determination to resist the perceived threat from the Soviet Union at all costs.

The deepening dispute between the Soviet Union and the western democracies took on that profoundly dangerous 'ideological' character which marked politics of the late 1930s, and which – arguably – played a vital part in the genesis of the Second World War. Many people pushed the historical parallel to the point of arguing that Hitler could, and should, have been checked at an early point in his international career by an unambigious threat of war if he proceeded further; that failure to do this, so far from averting war, had been one of its major causes; and that similar conditions currently prevailed in relation to Stalin. Certainly there were risks in attempting to stop him; but these risks were small by comparison with those which any other course of action would involve.

It was in 1948 that the first indications appeared to show that communism and Soviet domination were not necessarily coterminous. In the early part of the year there were signs of differences between Tito's Yugoslavia and the Soviet Union. At first these signs were too subtle to be appreciated by most observers; but at midsummer it was plain that the dispute was real and deep. Charges and counter-charges both on practical matters and on questions of Marxist ideology were exchanged between Belgrade and Moscow. The Russians probably expected either that Tito would recant, or that they would be able to destroy him without much effort. No doubt many people in the West anticipated that Tito's example would soon be followed elsewhere in eastern Europe. Both expectations were disappointed; and it is not difficult today to understand why. Tito had 'made his own revolution'; the other communist leaders were puppets installed by the Russians and removable by the Russians. The western democracies had the good sense not to set pressure on Tito to accept their own kind of political or economic system; but both he and they saw advantages from Yugoslavia participating in the European Recovery Program.

The immediate consequences of Tito's revolt were considerable, and not all of them had been easily predictable. The Greek insurgents were still very active in 1948, and had long looked to Yugoslavia as a valuable source of weapons and a refuge to which they might turn if hard-pressed. Now Yugoslavia, having no intention of helping Russia to promote her own cause in a contiguous Balkan country, ceased to offer such services, and the task of combating the Greek rebels was greatly simplified. The Italo-Yugoslav dispute took on new aspects. The 'Free Territory of Trieste' existed as a visible monument to the failure of major allies to agree about the fate of the city and its environs. The Russians had backed Yugoslavia in the hope of advancing the interests of a client state; the western democracies had backed Italy largely in the hope of embarrassing Italian communists. But now that Yugoslavia was in revolt, why should Russia continue to cause difficulties for her supporters in Italy? In fact the Russians were caught both ways. They still believed – or hoped – that they could bring down Tito and restore

Yugoslavia as a reliable ally, and so for a long time were unwilling to execute the volte-face which might have helped the Italian communists. Not until 1954 did the major powers come to agree that Trieste should be returned to Italy; but by that time Stalin was dead, and the tide of Italian communism had abated greatly.

By the latter part of 1948 there were signs of stabilisation in Europe. Perhaps the risk of war had never been as great as it seemed, and the Russians had really been testing the determination of the West to defend existing frontiers between communist and non-communist areas of Europe. There were also signs of returning political stability in the United States. In the Presidential elections of 1948 Truman was challenged not only by a strong Republican contender but by two distinct splinter groups from his own Party: by Wallace, who was nominated by the pro-Soviet 'Progressive Party' on the 'left', and by a substantial breakaway from the Southern Democrats, the so-called 'Dixiecrats' on the 'right'. Nevertheless, Truman was returned with a comfortable majority to sustain him until 1952.

Yet almost immediately Truman lost his great Secretary of State, George C. Marshall, who fell ill at the end of 1948 and resigned in the following January. Happily Marshall was later able to return to public office in a somewhat less exacting role. But he had really done his work, and had set clear lines of foreign policy which his successor, Dean Acheson, would follow for the ensuing four years.

By this time the fate of Europe had really been decided. 1949 saw many important events, but these were to a large extent natural developments of processes which had already been set in motion. The Berlin blockade was proving a considerable nuisance to everybody. Russia's original objective, to make the position of the western allies in the capital untenable, had plainly failed, and was profoundly counter-productive. The western allies took much comfort from the success of the airlift. Germans, who until recently had been disposed to regard all occupying forces alike as haughty enemies, were coming to see the Russians as people who sought to bring starvation to their capital city; while the Anglo-Americans had brought in supplies at high cost to themselves. On the other hand that cost was so heavy that the Americans, who bore the brunt, and the British, who paid a smaller but still substantial share, were very eager to be relieved of it.

In spring 1949 there were signs that the Soviet Union might be prepared to lift the blockade. *Amour propre* demanded that some sort of reciprocity should be seen to occur, and the Russians set out terms which required that a new meeting of the Council of Foreign Ministers should be convened, to discuss future policy for Germany as a whole.[7] This required no more than a promise to talk, and could do little harm. The West accepted, and on 12 May the blockade was lifted.

Very likely there had been a lot of shadow boxing over the German question. It was in the interest both of the Anglo-Americans on the one side and the Soviet Union on the other to represent themselves as the people who really sought German unification, in which objective they were being frustrated by the other. Both sides could see advantages from a permanent division of Germany, but neither cared to make the bad propaganda involved in saying so. One of the curiosities of the 'Cold War' is that the very hostility of the former allies helped them towards solution of a problem which would otherwise have been inordinately difficult to solve.

Not much emerged from the meeting of the Council of Foreign Ministers, which was held in May 1949. Both sides were already making contingency plans for their own part of Germany. Since the middle of 1948 a German body had been drafting a constitution for the western side of the country, and that constitution came into effect with approval of the western allies in September 1949. Similar plans were set in motion for the establishment of an east German state, and in October the 'German Democratic Republic' was established. Both successor-states were anxious to maintain the façade of being the lawful government of the whole country, to which all Germans owed allegiance; but in practice the division was complete and irreparable.

The permanent division of Europe was acknowledged in other ways as well. In the immediate aftermath of the bleak events in Prague in February 1948, British official circles had been near to panic. There were deep apprehensions about possible Soviet designs against Norway, while both British and American ambassadors in Oslo were instructed to do what they could to stiffen the Norwegian Government. The 'Brussels Pact', concluded in March 1948 between Britain, France and the Benelux countries, hurriedly set up what was called the 'Western European Union'. Despite its grandiose name, the Union had few teeth, and Bevin began to press Attlee and Marshall for a much more comprehensive 'Atlantic Security System' which would include the United States.[8] It is rather striking to note that the American Chiefs of Staff, so far from taking such approaches as the cue to press for large-scale rearmament, argued that the cost of a rearmament programme would damage the European Recovery Program, and thus foster rather than deter the growth of communism.

By early 1949, however, the Americans were ready to press ahead with a policy of integrated western defence. The notion, in its original form, was to establish a defensive alliance between the United States, Canada, the 'Western European Union' countries, and – for essentially strategic reasons – Norway, Denmark, Iceland and Portugal. As negotiations proceeded many complications emerged. Sweden sought to attract Norway and Denmark into an alternative 'league of neutrals'. The Italian Government was 'almost hysterical in its demand for membership',[9] and was strongly backed by the French. To accept Italy, however, was to invite trouble with Yugoslavia, and might even drive Tito back into the arms of Stalin. Nevertheless, the alternative was to alienate the French, and perhaps dispose them to veto Norway. Greece and Turkey sought admission. At one moment it seemed possible that the Republic of Ireland might be included, but Dublin made trouble over the old 'partition' issue, and was excluded. In the end Italy was brought in, but Greece and Turkey were excluded until 1951. There was considerable trouble in the legislative assemblies of some proposed members. By far the most serious problem was Congress, where at one moment in the middle of February it looked as if any formal commitment to military action in defence of the European allies might be blocked; but strong pressure from Acheson eventually overcame that problem. The treaty, which set up what would be known as the North Atlantic Treaty Organisation – NATO – was signed in April 1949 and ratified by the various members later in the year.

Thereafter, something like stalemate prevailed throughout Europe. Neither the democracies nor the Soviet Union could make serious incursions at the expense of the other without a very high risk of real war, whose outcome no one could predict. Whatever anticipations the Russians may have entertained about Marxist revolutions in western Europe could be postponed to the Greek Kalends. Conversely, the western Europeans had for practical purposes lost all contact with the eastern side of the continent, and there was a deep measure of shame and humiliation felt over the fate of Czechoslovakia and Poland in particular. Unsatisfactory as the arrangements were from many points of view, people could go on living with them indefinitely. On both sides of the Iron Curtain a period of consolidation began: economic, military and ideological. Within the Soviet Union itself, the relative ideological laxity which had been permitted in wartime (when the theory of the 'Great Patriotic War' was developed), now gave way to a renewed campaign against the traditional enemies of the Communist State. There were signs of a return to the anti-religious policies of earlier days; a campaign was waged against western art and culture; while growing opposition to 'cosmopolitanism' seemed to contain a considerable element of anti-Semitism. However much the western countries might deplore these tendencies, there was reason to think that, for a considerable period to come, the Soviet Union would be a good deal more concerned with its own problems, and the problems of the dependencies it had recently acquired, than with problems of external expansion – at least in Europe.

15 The Deepest Danger

As Europe was beginning to settle down into comparative quiet after two decades of turmoil, so did new troubles flare up in many parts of Asia. Some of these problems had considerable 'Cold War' overtones, but many of them were difficult for either side to evaluate in simple and familiar 'Cold War' terms. The emerging regimes of Asia presented many problems for the formulators of policy in western countries. Traditionally the United States had favoured withdrawal of imperial control from colonial dependencies: a policy she applied in the immediate aftermath of war to her own territory, the Philippines. For such reasons British policy towards possessions in and near the Indian subcontinent was approved in Washington. The Dutch, however, took a very different view of nationalist movements in the Netherlands East Indies, which they continued to fight – against the advice of British and Americans alike – right into 1949, when at last Indonesia achieved effective independence. Already, in the late 1940s, the long, complex and exceedingly dangerous conflict in French Indo-China and its successors, Vietnam, Laos and Cambodia, had commenced.

Just as there were considerable differences between the western democracies over the fate of colonial territories, so also were there deep difference about attitudes towards developments in China. Once it became clear that Mao Tse-tung had won control over the mainland – the People's Republic of China was formally proclaimed in October 1949 – the British Government was disposed to extend recognition, and wished to have the new China admitted into the comity of nations. No doubt there were various reasons for this: a desire that the *de facto* position should be recognised as soon as possible *de jure*; desire to trade with the new China; and the judgement that China was much less likely to become associated with Russia in a hostile *bloc* if the regime was swiftly acknowledged than if it was treated as an international pariah. The Americans, however, took a very different view, and their reasons were rooted in a sense of moral commitment as well as calculations of interest. Their association with the 'nationalist' leader Chiang Kai-shek had commenced long before the communists became serious contenders

197

for power in China. Although the mainland had fallen more or less completely into communist hands, Chiang's forces were still in occupation in Formosa – now Taiwan. Chiang evidently thought that the civil war was by no means over; that reconquest of the mainland from his base on Formosa was still possible. In 'Cold War' conditions many Americans considered that the whole world was engaged in a struggle which was at root ideological, and which might turn into a 'shooting war' at any moment. Why give unnecessary hostages to fortune by recognising an odious regime, when the Chinese civil war might soon be subsumed into a wider conflict? There is a curious parallel here with the attitudes of many supporters of the Spanish Republic early in 1939, who also had refused to acknowledge clear defeat in an existing civil war, because they thought the lesser conflict would soon become part of a general war.

On the other side the Russians made an equally deep point of principle that Mao must be recognised – and, specifically, that the place allocated to China in the United Nations should be occupied by representatives of the new regime. This marked a considerable change of front by the Soviet Union. How far it was motivated by recognition of the *fait accompli*, how far by an ideological reassessment of the Chinese communists, and how far by a desire to ingratiate themselves with the new rulers is debatable. By contrast, the American attitude was inevitably seen by the Chinese as a mark not merely of political disapproval but of fundamental hostility, conjoined with a determination eventually to overturn the revolution in favour of Chiang. The British and American Governments made no secret of their own mutual disagreements, but were not disposed to inject acrimony into the matter. Towards the end of 1949 it became clear that the United Nations would not give Mao's Government the place allocated to China, and the Soviet Union withdrew angrily from participation in United Nations deliberations: a gesture which they would later have great cause to regret.

This diplomatic quarrel bore closely on great events which followed not long after in Korea. The strategic importance of that country was considerable. It has a long frontier with the Chinese province of Manchuria, and a very short frontier with the Soviet Union; but the particular importance of Korea is that it commands approaches to the Yellow Sea and thus to Peking; while it also comes very close to Vladivostok, and within a couple of hundred miles of Honshu, the principal island of Japan. Korean independence had been extinguished by Japan long before. Japanese rule was widely resented, and during the Second World War the allies promised that the country would recover independence after Japan's defeat. It will be recalled that the line 38°N was fixed as the boundary betwen American and Soviet occupation without any deep premeditation. Everybody seems to have taken it for granted that both occupations would be brief, whereafter the country would recover both unity and independence.

Most of the industry of Korea lay in the north, and the Russians were in a position to repatriate the many Koreans who had long lived in the Soviet Union, who may be presumed to have imbibed something of Soviet ideology. It appears a fair guess that the Soviet Union was hoping to consolidate the position of their own sympathisers in the north, and then reunify the whole country under the leadership of those people. Thus the various efforts which were made in 1946–47 to secure agreement between Russians and Americans about the country's future were foredoomed to run into the sands. The Americans would not contemplate unification on terms which would leave the communists in control; the Russians would not contemplate unification on any other terms. In November 1947 the General Assembly of the United Nations set up a Commission, charged to supervise elections throughout Korea. The Soviet Union refused the Commission entry to its own zone, and so elections were confined to the South. Thereafter the two parts of Korea were organised under separate civil administrations, each claiming to be the sole lawful government of the whole country. Both the Americans and the Russians withdrew their occupying forces, but each left behind substantial numbers of military advisers. The diplomatic position was anomalous. The Soviet bloc recognised the regime in the north as government of all Korea; most other countries recognised the regime in the south as government of all Korea. This somewhat technical point would prove of much practical importance later on.

The dominant figure in the South was the elderly President, Syngman Rhee, whose 'political personality suggested Chiang Kai-shek'.[1] This presaged considerable embarrassment for the United States. Within a week of America's recognition of South Korea the Korean representative received a very pointed warning from the Americans that Chiang's experience should be treated as a warning, not as an example.[2] As time went on, neither Korean Government left much doubt about its wish and intention eventually to unite the whole country under its own kind of regime.

On 25 June 1950 war broke out in Korea. Each side claimed that the other was the aggressor, but there is today little doubt that the attack came from the North; that it was a major assault all along the boundary, designed to destroy the South Korean state entirely. Nor was there long much doubt that the North Korean forces were more numerous and better equipped than the Southerners; that a great many of the North Koreans had received training in the Soviet Union; that if the Koreans were left to their own devices, the North would soon achieve total victory. Although there is some room for doubt how far the Soviet Union actually promoted the attack, and the Russians kept a rather low profile throughout the Korean war, the Soviet Union did almost immediately afford strong moral support to the North, and it was universally recognised that victory for that side would constitute a very important moral triumph not only for 'communism' but also for the Soviet Union. The Korean war represented, right from its inception, a radically new development for the 'Cold War' in several directions. For the first time troops backed (morally at least) by one 'Super-Power' were fighting troops backed by the other; and with this departure the technique which became known as 'aggression by proxy' was developed to a far greater extent than ever before, with limitless possibilities for the future.

The governments and – so far as one can determine – the peoples, of the democracies were united in the view that the attack should be resisted by those means which came most readily to hand. The Korean question was referred to the United Nations, and military assistance demanded for the South, as the victim of aggression. The appeal had to go before the Security Council, where the Soviet Union had a permanent place, with the right to veto any action which might be proposed. Yet – as we have seen – the Soviet Union was currently boycotting United Nations deliberations because of the dispute over China. The operative question was whether Russia could swallow a measure of pride, and return to the Security Council in time to block United Nations actions over Korea. Probably for internal reasons, the Soviet Union was incapable of executing the necessary swift volte-face, and in Russia's absence the Security Council accordingly resolved to grant military assistance to South Korea, which thus took on the official character of United Nations rather than United States intervention. Americans formed by far the greater part of the United Nations forces who eventually arrived in Korea; but the British Government and fourteen other close allies of the United States soon resolved to send forces to assist.

Almost at once stern action was taken to prevent escalation of the conflict in a direction where neither the United States nor the Soviet Union would have much control over events, should trouble start. There was a serious risk of either a communist attack on Formosa from the mainland, or a Chinese 'nationalist' attack on the mainland from Formosa; and either movement could lead to the most appalling consequences. So the United States Seventh Fleet was sent to 'neutralise' Formosa: to prevent invasion from either direction.

At first the Korean war went so badly for the South that it seemed likely that the Northern forces would come to control the whole peninsula. Then the tide of war turned and converse problems, no less serious, began to vex the United States and her allies. The line 38°N was not a military frontier, and if the enemy was to be cleared from South Korea it would be necessary to take military action north of the line. There was also a serious problem about the whole character of the war. As some countries recognised one Korean Government and other countries recognised the other, the 38°N dividing line did not, according to either theory, exist at all; indeed, it never had existed as anything more than the limit between two zones of a military occupation which had already ceased. Thus both sides, officially at least, saw the Korean war, not as a contest between two sovereign states, occasioned by aggression of one upon the other, but as action by a lawful goverment against rebels who were seeking to usurp its authority. The two sides, of course, disagreed as to who was the lawful government and who were rebels; but both were forced by a sort of twisted diplomatic logic to recognise an international conflict as a kind of civil war. As for the Koreans themselves, about the only important matter on which there was total agreement was that nobody, North or South, wished the country to be divided.

When people pretend to take a deep moral stand on a position which everybody knows to be a lie, the moralist will not be surprised to learn that trouble is likely to ensue. The Korean War had started in vindication of the Northern myth that the Southerners were rebels with no proper *locus standi*; the Korean War now proceeded to become deeper and more dangerous because of a corresponding Southern myth about the Northerners. The Koreans were not disposed to treat each other as honourable enemies. The Great Powers who stood in the background had much cause for embarrassment from the behaviour of their 'own' Koreans. As the British Cabinet minutes record, 'there was little doubt that the Koreans on both sides had conducted the war in a barbarous fashion'.[3] This is amply confirmed. At an early stage of the war General MacArthur, commander of the American forces, formally (and effectively) threatened North Korean commanders with personnal accountability if atrocities against United Nations prisoners were not stopped; while on the other side British troops in Korea found themselves on at least one occasion forcibly disarming a South Korean firing squad which was in the process of massacring prisoners. Published United States documents contain evidence that Americans also were from time to time sickened by Korean atrocities on both sides.[4]

As early as July 1950 the argument about whether United Nations forces should halt at the 38th Parallel, or attempt to establish control over the North as well, became of practical as well as theoretical importance.[5] Throughout August, and far into September, that argument continued to rage. As time went on the military side of the question more or less settled itself, for it was clear that so long as North Korean forces remained in being, the threat to the South continued. Thus there was not much doubt that the instructions issued to MacArthur on 26 September, to seek 'destruction of the North Korean armed forces', with authority to operate north of the Parallel, were inherently reasonable. Those instructions, however, were subject to the very important qualification that if either Soviet or Chinese forces should enter Korea in strength, or indicated their intention of doing so, the General should await further orders.

It is one thing to operate across a frontier in order to remove a continuing military threat; but it is a very different matter to seek to obliterate the enemy regime altogether. For a time, however, United Nations forces halted at the Parallel, and MacArthur broadcast a final appeal for the North Koreans to surrender. Predictably, there was no response, and on 1 October South Korean troops crossed the line – encountering no resistance. For some time the United Nations forces did not follow this example.

The political question of whether to attempt suppression of the North Korean state remained unresolved. On 7 October, through a British initiative, the United Nations adopted a resolution calling for all necessary measures to be taken – including elections throughout the country – to establish a unified and democratic government for Korea, and to rehabilitate the country. The crucial resolution contained no express demand that United Nations forces should enter North Korea, but this was taken as implicit. The voting was significant, for it was carried by 47 votes to five, with eight abstentions. The Soviet Union had by this time returned to United Nations deliberations, and communist bloc opposition was predictable. Abstentions were more important, for they included not only Yugoslavia but also India – clear indication both that the Commonwealth bloc was crumbling and that a new, 'neutralist', group was beginning to appear. Howbeit, the necessary authority had been provided, and on 9 October MacArthur ordered troops under his command to cross the Parallel. Thereafter, those troops surged forward with considerable speed, and by 22 November had reached the Yalu River, which divides Korea from Manchuria.

MacArthur's instructions, we have seen, expressly warned against the possibility of intervention from either Russia or China. Direct conflict between Americans and Russians on a large scale – whether or not the former were officially agents of the United Nations and the latter 'volunteers' – would probably escalate rapidly into general war; but the same dire result need not necessarily follow if the Chinese were to intervene.

Almost immediately United Nations troops crossed the Parallel, the Chinese Government began to issue public warnings to the effect that they could not 'stand idly by' while the 'invasion' proceeded; but nobody was sure how far this was bluff. At a Conference on Wake Island on 15 October, MacArthur told Truman that the chances of either Chinese or Soviet interference was 'very little', and the General's own later account suggests that the others present required little persuasion from him in reaching the same judgement.[6]

In the light of after-knowledge it looks very much as if the Peking Government was more or less indifferent when only South Korean troops crossed the Parallel, and perhaps did not care very much if Americans did so as well, provided that they kept well clear of the Chinese frontier; but that they were appalled at the prospect of American forces coming right up to their own borders. Perhaps they feared that in such circumstances there might be a renewal of their own recent civil war. The American Government acted as if they were conscious of apprehensions in that direction, and took good care – despite strong pleas from MacArthur – to avoid the ultimate provocation of accepting Chinese Nationalist troops from Formosa for service in Korea.

As United Nations troops advanced northwards, the prospect of Chinese intervention increased. The British Government continued to maintain that the risk of trouble from that direction would be less if China were admitted to the United Nations; for this would imply that no one contemplated hostile action against the Chinese Government. There is some evidence which suggests that the acute phase of Chinese hostility dates, not from the moment when United Nations troops crossed the Parallel, but from when China was again refused admission to the United Nations.[7] At all events, by mid-November it appeared that something like 35 000 Chinese troops had already infiltrated into Korea – although for the time being they had made little contact with United

Nations troops. By this time Bevin,[8] and many other Europeans as well, were beginning to feel deepening apprehensions of risks involved in the Korean conflict. The problem was not just the old peril that Russia and possibly China might have resolved on a course of aggressive action which would compel the democracies either to capitulate or go to war. There was also a very deep risk that they might become involved in an unnecessary war, fought in the wrong place from both strategic and moral viewpoints. If the Korean War escalated into general conflict, the Americans could well be bogged down in an incredibly costly campaign with very dubious prospects of victory, in alliance with Asian associates of unattractive character and doubtful military value; while western Europe, starved of both military and economic assistance through this new American preoccupation, might gradually collapse into chaos – and very likely into communism.

Towards the end of November MacArthur prepared a new offensive whose declared objective was to 'end the war' by destroying North Korean resistance. Simultaneously the Chinese prepared their own offensive with the converse objective, and before the month was out the two offensives 'ran into each other'. According to MacArthur, the forces ranged against him were 200 000 Chinese and only 50 000 North Korean 'fragments'.[9] Just four days after MacArthur's call for the final victory offensive, he made an equally famous declaration that 'we face an entirely new war'.

Almost immediately Truman made a critical situation far worse by a highly injudicious statement, which generated great alarm both in his own country and among his European allies. Under the barrage of questions at a Press Conference – never a good atmosphere for reflective and statesmanlike thought – the President declared that the use of atomic bombs in Korea was under consideration; furthermore, that the choice of what weapons to use lay with MacArthur. The first part of the statement was technically both true and unexceptional; for any government involved in any conflict must at all times be 'contemplating' which of its available weapons should be brought into use; but journalists avid for sensation, and politial commentators in the United States and elsewhere, found it easy to read into that statement a broad hint that the United States was actively considering the use of atomic weapons in Korea in the near future. The second part of the President's statement was factually erroneous; for only Truman himself was legally entitled to authorise use of atomic weapons, and a correction was issued almost immediately. In 1950 concern over atomic bombs was both deep and general; but nuclear weapons did not carry quite the emotional significance they bear today. Nevertheless, America's allies, and particularly the British, were at no pains to conceal their profound concern at the trigger-happy attitude which this incident seemed to reveal. Attlee travelled to Washington early in December for conference with Truman. The necessary reassurances were given; but the damage to the President's prestige was considerable.

At the turn of 1950–51 there was every reason for profound concern both over the Korean War itself and over its possible repercussions. Chinese and North Korean troops advanced so rapidly that again the serious risk appeared that United Nations forces would be driven from the whole peninsula – or, in the alternative, that very costly and very risky action would be taken in order to keep them there. The American Government, caught between MacArthur and domestic fire-eaters on one side, and their European allies on the other, seemed in a condition not far short of panic. Instructions issued to MacArthur at the end of December clearly envisaged the possibility that the whole Korean peninsula would soon prove untenable, and evacuation of American troops to Japan would become necessary.[10] Elements of the Press, both in America and in Europe, made this eventuality appear highly probable. MacArthur's own account indicates that this deeply defeatist attitude persisted at Washington until, suddenly, a message from the President on 14 January 1951 enabled the Commander to assure his staff that 'there will be no evacuation'.[11] These changes of attitude were, of course, closely related to fluctuations in the military position. Whether for logistic, or, for the diplomatic reasons, the Chinese did not push their initial rapid advance to its limits and make a serious effort to drive United Nations forces from Korea.

No less remarkable was the curious forbearance of the Soviet Union. North Korea, after all, had been a Russian, not a Chinese, satellite; and if United Nations forces took over all Korea they would be much closer to Vladivostok than to any major centre in China. So why were the troops which saved the North Korean Government at its last gasp Chinese, and not Russian? No doubt the Russians were as conscious as anyone of the dangers of general war if Soviet troops intervened; and perhaps also they viewed favourably the prospect of a mutually destructive conflict between the United States and China. If so, the Chinese were not willing to comply with Soviet wishes. Thus United Nations troops in Korea, and the American Government, were not faced with the terrible dilemma of either accepting a most humiliating defeat whose world-wide consequences could prove shattering – or, in the alternative, of involving men and resources to an almost unlimited extent in defence of a peninsula which – should general war supervene – would almost certainly be abandoned at an early stage. Nevertheless, a considerable time elapsed before anybody in the West could feel reasonably confident that the fearful choice could be avoided. Before that happened great new problems arose.

In the early months of 1951 United Nations troops in Korea began, at first very slowly, to push northwards again. Then the old question recurred: whether they should attempt to advance into the North should opportunity arise. The British view on the matter was soon made clear, and was very different from the opinion expressed in the heady days of the previous autumn. Buttressed with advice from the Chiefs of Staff that a defensible line existed across the 'waist' of Korea, and following roughly, though not exactly, the 38th Parallel, the British Government publicly announced its view that United Nations troops should halt on the Parallel 'subject to such local variations as the tactical situation might require'.[12]

The Truman administration was probably glad to learn the British view, not least because it helped them deal with extremist opinion in their own country. By mid-March United Nations troops were back on the Parallel, and the issue became of immediate practical importance. Luckily for the American Government, General MacArthur, principal exponent of the contrary view, gravely misjudged the strength of his own position.

On 6 December 1950, in the aftermath of the President's own indiscretion over atomic weapons, an order had been issued to the effect that public statements by MacArthur should be cleared with Washington before they were issued. On 24 March, however, MacArthur issued a statement deeply disparaging Communist China's military power, but indicating his own willingness to confer with the enemy Commander in order to avert future bloodshed. That statement ran counter to the President's instructions; while, to make matters worse, a 'routine communique' – MacArthur's expression – was issued on the same day, which could be taken to imply that the Parallel would be crossed by ground troops as and when military convenience so prescribed. On 5 April a letter written some time earlier by MacArthur to a leading Republican Congressman was published, making even more plain the General's dissent from Presidential policy. MacArthur's defiance was palpable, and there was no doubt that Truman had the legal right to dismiss him. Yet the General's prestige both as a wartime commander and as post-war controller of Japan was immense, and he had many supporters for his current line over Korea and China. There was serious danger that Congress might baulk at passing military appropriations if MacArthur were dismissed. At last, however, Truman took courage in both hands, and on 11 April removed the errant General from command. Great political turmoil supervened; but the essential point had been made. Truman proposed to control policy himself, and not to be manoeuvred into serious dangers of a global conflict by an insubordinate soldier, however distinguished.

While the MacArthur crisis was moving towards its climax, the precarious health of Ernest Bevin finally broke down. In March the great Foreign Secretary resigned, to be succeeded by Herbert Morrison. Bevin remained briefly in the Cabinet with non-departmental duties; but in mid-April he died. Personal relations between Bevin and Morrison had been notoriously bad, but the newcomer had little chance in practice to depart from his predecessor's policies. The essential guidelines were ineradicably defined.

As 1951 advanced the military situation in Korea seemed to be moving towards a kind of stalemate, with both sides establishing entrenched positions not very far from the 38th Parallel: in places a little to the north, in others a little to the south. Did this state of affairs point the way to an acceptable solution? The new line was a defensible military frontier from both sides, much less costly to protect than the old, arbitrary, boundary; and yet it gave no overall advantage to either side by comparison with the Parallel. The United States – indeed, the United Nations – had made the essential point that aggression did not 'pay', for the aggressor had not improved his position. The Chinese had made their essential point that American forces should keep well clear of the Manchurian border. The Russians had not suffered any intolerable loss of prestige, to the benefit of the West, although they had certainly suffered a significant loss of influence, to the benefit of China. The South Korean Government, which continued to proclaim the essential unity of Korea, was disgruntled, and it may well be that the North Korean Government was not very pleased either. What ordinary Koreans may have thought on the matter, nobody bothered to enquire.

Although the main fighting in Korea had finished, the war was less than half way through. Negotiations soon commenced with view to a settlement, but they ran into great difficulties. Perhaps the most serious stumbling-block was the question of repatriation of prisoners-of-war. Just over half the prisoners and internees held by the United Nations forces did not wish to be returned,[13] while considerable numbers of South Koreans held by the Northern forces were equally reluctant.

Old and ugly memories were stirred. In 1945 a great many Soviet citizens had been repatriated against their will by the western allies. A lot of people destined for repatriation had pleaded and struggled to avoid the fate which they knew, or guessed, awaited their return, and some had even committed suicide. Many repatriated prisoners were put to death on their return, and many others suffered appalling punishments – with little effort being made to distinguish the innocent from the guilty. If, in current circumstances, North Korean prisoners were forcibly repatriated, the most tremendous storm would burst in America and Britain. On the other side, the South Korean authorities were not likely to show much humanity to those of their own repatriates who had demonstrated sympathy for the North: a matter which would also cause awkward questions to be raised in the democracies.

The wrangling continued, and so did the military stalemate. Neither side wished to return to the fluid and perilous condition of the previous year, yet neither felt any pressing urge to settle. In fact no armistice was concluded until the summer of 1953, after Stalin was dead. Korea, however, was no longer the centre of international attention, the fuse which might detonate Word War Three. The risks of such a war occurring could not be excluded; but once MacArthur was safely out of the way Korea was no longer a likely place for it to start.

Today we are sufficiently distanced from the Korean war to see matters in a better perspective than could easily be done in the early 1950s. Neither Korean Government was particularly attractive; but the principle that a boundary, however arbitrary, must not be changed by force was an important one; and we may reflect that the prospect of general war sooner or later would have been increased and not reduced if the United States had not taken the lead in accepting the challenge; while if Britain had failed to follow that lead the Americans might well have been unable to maintain effective resistance to the attack.

The Korean War may be seen as the last episode of the territorial settlement directly consequential on the Second World War. Spheres of influence between the allies in former enemy territory had been defined. The West tacitly acknowledged from the start that the line could not be pushed back to the disadvantage of the Soviet Union. However much they might disapprove of what was happening beyond that line, the democracies could only change matters by war or the unambiguous threat of war, which they had no intention of issuing. The Soviet Union, doubtless perceiving much confusion and disunity in the western camp, and possibly anticipating assistance from revolutionary forces in some countries within the western sphere of influence, made several attempts by various means to extend beyond that line – through encouragement to communist parties in France and Italy; by supporting military uprising in Greece; by the Berlin blockade, and eventually by giving some sort of moral backing to the North Koreans. In all cases the Soviet Union backed down in face of determined resistance. To say that, however, is very diffent from echoing MacArthur's argument that the Soviet Union, and the communist forces in China, could be compelled by a sufficiently determined show of force actually to retreat from ground which they had already consolidated. In the second phase of the Korean War – the advance up to the Manchurian frontier in the early autumn of 1950 – there was a somewhat half-hearted effort by the West to test the communists' nerve. The attempt miscarried badly. It is, of course, possible that with more determination that attempt might have succeeded. It is also possible that it would have pushed the communist powers to a point where they considered that retreat would bring total destruction, and they would have chosen to risk general war. We do not know which would have happened, and probably never shall know.

So the general conclusion of the war in Korea was rather like the general conclusion of the 'Cold War' in Europe. Very likely, wiser policies at an earlier date would have set different frontiers for communism, whether in Europe or in Asia; but there was intolerable peril in seeking to reverse the situation which had established itself by the late 1940s. But western statesmen decided that existing limits must be maintained, and countries in sensitive areas still lying outside the communist orbit must be adequately defended, both militarily and economically, against further incursions. Either provocation at one extreme, or pusillanimity at the other, would create that uncertainty about what was bluff and what was not bluff which has on many occasions in the past led to war. Marshall and Bevin both had the wisdom, which was not vouchsafed to all their successors, to perceive that mere 'anti-communism' was not enough; that corrupt, reactionary regimes provided no security for anybody; that in the long run the best way of countering communism was by offering an alternative more attractive to the masses of the people. The acute phase of the 'Cold War' – from the middle of 1948 to the middle of 1951 – may be seen in retrospect as the period in which policies originally evolved by Marshall and Bevin were tested, and proved wise.

Britain had considerable influence on these events, and without that influence their course could have been very difficult. Without British participation in Korea it would have been difficult to represent the miscellaneous forces which supported the South as a credible 'United Nations' as opposed to an American contingent; while visible British concern about MacArthur's policies gave real help to those Americans, from the President downwards, who felt similar concern on their own account. Yet it was Britain's swan-song as a Great Power. Her refusal to come to terms with Germany in 1940 had sprung from the belief that the United States and the Soviet Union would both become involved if she held on, and she had been vindicated in that judgement. In the aftermath, Britain had urged the United States to meet the new perceived threat of rampant communism, and again it is arguable that British influence was of critical importance. But Britain had also demonstrated that she no longer retained the strength to act as one of the great protagonists in world affairs. If any doubt remained on that score, it would be removed a few years later.

16 Withdrawal from Empire

The period of acute international tensions which followed the Second World War also witnessed profound changes in British attitudes towards the Empire and towards other places where British influence was strong. Some of the more spectacular changes have already been considered, but many other developments were taking place at the same time. They do not all follow a consistent pattern – partly because of the diversity of the Empire, partly because the British Government's view of its role underwent considerable modifications as time went on.

During the wartime Coalition period it became generally accepted – in the words of the Colonial Secretary of the day – that it would be Britain's task in the aftermath of war 'to guide colonial peoples along the road to self-government within the British Empire'. The underlying assumption, of course, was that they would wish to remain in the Empire if properly 'guided'. Even before the 1940s were out, this assumption came under challenge. When Britain was in the process of granting independence to India, she could hardly fail to make similar offers to peoples of other parts of Asia with equally distinctive civilisations. Ceylon (Sri Lanka) presented few problems, and plans were made to grant Dominion status in the course of 1948. Burma proved more difficult; for whereas the Burmese negotiators were apparently willing to accept a similar solution, there was – so they declared – 'no prospect that either their own supporters or Burmese opinion generally could be brought to accept anything less than independence outside the Commonwealth'.[1] There was no point in resisting this demand; for if Burma were constituted a Dominion she would acquire the immediate right to secede from the Commonwealth if she chose, under provisions of the Statute of Westminster. Thus, when Burma received independence on 4 January 1948, the country was constituted a Republic outside the Commonwealth, and for the first time for many years a dependent territory broke all former links with Britain through its own action.

Malaya required different treatment from Britain's larger Asian possessions. The country's constitution was complex. The Straits Settlements ranked as a Crown Colony; the nine Malay States were more or less independent Protectorates under their own rulers. The population of Malaya was only about six millions, but the ethnic mixture was profound. Malays and Chinese were present in approximately equal numbers, and there were rather fewer than a million Indians. There had been little 'nationalism' before the war, although the Chinese population had been to some extent influenced both by Kuomintang and by the communists. The Malays had tended to look to the British for protection against the growing number of immigrants.

The Japanese capture of Malaya had been very swift. During the occupation period the invaders ingratiated themselves with the Malays, encouraging them to regard the Chinese, and particularly the communist Chinese, as the enemies. A few of the communists escaped to remote areas, where some guerilla warfare was maintained. Apparently the insurgents had planned to take over the country after the war, but in fact the British were able to reassert themselves with relative ease after the Japanese surrender.

During the war the British planned that Malaya should be divided after victory. Singapore would be a separate Crown Colony, while the remainder of the country would be constituted the Malayan Union. The role of the rulers would be more or less honorific, while the country gradually advanced towards independence. With visible reluctance the rulers accepted their new status, and in 1946 the two new Constitutions came into force. The arrangement, however, was not popular, particularly among the Malays, and soon broke down. In 1948 a new Federal constitution was promulgated; whereupon the communists broke into open revolt, and there commenced a 'State of Emergency' which was destined to last for twelve years. A pattern of guerilla warfare developed, which would soon be emulated elsewhere. The insurgents were never more than about 5000 strong, but losses were replaced by new recruitments. It was no doubt fortunate for the authorities that the rebels were almost exclusively Chinese, for this more or less guaranteed Malay support for the government forces. There soon appeared a strong anti-communist movement among the Chinese themselves, which came to co-operate with Malay political groupings. The burden of resisting the rebels was borne partly by British forces, but also to a large extent by the local population.

Thus a remarkable pattern developed in Malaya in the three years following the Second World War: a pattern quite different from that predicted in all familiar theories about colonial 'wars of liberation'. The colonial power had first sought to press the subject people towards independence a good deal faster than many of them wished to go. When it resiled from that position, civil war developed with an astonishing line-up. The British, strongly supported by almost all the autochthonous population and a large proportion of the comparatively recent incomers, became engaged in a seemingly endless conflict with what might be described as a minority among a minority, whose strongest asset was not their own popularity, or the unpopularity of their opponent, but their capacity to terrorise other colonial subjects.

The continuing ethnic struggles within and between the new Dominions of India and Pakistan, after the grant of independence in 1947, lie outside the present story; but one of the consequences of independence was a remarkable constitutional expedient which was later to be emulated widely in other parts of the Commonwealth. Down to 1948 it was generally considered that the essential formal link between independent Commonwealth states was the acknowledgement of the British Sovereign as Head of State. This idea long survived the demise of the doctrine of 'unity of the Crown' in 1939. In conformity with established notions, it was generally acknowledged that countries which found the Crown link irksome had no alternative but to leave the Commonwealth – as Burma did.

Long before India achieved independence there were substantial numbers of people who wished the country to be become a Republic. They were prepared to accept Dominion status as an interim measure, because the Statute of Westminster would then permit them to withdraw whenever they chose. Other Indians perceived practical advantages from Dominion status. There was no compulsion to underwrite British policies, and yet India was in a position to exert considerable influence over the policies of Britain and perhaps other Commonwealth countries as well, notably in fields like trade and immigration. Yet the word 'Republic' possessed an emotional allure for people with a long tradition of national struggle against the British.

From Britain's point of view emotional aspects could not be wholly ignored. The idea of the British Empire or Commonwealth as the focus of national pride and interest was strong. Not many people felt much emotional wrench when India became a Dominion, although some judged the action unwise. Many, no doubt, regarded the process as a vindication of enlightened imperialism. Yet most Britons would certainly deplore any final renunciation of the Indian link: a matter which could have repercussions on domestic politics. India had the undeniable right to become a soveriegn Republic and to break all links with Britain; but it would be hard to deny that Britain had a corresponding right to seek to dissuade her.

In the course of 1949, the Indian Constituent Assembly was engaged in the task of drafting a new Constitution. To meet the constitutional dilemma, a new category of Commonwealth membership was invented – 'Republic within the Commonwealth'. In January 1950 India became the first country to come within that category. Unlike the Dominions, India did not recognise the British Sovereign as head of State; but the King was acknowledged as 'Head of the Commonwealth'. In later years many other Commonwealth countries adopted the same position as India had taken in the matter.

Even before she became a Republic India was striking a distinctive line in international affairs. When the forces of Mao Tse-tung secured control of China, India was the first Commonwealth country to send an Ambassador to the new government. At an early stage of the Korean war India took a line very much of her own. Thereafter, India came to be a major inspiration for a 'Third Force' in world politics, which refused to associate itself closely with either the western or the Soviet bloc.

The Indian lead was followed to a considerable extent by other Asian Commonwealth territories. In the long run most of them became Republics, whether inside or outside the Commonwealth. Even before that process had become general, an important Conference was held in 1950 at the Ceylonese capital, Colombo – and was attended by Foreign Ministers of the Asian and Australasian Dominions. This signalled a temporary disposition of Commonwealth countries in the Pacific area to look at their own problems together without too much reference to the British. This disposition, however, did not continue for very long, and in the Korean war and afterwards the split between Australia and New Zealand on one side and the Asian territories on the other became increasingly apparent.

While the bonds of Empire were being rapidly loosened in Asia, a strange concatenation of events much closer to Britain marked yet another phase in the process of imperial disintegration. In southern Ireland, De Valera's Fianna Fáil had been by tradition the 'separatist' party; but the long political reign of Fianna Fáil ended with the Irish General Election of February 1948. Fianna Fáil remained the largest single group in the Dáil, but a ramshackle coalition headed by John Costello's Fine Gael was able to amass a composite majority. In September that year, Costello, then in Canada, suddenly declared for repeal of the External Relations Act – the measure which, in effect, kept Eire within the Commonwealth. Some altercation with the less-than-tactful Governor-General of Canada, Viscount Alexander, appears to have played a part in precipitating the announcement. The necessary legislation was set in motion, and before the year ended had passed the

Dáil. Thus the 'semi-Dominion' of Eire became the Republic of Ireland; and early in the following year, 1949, the British Parliament gave formal acknowledgement to the country's new status.

Wisely or unwisely, the developed parts of the British Empire were moving more and more towards total separation from Britain in the 1940s, and for the most part the process derived from an internal dynamic in the countries concerned. Yet in 1945 there was little sign of a parallel movement in British colonies in most of Africa, where there were few people possessing the education required for national leadership of that kind. The British Government, however, resolved to make public money available on a much larger scale than hitherto for colonial development. Civil engineering works and education both absorbed a good deal of that money. Other colonial development schemes were directly related to the anticipation that African territories, like much of the Middle East, could become an important source of food for the British people. The money lavished on schemes for ground-nuts in Tanganyika and for eggs in Gambia became the subject of considerable opposition criticism at home.

Parallel plans for political development were produced. At the beginning of 1948 Colonial Secretary Creech Jones reported to the Prime Minister in favour of 'quick and vigorous development' with the 'long-term aim . . . that when the African territories attain self-government they do so as part of the western world'. Communism, explained the Colonial Secretary, 'has so far made only limited progress in our territories, but there are incipient nationalist movements in Nigeria and Kenya'. Thus, even in 1948, there seemed little reason to anticipate any early challenge to Britain's ascendancy in Africa: indeed, Britain appeared more anxious to force the march towards independence than to hold it back.

Troubles there certainly were about this time in colonial territories – serious riots in the Gold Coast (Ghana) in 1948, and in Nigeria in the following year – but these could be related to industrial rather than political complaints. In the course of the next couple of years or so a great deal of work was done, with active British stimulation, to consider possible constitutions for colonial territories like the Gold Coast and Nigeria; while, in another part of the world, comparable plans were devised for the creation of a Caribbean Federation from British territories in and near the West Indies. By 1950 there were signs of a strong local response to the initiative in some places. Thus, the Convention People's Party of the Gold Coast won sweeping victories in the local election at the capital, Accra. Indeed, Africans were already taking matters so much into their own hands that the colonial authorities found it necessary to proclaim a State of Emergency, and send several of the local leaders to prison.

At the same time plans were being devised for the political future of British African territories where – unlike the West African colonies – there were substantial numbers of white settlers. Towards the end of 1948 the Governor of Kenya looked forward to the time when his charge should become a Dominion; yet he derided as 'fantastic' the notion that it might come under African self-government in the foreseeable future. Within the next year or so there were indications both in Kenya and in Tanganyika that the ethnic triangle of indigenous Africans, white settlers and Asian immigrants was producing considerable restiveness about constitutional developments which were currently under discussion.

In fact a very different pattern was appearing in the areas of ethnic mixture from the comparatively straightforward progress towards independence which marked those colonies whose residents were nearly all of African stock. The Union of South Africa, although an independent Dominion ever since 1910, provided an extreme example of these problems, and exerted a great influence throughout Africa. Right down to 1948 exponents of what might be called 'enlightened imperialism' were disposed to extol the Union as a splendid example of the manner in which once-antagonistic societies – the British and the Boers – could be reconciled by wise and far-seeing statesmanship; and there seemed considerable prospects that in time the non-European communities would participate as equals. Neither the British nor the Boers deserve much credit for their attitude either to the Africans or to the various Asian immigrants; but there was some hope that their attitudes might gradually soften with time. In truth, the cleavage between British and Boers was not really healed either, even though Prime Minister General Smuts was a Boer presiding over a predominantly British Party; but that fact was less clear at the time.

In early 1948 political pundits anticipated a General Election in the Union, but felt little doubt that Smuts's United Party would maintain control.[2] In March of that year a South African Government report stirred the very sensitive question of racial relations. The Nationalist Opposition leapt to the attack, criticising the government for being too liberal on the native question, and recommending instead a policy of 'apartheid' – ostensibly, separate development for black and white races in South Africa; in practice white domination even sharper than hitherto. At the General Election of May 1948 the Nationalist Party, headed by D. F. Malan, won rather more seats than the United Party, and, with assistance from the Afrikaans Party, secured an over-all majority. The United Party retained a substantial majority of the popular vote, but this was ineffective. Smuts himself was one of the electoral casualties. The Nationalist Party, whose support came overwhelmingly from the Boer rather than the British section of the white population, included many members who had adopted a neutralist attitude during the war, and many who wished to leave the British Commonwealth.

The South African electoral result was generally deplored in Britain, and it presented any government, whether Labour or Conservative, with the prospect of very difficult decisions in the future. Economic considerations – notably the great gold resources of South Africa – made the British unwilling to encourage any serious rupture, and the country was perceived to have strategic importance. There was also the emotional tie that many British families had relatives in South Africa, while the idea that the British Commonwealth was an essentially united body, capable of tolerating aberrations among some of its members, had diplomatic as well as sentimental overtones. Conversely, any disposition to work closely with the new South African administration was certain to alienate a large body of opinion in other parts of Africa, and might seriously damage relations with India and Pakistan. There was also a vociferous body of critics in Britain – some, but not all, of them government supporters. Nobody was very sure how long the new South African Government would last, and there was honest doubt whether Britain would serve the interest of the black peoples and moderate whites in South Africa better by co-operating with that government and attempting to influence it in the direction of milder policies, or by a root-and-branch challenge.

The nature of Britain's difficulties was well illustrated by a problem, seemingly unimportant, which attracted much public attention in the early 1950s and was the subject of many Cabinet discussions and memoranda. Bechuanaland was a British Protectorate, surrounded on three sides by South African territory. In the middle lay the Bamangwato reserve, an area with a total population of about 10 000 and of no economic or strategic importance. Chieftainship of the Bamangwato was hereditary, and the incumbent, Seretse Khama, succeeded during his minority. He then travelled abroad on studies, while his uncle Tshekedi Khama, acted as regent. While away Seretse married a white woman; and the question arose whether he should be allowed to assume the rights of chieftainship on his return. Deep controversey was stirred in many places. There was some opposition to Seretse among the Bamangwato themselves at the beginning, through this soon died down; while some other African chiefs remained unhappy. There was predictable uproar among the whites in South Africa and Southern Rhodesia (Zimbabwe). The British were beginning to consider the problem before Labour left office, but it soon hit the new Conservative Government with full force. Various inducements were offered to Seretse to abdicate his claims – but without success. Eventually the government decided to exclude both Seretse and Tshekedi and their heirs from chieftainship. Needless to say, the whole episode attracted much controversy in Britain and wide international interest – which could hardly fail to weaken Britain's moral authority among a large section of the Commonwealth, whatever was done. Seretse eventually returned to the scene as the very-successful President of a newly-independent Botswana; but this lay well in the future at the time under consideration.

Meanwhile, the South African apartheid policy put the British Government in a quandary in other directions. In the autumn of 1952 a critical resolution was being prepared for the General Assembly of the United Nations.[3] The British Government was distinctly apprehensive. In the first place there was concern lest the United Nations should establish a 'right' to intervene in the internal affairs of a member-country. On this point, no doubt, other major powers felt a quiet and unexpressed sympathy, for none of them would wish too much publicity to be beamed on the darker places of their own rule; and a precedent might prove dangerous. Yet, from Britain's point of view, there were the particular difficulties of balancing her desire to appear 'as a champion of liberal western civilisation' – not least in front of her colonies – with her desire to keep on good terms with South Africa. In the end she got the worst of all worlds. A resolution was carried by the United Nations, calling for a commission to examine the racial situation in South Africa. A counter-resolution, declaring the matter one of domestic jurisdiction and outside the competence of the United Nations, was overwhelmingly defeated; but Britain found herself in the small minority supporting it. She had not maintained her 'liberal' stance; but she had also failed ignominiously to render useful assistance to South Africa.

There were indications that some of these baleful developments in South Africa did not just represent a peculiar local phenomenon, attributable to the country's earlier history – ghosts of the Boer War walking, as it were – but a more general problem. It will later be necessary to consider manifestations of that problem in Central Africa.

In Kenya, however, ethnic problems followed a distinctive course. There was a longstanding complaint among the black peoples that much of the best land had been taken by the whites. About 1950 disturbances associated with a movement called 'Mau Mau' arose. Throughout its course Mau Mau was almost confined to the Kikuyu tribe: a matter of considerable surprise to the British Colonial Office, for tke Kikuyu were not regarded as warlike, and were by no means the worst sufferers from 'land hunger'.[4] The Colonial Office was told little about those trouble in their early stages, and its Secretary complained in Cabinet that:

> The Government machine in Nairobi was out of touch with many of its officers, even its senior officers, in the field and sometimes information which told them what they did not want to know was discarded.

By late 1952 Mau Mau had developed characteristics which have been compared with the Irish 'Land War' of 70 years earlier. There were murders of British settlers and mutilations of cattle, largely by night raids on scattered farms; yet in other places not far distant everything was quiet. Far more casualties, indeed, occurred among the Kikuyu themselves, where reluctant tribesmen were terrorised to give support. There is little indication that the British Government had seriously analysed the causes of the disturbances, still less that they had proper plans for dealing with them. Although Jomo Kenyatta was already beginning to emerge as leader, it was by no means clear whether he was morally the author of the sporadic and often sickening crimes of violence, or whether he was really a force of moderation, frustrated by the crude barbarity of his putative followers.

Mau Mau was in many ways an aberrant development, peculiar to a region within Kenya, and it would be most dangerous to draw too many wider parallels; but in one respect at least it provided good lessons for Africans and Europeans alike throughout a large part of the continent. The old pattern of settlement, in which tiny minorities of white people lived in conditions of relatively enormous affluence among great numbers of Africans, could not possibly be maintained unless the vast majority of the native population willingly accepted it.

Although the British Empire was distintegrating rapidly by the early 1950s, Britain continued to exert substantial control over events in many places. 'The United Kingdom still commands on the whole more influence and goodwill in the Middle East than any other foreign Power', wrote Herbert Morrison, briefly the Foreign Secretary, in a

Cabinet memorandum of March 1951.[5] Much can be said for the view that this statement was aready wrong when it was written; but the fact that it could be written at all for that sort of readership, without conscious irony, serves to illustrate the important fact that British power in the Middle East was still enormous, six years after the Second World War.

Even the Palestine débacle had not destroyed that influence; but it was highly relevant to the collapse which followed soon afterwards. In the last few months of the Mandate, the two sides contended with growing violence in preparation for the military showdown which would necessarily follow British withdrawal. At midnight on 14 May 1948, as British administration came to an end, Jews announced the establishment of the State of Israel. Within hours the new country was invaded by its Arab neighbours. No doubt some had anticipated that the surrounding countries would destroy the infant Jewish state at its birth. This was not to be. The Arab areas of Palestine were occupied or annexed by neighbours: Gaza and its vicinity by Egyptians, the Arab area of the West Bank by Transjordan – now renamed Jordan. The King of Jordan was formally proclaimed King of Palestine as well. A long period of intermittent warfare began, with the familiar and tragic pattern of mutual crimes and atrocities, and the diplacement of vast numbers of refugees. According to United Nations estimates, some 725 000 Arabs fled Palestine; while British estimates were even higher.

For some years there had been signs that the Egyptian Government was moving towards the conclusion that its best chance of surviving against internal opposition lay in leading a national movement against the British. At the end of 1945 they had served notice on Britain – as they were entitled – requesting revision of the 1936 treaty. The initial concern was primarily to clear British troops out of Egypt. The British Government felt considerable ideological sympathy with this objective: indeed, if Egypt proved friendly this would remove a considerable burden. The Chiefs of Staff demurred; but, after considerable discussion, the Cabinet decided to inaugurate the negotiations by an offer to withdraw all British troops from Egypt over the next five years. This offer was not received with the gratitude which had perhaps been anticipated, and Egyptian negotiators easily pushed their British counterparts to accept the view that evacuation should be a good deal more rapid.

What eventually wrecked the Anglo-Egyptian negotiations was not British imperialism but Egyptian. Cairo talked of 'unity of the Nile Valley' – a high-sounding expression which meant, in practice, that the

Sudan should be brought under the Egyptian Crown, whatever might be the wishes of the people living in the area. On this point the British Government dug in its heels. By January 1947 there was no outstanding difference between the British and Egyptian Governments on terms of the treaty directly affecting Egypt; but there was total deadlock on the 'Sudan Protocol'.[6] Within a few months, the British Government began to make its own arrangements for constitutional reform in the Sudan, which would eventually lead to independence – but without the benefit of Egyptian approval or assistance. No doubt there had been honest concern for the Sudanese in the British intransigence, but interest was involved as well.[7] The Sudan was of strategic importance 'as protecting the backdoor to Egypt and as an important source of manpower'.

Although the inability of Britain and Egypt to reach general agreement on revision of the 1936 treaty could be considered to invalidate the original offer to remove British forces from the country, in practice the evacuation continued nothwithstanding, and by April 1947 British troops had been withdrawn from all of Egypt save the Canal Zone: an area which would later form the subject of deep antagonism.

The precipitate British evacuation of Palestine, and the troubles which followed, gave new animus to the dispute. On one hand it had been shown that Britain could be displaced from a Middle Eastern foothold by internal forces. On the other hand the Palestine affair presented Egypt with new difficulties and new grievances. The intervention of 1948 had failed in its primary objective of destroying the Jewish state, and this dealt a serious blow to the governments of the Arab powers – not least Egypt; for 70 000 Arab refugees had fled to Egypt and to the 'Gaza strip' which she occupied. Neither the British occupation of the Canal Zone, nor the question of the Sudan, had been resolved, and the Anglo-Egyptian dispute spluttered on. Just possibly the intensity of the 'Cold War', and the serious possibility of a general war, held back Egyptian animosity to a degree; for, little as the Egyptians liked the British, they certainly did not wish to exchange them for the Russians. Then, in April 1951, the Egyptian Government demanded that British forces should be evacuated from the country within a year. On 15 October Egypt pushed matters a great deal further. The 1936 treaty was formally abrogated, and with it the 1899 Convention which had established the Sudan as a condominium; while at the same time Farouk assumed the title 'King of Egypt and the Sudan'. This did not make much immediate difference, but it was clearly intended to heighten the dispute.

While the Anglo-Egyptian dispute was gradually coming to the boil, an old problem at the other end of the Middle East followed a more erratic course. By an agreement reached in 1942 the major allies had agreed to withdraw troops from Iran within six months of the end of the war. The British pulled out; but the Russians set up a satellite regime in the adjacent provinces of Azerbaijan and Kurdistan. There followed considerable altercations in the United Nations; and then, in the spring of 1946, Soviet troops were suddenly withdrawn. By the end of the year the Shah's Government had recovered control over those remote areas. Just what had happened to persuade the Russians to go? It is difficult to believe that they had yielded to moral pressure, and nobody was in a position to drive them out by force. Just possibly this was part of some obscure package-deal concluded between Byrnes and Molotov; but it appears not unlikely that the dominant consideration on the Soviet side was an agreement which had just been concluded, though not ratified, under which the Iranian Government would make oil concessions to the Soviet Union. Thereafter there was considerable delay; but in October 1947 the Majlis, or Parliament, of Iran refused, by a large majority, to ratify the agreement. Relations between the two countries became frigid. In 1949 the communist-orientated Tudeh Party was proscribed. There was a brief reaction in Russia's favour early in the following year, but this was soon reversed. In the 'Cold War' context of the time, it was significant that Iran received military missions from the United States. The Iranians, one may reflect, had suffered from attempted encroachments from both Britain and Russia for many years, and there was widespread hostility to both countries for national as well as political reasons; but there was no similar tradition of hostility towards the United States. Far from it; the Iranians eagerly sought both military assistance (which they got) and economic assistance (which was refused) from that quarter.

Wartime concern over Iran appears to have played a considerable part in exciting American interest in countries around the Persian Gulf. The British in Iran sought United States technical advice; and thereafter the potential both of Iran and of nearby countries came to be appreciated. Among those countries Saudi Arabia had long been a sort of backwater in the Middle East, with its ruling dynasty on notoriously bad terms with the Hashemite Kings who ruled in Transjordan and Iraq. At the end of 1950 the Arabian-American Oil Company (ARAMCO) concluded an agreement with Saudi Arabia, under which oil incomes would be equally divided. The Iranians could hardly fail to contrast that agreement with the one they were being invited to sign with Britain, by which only 25–30 per cent of the income would go to themselves. In March 1951 the Iranian Prime Minister was assassinated, and a month or two later the office was taken by a politician who had for many years played an important part in his country's development, and who had been particularly concerned with the oil question – Mohammad Musaddiq. Curiously it was Musaddiq who a few years earlier had led the Majlis in rejecting the proposed treaty with the Soviet Union; but he now ran into head-on conflict with Britain. Legislation was swiftly passed nationalising the country's oil industry, thus seizing the oilfields of the Anglo-Iranian Oil Company (AIOC). Terms of compensation – if any – were not specified. The Iranians required masters of tankers who collected oil from the refining port of Abadan to sign receipts acknowledging in effect the right of the new 'National Iranian Oil Company' to dispose of it. The great majority of the tankers were British, and the British Government instructed the Masters to refuse to sign. So oil shipments virtually ceased.

The British Government now appealed to the International Court at The Hague, for a ruling to the effect that the Iranian action was unlawful. The Court, which was far from certain whether it had jurisdiction in the matter, urged both parties for the time being to refrain from action prejudicial to the other, specifially ordering that the AIOC should be permitted to function until a decision could be taken on the point. This was naturally hailed by the British Government, but had no efect on the Iranians. The United Nations sat on the fence: they acknowledged Iran's right to nationalise her oil, but denied her authority to denounce the agreement with Britain unilaterally.[8] The British Government decided that there was little prospect of persuading the Security Council to give teeth to this decision and coerce the Iranians, and at first declined even to make the attempt. Later, as matters became more desperate, an appeal was made; but with no success. As for the International Court, it continued to argue ineffectually for a further year, and eventually decided, in July 1952, that it had no authority in the matter.

If appeal to international law was useless, and appeal to the United Nations unproductive, then what alternative remained? The possibility of using force was seriously disussed by Ministers in the dying Labour Government, and at one point seemed to attract Morrison:[9] but such action would have – to say the least – considerable disadvantages. The Soviet Union might well regard it as the justification, or pretext, for invasion from the north. The United States would deplore it. So there was little to do except continue the economic boycott, and handle contingent problems as they arose. In June British women and children were evacuated from the danger area; in July Truman sent the distinguished American diplomat Averell Harriman to attempt mediation; in August the British sent a member of the Government, R. R. Stokes, on a conciliatory mission. Not much emerged from these efforts; and when the Labour Government collapsed in October the issue was still unresolved.

Whatever might be the outcome of the current disputes with Egypt and Iran, whatever might be the future of the British Commonwealth, there could be no doubt whatever in the autumn of 1951 that the visible manifestations of British power had declined enormously within a few years, and were likely to decline further in the foreseeable future. It is important, however, to look at the positive side of the 'retreat from Empire'. The historian, like the journalist, is disposed to observe dramatic events where deep dissensions occur; but the truly remarkable feature of the 'retreat' is surely the fact that it was so smooth. After the Second World War the British made no attempt to hold on obstinately to imperial territories which were in the long term untenable. Even in Kenya and Malaya, where the British were engaged in prolonged conflict with indigenous rebels, the issue was completely different both in character and in upshot from the colonial wars which the French waged in Indo-China and the Dutch in Indonesia. There was certainly bloodshed on a vast scale in India; but it was bloodshed between Hindus and Moslems, not bloodshed between Britain and Indians. Credit for the smoothness of the imperial withdrawal should go to many places. Both the Labour Government and its Conservative successor decided that the process was inevitable, and set out to make it as smooth and painless as possible for all concerned. Colonial administrators during this period showed a real sense of responsibility for, and duty towards, the people whom they ruled – an attitude which contrasts sharply with the selfish follies which some leading administrators of India sought to impose on successive British Governments. This sense of responsibility was not a new thing, called into being when the British Government decided that withdrawal was imperative; but it had pervaded the colonial administation at a time when the Empire appeared a permanency. Nobody could have made the speedy and relatively smooth transition from colonial rule to independence if the facts had been otherwise. Whether the British were equally far-sighted and humane in their handling of Egypt and Iran was another matter; but neither of those stories had yet reached its conclusion.

17   A Calmer World

The eighteen months from October 1951 to March 1953 witnessed changes in the governments of all of the wartime 'Big Three' countries. In Britain the General Election of October 1951 replaced the tiny Labour majority by a Conservative majority not much larger. Yet – with Winston Churchill again at the helm, and with Anthony Eden – a prestigious figure in those days – again at the Foreign Office, would Britain somehow reassert her former authority? People who had hoped for, or who had feared, dramatic changes in policy would soon perceive a remarkable measure of continuity, both in domestic and in international matters. The new Prime Minister's language was more ferocious than that of his predecessor, and other Ministers from time to time gave indications in Cabinet that they disliked the constraints now imposed upon Britain; but in general they had no choice save to follow lines of policy already prescribed.

By the time the new British Government took office the Iranian problem had reached the stage where no immediate action was required, and the two sides coud do little but wait and see how matters would work out. The Iranians had evidently overestimated their current international importance, for new oil-producing countries were developing rapidly. Furthermore, the great international oil companies stuck together, and refused to handle Iranian oil under the new administration. With the exceptions of the Iranian market itself, and minor leakages to Japan and Italy, the nationalised company found few sales. In 1950 Iranian oil production was over 240 million barrels, or 6 per cent of the world's total. This dropped to 10.6 million barrels in 1952.[1] Beyond doubt, Iran was suffering more acutely than Britain from the dispute. Early in 1952 draconian measures were taken by the Iranian Government to reduce imports, and great hardship soon developed. On the face of it, there seemed much wisdom in Eden's judgement that Mussadiq would fall, and would be succeeded by a more 'reasonable'[2], that is a more amenable, government

This assessment made little allowance for the vast changes which had taken place both within Iran and within many other countries since Eden was last in office. What worried the Americans far more than it worried the British was the prospect that Mussadiq's successor would be a communist, rather than a supporter of the 'reasonable' policies Eden desired. Early in 1952 Mussadiq's 'National Front' secured a relative, but not an over-all, majority in the Majlis elections. At first the Premier relied for support on religious fundamentalists; but soon he found himself in dispute with the Shah over control of the Ministry of Defence. The religious party sided with the monarch, and on 17 July Mussadiq resigned. This seemed exactly the upshot which both Eden and his Labour predecessor had sought; but British rejoicing was short-lived. A General Strike brought down Mussadiq's ephemeral successor; and the Premier was back after only five days' absence.

The Mussadiq restoration brought on a new problem; for during the brief internal crisis his support had come largely from Tudeh. In all probability the Premier saw his new allies as a valuable asset in encouraging the Americans to render financial and moral support, lest worse should follow. But the United States Government did not see things that way at all; rather did they decide that he was no longer trustworthy. The State Department thus found itself increasingly in agreement with the British about the need to bring down Mussadiq – although for different reasons – and was therefore disposed to seek agreement between world oil interests which might help that development. At this point, however, they ran into conflict with the United States Department of Justice, which was engaged in 'trust-busting' – a process for which those same oil interests were a prime target. So Mussadiq, like his opponents, was compelled to await events; and by the time those events took place, in the late summer of 1953, developments of greater world significance had already changed radically the context into which they had seemed to fit.

The problem of Iran, the problem of Palestine, and the problem of Egypt (which demands a whole chapter to itself) are part of the story of British withdrawal from the Middle East, which in many ways proved more difficult than withdrawal from places formally acknowledged as part of the Empire or Commonwealth. No doubt forces had been at work for many years which prescribed that Britain must eventually execute general withdrawal from the Middle East. Down to the war, however, Britain appeared to have control over the speed and manner in which that withdrawal would take place, with reasonable expectation that the transfer of power would be very gradual and probably amicable. The Second World War imposed both military and economic burdens on Britain which would prove in the long run intolerable, and at the same time set in motion processes within the Middle East itself which brooked no such slow and planned withdrawal. The collapse of Britain's power in the area was precipitate, confused, demoralising, and accompanied by much illwill. That collapse was by no means complete at the turn of 1952–53.

1952 was another American Presidential election year. Truman was not a candidate for re-election, and the new President, whoever he might be, was likely to give important new twists to American foreign policy. In November Dwight D. Eisenhower was elected on a Republican ticket, while his Party held majorities in both Houses of Congress. Thus ended an era of twenty years, during which the Democrats had held the Presidency throughout, and control of both houses for most of the time. There followed a substantial period of moral, though not legal, 'interregnum', but in January 1953 the new President assumed office. Within a couple of months a much more dramatic change occurred in the Soviet Union: the death of Stalin on 5 March.

The importance of Stalin's death both to his own country and to the world would be difficult to exaggerate. His influence had been of the most massive kind. Stalin had taken the major role in industrialising the Soviet Union, and had encompassed the deaths of millions of peasants in the process. A little later he had pulled the country from its diplomatic isolation, and shortly afterwards promoted the purges which eliminated something like two-thirds of the Soviet High Command and vast numbers of civil administrators. During the immediate run-up to war, and during the war itself, his personal command both of foreign policy and of the country's internal organisation had been about as complete as that exercised by any man anywhere in human history. In the aftermath of war Stalin had been the chief instrument of Soviet expansion; and it was to counter that expansion that the 'Cold War' began. Just before his death Stalin seemed on the point of inaugurating another purge in the Soviet Union: a purge with strong anti-Semitic overtones, which seemed likely to be as terrible as its predecessor, and from which nobody, from the highest ranks of the Politburo downwards, would be safe. To top all this, Stalin was developing a cerebro-arterial condition which added significantly to the risk of war by caprice. There can have been few people occupying important positions in any country, and least of all in the Soviet Union itself, who received the news of Stalin's demise with anything less than ineffable relief.

The death of Stalin did not end the Cold War; indeed, in a sense the Cold War is still with us today. But it did reduce substantially the

imminence of the danger of a 'shooting war'. The new masters of the
Soviet Union, whoever they might be, would have their work cut out to
establish and maintain power in their own country, and would not be
likely to enter wantonly on external adventures. There was abundant
evidence of a power-struggle. Official obsequies at Stalin's funeral were
pronounced by Molotov and by two less familiar figures, M. G. M.
Malenkov and L. P. Beria. Such arrangements usually provide an
indication of where power currently resides, and for a short space that
triumvirage ruled. Extensive amnesties were soon proclaimed; the
mythical 'doctors' plot', on which Stalin seemed to be founding his
forthcoming reign of terror, was forgotten, and the spurious charges
withdrawn. Negotiations to end the Korean War, which had been
suspended for months, were soon resumed, and in July an armistice was
at last signed. Another potential threat to world peace vanished when
two Caucasian Republics of the Soviet Unon, which had been making
territorial claims against Turkey, withdrew their demands. The one man
who might have aspired to a large share of the former dictator's power
inside the Soviet Union was Beria, controller of the secret police. He fell
into disgrace during the summer, and a few months later was shot. None
of the Soviet leaders could afford to take the smallest risk of another
Stalin emerging.

For all that may be said about the importance of Stalin's death in
reducing the imminent risk of war, it would be wrong to suggest that
1953 marked a great and immediate surge of international goodwill. The
new Soviet leaders dared not be seen to 'weaken'; not only would this
have made their domestic position impossible, but it would have
produced a sudden and dangerous international imbalance. The first
Soviet hydrogen bomb was tested in 1953. For years to come, leading
statesmen in the West periodically issued warnings to their own peoples
to the effect that the Soviet leopard had not changed its spots. It would
be fatuous to deny that the new Soviet leaders had been participants at a
high level in Stalin's crimes.

Yet by 1954 the whole climate of international relations had changed
greatly in another respect. The new administration in the United States
was regarded with considerable alarm. British officials were not
antipathetic towards the President, with whom they had co-operated
extensively during the War; but there were many signs of concern over
policies linked with his Secretary of State, John Foster Dulles. Thus, in
the summer of that year there was quite a savage and protracted
argument in Cabinet over an attempt by Churchill to establish a kind of
'personal diplomacy' with Malenkov. The details of this dispute are
irrelevant here; but during its course Lord Salisbury, a figure well to the

'right' in Conservative politics, delivered himself of the opinion that the 'greatest threat to world peace' no longer came from Russia, but was 'that the United States might decide to bring the East-West issue to a head while they still have overwhelming superiority in atomic weapons'.[3] The record of the discussion does not suggest that Salisbury's colleagues took deep issue with this assessment. Later in the year there was much concern over American policy towards China, and fear that commitments would be entered with Chiang which might visibly increase the risk of a new war in Asia.[4] Perhaps it is not fanciful to see the 1954 decision to manufacture a British hydrogen bomb as conditioned, in part at least, by a desire to speak from strength towards the United States as well as the Soviet Union.

When the immediate threat of war through Soviet action was removed by the death of Stalin, more attention became focused on the disintegrating empires of Britain and France. Several of the most important questions of the period turned on the capacity of those two European Powers to preserve for a time some part of their former influence in places where the major challenge to the status quo came, not from other Great Powers, but from the indigenous peoples. In Britain's case the real trouble was not so much with territories which were acknowledged parts of the old Empire, but with countries formally recognised as independent states, yet which were under strong British economic or diplomatic influence.

In 1953 the British disputes with Egypt and Iran were unresolved, but there were pointers towards solutions. The Anglo-Egyptian Treaty of 1936 was due to expire in 1956, and thereafter Britain could not lawfully maintain troops in any part of Egypt without renewed assent of the Egyptian Government: assent which would certainly not be given. It was equally evident that Iran would be able to claim a far greater share of proceeds from her oil resources than she had obtained before Mussadiq, whatever the outcome of the current dispute. The British, however, had not scrupled to advance 'Cold War' arguments in an attempt to win some support from the United States, which could to a degree influence matters in their own favour. They were not very successful in pressing the argument that Egypt was vital for protection of the Middle East against a possible Soviet attack – with the implication that their own remaining authority should therefore be underwritten. They were rather more successful in relation to Iran. At the commencement of the dispute the Americans adopted a stance of fairly strict neutralism. When Mussadiq seemed likely to come under a degree of communist influence, the Americans tilted in Britain's favour.

There was, nevertheless, a considerable difference between British and American attitudes on the Iranian question. The Americans, particularly after Dulles's arrival at the State Department, were preoccupied with the dangers of communism. Might Mussadiq be compelled, if too much pressure was exerted, to rely on the Tudeh; or, alternatively, if he fell, would this create conditions of chaos which would enable the communists to take over? Thus the Americans were anxious to achieve an early settlement in order to avert either calamity. This rather cut across the British policy of leaving the Iranians to stew in their own juice. Furthermore, the British were disposed to discount the danger of communism in Iran – perhaps because their own interests were more deeply involved in securing adequate compensation than in the country's political future. Thus, to the British, the Americans seemed weak and vacillating; while to the Americans the British appeared foolhardy in the face of overwhelming risks.

Common interests were nevertheless strong enough to compel the two countries to work together more or less closely, and an urgent appeal made by Mussadiq in the summer of 1953 for aid from the Americans was rejected. In August the Shah dismissed Mussadiq, replacing him as Prime Minister by the less intransigent General Zahidi. Before the year was out Mussadiq was in gaol, and Zahidi's government appeared to have established normal relations with Britain, and also to be in control of the internal situation. In the following year a new oil agreement was negotiated; but the arrangements were markedly different from those which had existed before nationalisation. Future oil profits would be shared between the Iranian Government and an international consortium; while the Anglo-Iranian Oil Company, now meta-morphosed into British Petroleum, would receive compensation. The agreement squeezed through the Iranian Majlis and Senate with desperately narrow majorities. The Iranian crisis was over, and the British might reflect that they had won a kind of victory, though a costly one. Britain's position in the world oil market had declined considerably, and the Americans were now an important element in Middle Eastern oil politics.

In the early 1950s France was also struggling with the vestiges of an imperial legacy. She had already been compelled to admit that Indo-China could no longer be treated as a colony. The new status of the successor-countries – the 'Associated States' of Vietnam, Laos and Cambodia – was widely regarded as a mere subterfuge for France to retain some share of her former colonial authority; but she certainly did not retain all of that authority, and it seemed likely that she would lose control altogether in the not-too-distant future. Nevertheless, the

French still hoped – at worst – to be able to withdaw in circumstances which would not do too much damage to their prestige elsewhere,[5] and this necessitated American support. Before the war the Americans had taken a baleful view of French behaviour in Indo-China, but they could hardly allow the former colony to come under control of communists, who were increasingly important among the local rebels. This applied especially to Vietnam, where Ho Chi-minh, principal challenger to French authority, was an avowed communist, while the playboy 'Emperor' Bao Dai, whom the French were currently supporting, was certainly not. The Americans were already being drawn into Vietnam before the Democrats left office; even in 1952 Secretary of State Dean Acheson had to point out to the French that the United States was defraying a third of the cost of the war in Vietnam.

The Russians, for their part, had no need to bring fuel to keep the flames going in these conflagrations which were engaging the British and French, and perhaps they were beginning to reflect that they had little real interest in their outcome. Vietnam and Egypt were both far too distant from Soviet borders from any real control to be exercised, whatever happened; while in Iran, Mussadiq was in no sense a more reliable tool for Soviet interests than for those of the West. The main value of the disputes, from the Soviet point of view, was that they attracted American attention which might have been directed elsewhere.

In the later judgement of Anthony Eden, 'the restoration of peace in Indo-China was the most dangerous and acute of the problems with which I had to deal during my last four years as Foreign Secretary'[6] – that is, in the period 1951–55. We may perhaps see a measure of afterknowlege in that assessment; but the fact that it could be made at all is a remarkable indication of the truly global character which the Cold War had assumed. Unlike past areas of dispute – Poland, Germany, Korea or even Iran – Indo-China was remote from the obvious spheres of influence of the super-powers, and also had little direct relation to Britain; yet it succeeded in drawing everybody into perilous involvements which would eventually produce even more costly repercussions.

Soon after Eisenhower became President of the United States he promulgated the 'domino theory', which was eagerly taken up by Dulles. Knock down on standing domino, and it dislodges the next, which, in falling, displaces a third, and so on. The importance of Indo-China, and specifically of Vietnam, was seen, not in terms of its own value – whether economic or strategic – but of its anticipated bearing on other places. Following that view, what lay at stake was not the fate of one country, but the fate of all south-east Asia; and it was not difficult to extrapolate the theory to include the remainder of Asia as well. If Asia fell, what prospects existed for the rest of the world? This line of reasoning could easily lead to the view that any territory anywhere in the world was of, literally, vital importance to the United States.

By the spring of 1954 the French hold on Vietnam was precarious indeed. Communist forces, known as Vietminh, invested the last great northern stronghold of Dien Bien Phu, which eventually fell on 7 May. Long before that date it was a foregone conclusion that only massive assistance from outside – which meant in practice from the United States – could save the French and their Vietnamese associates in the north. Further south the communist threat was less immediate.

The attitude of the powers towards Vietnam was complex. The United States was still not technically involved, save in the sense that they were carrying a great deal of the financial burden; for they had refused – despite the 'domino theory' – to succumb to French pressure to 'internationalise' the war. Although they saw their interests to lie in organising the general defence of south-east Asia against communism, they had no intention either of shouldering responsibility more or less alone, or of committing themselves to forlorn hopes. The British were perhaps influenced by Indian 'neutralism', and perhaps fearful for Hong Kong; they were certainly conscious of the financial and physical limits to their remaining power in the Far East, and would give no open-ended commitment. The French were plunged in political crisis, as their government came to be assailed from very different angles at home. On one hand they were conscious that France's prestige in Asia, and perhaps much closer to home, lay at stake; but on the other hand they could hardly wish the Americans to become too deeply involved in Asia, lest this should reduce United States concern in the fate of Europe. For various reasons, other interested powers came to see the merits of compromise, and in July 1954 a solution was agreed, by which Vietnam was divided into a pro-communist northern state and a pro-western southern state. For a few years peace was more or less preserved – until the dispute erupted again, in a different and far more lethal form, in 1959. That story, however, lies outside the present study.

More durable than the uneasy truce was the international body brought into existence as an indirect consequence of the Vietnam dispute: the South-East Asia Treaty Organisation, or SEATO. It is tempting to regard SEATO as an organisation comparable with NATO; but in fact the measure of commitment of the principal powers was far less than in Europe. There was considerable argument as to what countries should participate; but the eventual founder-members were the United States, Britain, France, Australia, New Zealand, the Philippines, Thailand and Pakistan. This excluded not only both Vietnams, but also the other successors of French Indo-China, and the Chinese Nationalist government still established on Formosa (Taiwan).

Despite the formation of SEATO, it was obvious by the 1950s that the countries of western Europe were in the process of gradually liquidating commitments outside their own continent, while at the same time the immediate threat to western Europe itself had largely disappeared. Yet the impetus towards European co-operation which had been engendered during the active phase of the Cold War was still not spent. Inspired to no small degree by the success of the European Recovery Programme, the democracies began to establish economic links with remarkable ease. In 1951 the European Coal and Steel Community was set up, involving France, West Germany, Italy and the Benelux countries. Co-operation between those 'Six' was to become increasingly important in the years to come. The problems of military defence were more difficult, despite the establishment of NATO and the deep American commitment which this implied. Nobody could be sure that this commitment would last for ever; and in any event the Europeans could hardly view with equanimity the knowledge that their survival depended on the willingness of an outsider, whose interests did not always correspond exactly with their own, to rush to their defence.

The first essay in that direction was the so-called 'Pleven Plan', promulgated by France in the autumn of 1950. This envisaged a European army in which Germans would participate. Recognising the real fear of German military revival which still persisted, the proponents of the plan insisted that specifically German units should not exceed battalion strength. The presence of German units would ensure that the Germans did not consider themselves powerless in their own defence, and would avert the danger that they might lapse into a kind of helpless apathy. German participation was also essential to ensure that sufficient men could be raised. On the other hand there was no risk of a specifically German army coming into existence.

The United States would not be involved as a direct participant in these new arrangements, although indirect American support was plainly necessary. Britain, however, was invited to participate in the 'European Defence Community' which the Pleven Plan proposed to set up. In fact, however, the offer was rejected by the dying Labour Government, and that rejection was confirmed when the Conservatives took office in the autumn of 1951. Britain, like the United States, welcomed the idea of the EDC, but the military implications of membership were quite unacceptable. Next the French themselves shied off. The proposal came for consideration at a bad moment, for national pride had been deeply wounded by the disaster at Dien Bien Phu. The communists, for obvious reasons, disliked the whole idea; while the 'Gaullists', who saw their eponymous leader as the man who might yet restore France to her distinctive and dominant position in Europe, were also hostile; and the German question was still very much a live one. Thus did the French Assembly narrowly reject EDC in August 1954.

The British, however, soon dreamed up a tolerable substitute. The effect of their proposal was that 'Western European Union' – devised by the Brussels Treaty of 1948 as (in theory at least) a means for countering a renewed threat from Germany – should be turned into an instrument establishing a defensive alliance against possible Soviet incursions. From the point of view of proponents of the original EDC idea, this had the disadvantage that no supranational authority was set up; but against that they could balance the fact that Britain, for the first time, had specific military commitments to continental defence. In the course of the ensuing winter and spring the legislatures of the 'Western European Union' countries endorsed the arrangements – though the French Assembly only gave a small majority. As for West Germany, her rehabilitation was soon practically complete. In the course of May 1955 the Federal Republic was first recognised as a sovereign state, and then brought into NATO.

These military arrangements were followed swiftly by further economic moves in the direction of western European integration. In January 1955 the OEEC countries agreed to increase the volume of internal trade which should be free from tariffs from 75 per cent to 90 per cent. At the Messina Conference of June, Foreign Ministers of the 'Six' gave rather tentative endorsement to the idea of a 'common market' which would cover all commodities. In the same year the proposal of a European atomic energy commission – 'Euratom' – was seriously bruited.

In Europe, as in Asia, the control of events had largely passed out of British hands. In Africa the British role was different, and less closely related to overtones of the Cold War. Decolonisation proceeded at an accelerating pace during the early 1950s. Nigeria and the Gold Coast were front runners. Both were large and populous countries, with rising standards of general literacy and emerging educated élites capable of taking on the responsibilities of government, and in neither country were matters complicated by substantial numbers of white settlers who wished to make the place their permanent home. In both, however, there was a serious problem reminiscent of the one which arose in the late phase of British rule in India. Ethnic minorities began to evince increasing apprehension about their own position when independence should eventually arrive. This problem was particularly marked in Nigeria, where a large proportion of the population in the north was Moslem. There were serious riots in the northern town of Kano in May 1953, when forty-six people were killed and many injured. It would plainly be necessary to devise some sort of federal system for the future. Nigerian politics took on an ominously 'ethnic' character in the elections of 1954, when the northern region gave a great majority to a local party, completely unrepresented in the remainder of the country. Resolution of the constitutional difficulties created by this situation would take time; and although in some ways Nigeria seemed the more advanced, it was the Gold Coast which developed more rapidly towards independence.

The Gold Coast was not completely immune from similar problems. Elections in 1951 showed a considerable contrast between the views of the north and those of the remainder of the country. Nevertheless a remarkable partnership developed between the leading African politician, Kwame Nkrumah, and the Governor, Sir Charles Arden-Clarke. By 1954 it was being taken as axiomatic in the British Cabinet that the Gold Coast would attain full independence in 1956 or 1957.[7] Nkrumah, now dignified with the title of Prime Minister, was associated with a formal demand for complete independence within the lifetime of the existing Parliament. In the event, a further General Election was held in July 1956. Although the North – and, this time, the Ashanti region as well – showed a signficantly different pattern from the bulk of the country, regional differences were less sharp than in Nigeria, and the largest political party – the Convention People's Party – did secure some representation in all parts of the country. In the immediate aftermath of the election the British Colonial Secretary made a conditional promise of independence for March 1957: a promise which was in fact fulfilled. Thus did the Gold Coast transform itself into Ghana, and become the first fully-independent negro state in the British Commonwealth. Nigeria would follow a few years later.

In British territories on the eastern side of Africa problems were of a different kind. There were fewer educated Africans; and there were numerous communities of white settlers, long accustomed to social and economic privilege, who wished to make the place their permanent home. Before the war Southern Rhodesia (Zimbabwe) had seemed well advanced on the road to Dominion status, and it appeared not unlikely that other colonies would follow. Now, in the 1950s, the larger West African colonies were shooting ahead towards full independence, and many people on the other side of the continent were anxious to see similar developments in their own countries.

In the closing years of the Labour Government plans had been inaugurated for establishing a 'Central African Federation' from Northern and Southern Rhodesia and Nyasaland. The Conservatives' intentions in the matter were set out in a White Paper published early in 1953, which included a statement that 'the association of the three Territories would enable the Federation, when the inhabitants of the Territories so desire, to go forward with confidence towards the attainment of full membership of the Commonwealth' – in other words, Dominion status. This was designed largely to allay fears in Southern Rhodesia, much the most advanced of the three Territories, that its own constitutional development might be prejudiced by joining the Federation.[8] It looked, at first sight, like adequate satisfaction of local aspirations; but serious problems were immediately raised. The nub of the difficulty was that the black majorities, noting the baleful trends in South Africa, feared above all things that their own countries would come under similar domination from minorities of white settlers. The British Government was too deeply committed by this time to resile from its plans, and the Federation was brought into existence later in the year; but the growing suspicions of the black population really foredoomed it from the start. Independence could not be granted against the not-unreasonable hostility of the bulk of the population; but, if independence was refused, the white settlers of Southern Rhodesia would complain that they had been tricked into acceptance of Federation in the first place.

Yet while the situation was deteriorating in Central Africa, it was improving further north. By the middle of the decade Mau Mau was more or less under control in Kenya. The scale of the trouble while the 'emergency' persisted had been very great; for some 11 000 people – the vast majority of them Africans – had lost their lives. Paradoxically, Kenya – like other East African colonies where white settlers were not very numerous – was able thereafter to advance towards independence a good deal more rapidly and smoothly than Southern Rhodesia, whose problems would plague the Commonwealth for many years yet to come.

Other difficulties impeded the smooth progress of 'decolonisation' elsewhere. In many parts of the world substantial numbers of Indians had settled in British colonies; and in some places they had constituted the bulk of commercial classes. Like the white settlers, they viewed the prospect of 'majority rule' with serious misgivings. The 'external Chinese' settled in British possessions of south-east Asia were also apprehensive of discrimination when the ethnic majority should gain control.

Sometimes the main problem of decolonisation had little to do with either economics or race. In many colonies the population seemed too small, or the proportion of educated people too low, to permit easy development towards independence. What could be done for a West Indian island whose population was no greater than that of a very moderate-sized English town; or for a territory like Gambia: a narrow riparian strip thrust deep into French-controlled Senegal? All kinds of expedients were proposed, sometimes turning on federation with other territories; but small territories were naturally apprehensive of domination by larger neighbours. Indeed, 'neighbour' was often a relative term, for sometimes the proposed units of a federation were hundreds of miles apart, and had had little contact with each other in the past.

In some remarkable cases the general pattern of Commonwealth development seemed to go into reverse. In South Africa the Nationalists' domination showed no signs of abating, and neither did the avowedly racial policies pursued. Many people, within the Commonwealth and outside it, who knew little of the subtleties of 'Dominion status', tended to hold Britain indirectly responsible for those policies. British spokesmen, conscious of their country's position as leader of the Commonwealth, sometimes felt themselves constrained to make what case they could for South Africa's 'right' to pursue policies which British opinion almost unanimously deplored. The economic importance of South Africa was undeniable; her strategic position could not be ignored. By the mid-1950s, however, South Africa was on one hand anathema to African and Asian opinion, and on the other hand an encouragement to white settlers in other places who wished to emulate her selfish and short-sighted policies. On balance, she was more of a liability than an asset; yet there was no precedent, and there was no mechanism, for driving her from the Commonwealth.

Britain's European possessions presented difficulties very much of their own. Gibraltar, Malta and Cyprus had been acquired at different times for strategic reasons, and the strategic problems of the Mediterranean had changed dramatically. Questions relating to the future of Gibraltar rather hung fire, because the only practical alternative to British rule was incorporation into Spain: a course which the peninsula's inhabitants plainly did not desire, and which few non-Spaniards cared to advocate while Franco remained in power. Malta was not unlike a detached British dockyard town with hinterland, and some Maltese advocated incorporation in the United Kingdom. This, however, would imply heavy and continuing contributions to Malta's defence, and the financial burdens of extending Britain's Welfare State to an island where living standards were much lower. Cyprus, unlike the other two, was still believed by many people in the 1950s to possess real strategic importance. Palestine had gone, the British foothold in Egypt was crumbling. It was widely thought that the eastern Mediterranean was still a vital British interest; and if that was so, Cyprus was very important. The island had a mixed Greek and Turkish population, and the two peoples had a very long history of deep mutual animosity. Greeks, who preponderated, began to press for 'enosis' – union with Greece – and at the end of 1954 serious riots in Nicosia and Limassol marked the beginning of a long and violent struggle between the British and Greek majority in Cyprus. Cyprus acquired the dubious distinction of becoming the last place in the world which Britain sought to hold against the demonstrable will of the majority of its inhabitants.

The pattern of development within the British Commonwealth was certainly very different from what had been anticipated at the end of the war, and the difference had little to do with the change of British Government in 1951. By the early 1950s it was plain that relations between Britain and the Asian members were radically different from relations with the old Dominions; while the African colonies, already on the verge of independence, would alter the character of the Commonwealth further. At one point members of the British Government were disposed to favour a sort of 'two-tier system', with different grades of Commonwealth membership; but close study convinced them that this was unworkable.[9] Churchill was still Prime Minister when, in December 1954, the Cabinet acknowledged the validity of these conclusions. Close co-operation on matters of defence and foreign policy could not really extend further than the 'white Dominions'; while among those Dominions themselves it was apparent that South Africa would soon present problems of an acute kind.

For all the anomalies and irregularities of pattern, the process of British withdrawal from Empire was proceeding, on the whole, with astonishing speed and smoothness. There was – and there remains – a strong argument for the view that, in many parts of the old Empire, the new dispensation was no improvement on the earlier one. What has been cynically called 'the right of all peoples to be exploited by their own nationals' implied that overwhelming power would pass to small local élites; or in some cases plunge the country into chaos and civil war as different élites struggled among themselves. A third of a century on from the main events of the 'decolonisation' period, we may fairly ponder whether the governments which now rule are more enlightened, or even more democratic, than the old colonial administrations had been. Yet, as has so often been observed, politics is 'the art of the practical'. For many different reasons, it was evident in the aftermath of 1945 that Britain could not hold on for long to her imperial ascendency. Having recognised the essential facts of the situation, the British then prepared to withdraw in a manner which would do the minimum damage both in the withdrawal period itself and thereafter. Broadly speaking they succeeded. Politicians seldom have a simple choice between good and evil; and in most cases here they probably chose the least of available evils.

One is tempted to make invidious comparisons between Britain's experience as she prepared to withdraw from her imperial authority with that of other European countries. The Dutch struggle, against all advice, to hold Indonesia, did no good to either the Netherlands or her colonies; while the French obstinacy in Indo-China not only led to discrediting failure in the short run, but in the long run destabilised south-east Asia, producing in the process unspeakable miseries, and terrible risks to the world at large, for a quarter of a century to come. Belgium's baleful rule in the Congo left very few people possessed of tertiary eduction, or qualified to accept the independence which was suddenly thrust upon a wholly unprepared country. Portugal, who had held colonies in Africa for longer than most others, also left a legacy of chaos when she departed.

Yet the course of events in what had been the British Empire was certainly different from what the British themselves had anticipated or intended. Romantic imperialists might bemoan the collapse of Empire; but domestic prosperity rose apace, and the man-in-the-street, suffused in a flood of consumer-durables, watched the process of dismantlement with indifference. Nor were prophets in the centre ground of politics much closer to the mark in their anticipations. Down to the very late 1940s it had been more or less taken for granted by democratic socialists, liberals and moderate conservatives that the eventual destiny of the British Commonwealth was to be a free association of ex-colonies who had evolved into self-governing Dominions, co-operating voluntarily in most vital matters of world concern. They would all be Westminster-type democracies with bewigged Speakers; with government and opposition parties divided into socio-economic lines, who would gradually spread education, and eventually full participation in the democratic process, to the less-civilised groups who lived within their frontiers. In few places indeed have events followed such patterns.

18 Suez

At the beginning of 1952 the already bad Anglo-Egyptian relations deteriorated further. The British military commander declared his intention to disarm and expel the Egyptian military police located in Ismailia. This led to fighting in which three Britons and forty Egyptians were killed. On 26 January great riots occurred in Cairo, where large numbers of business premises were destroyed. Churchill later told the Cabinet that there were 70 000 troops in the Canal Zone,[1] and so the British could hold the military situation; but nobody could hold the political situation in Egypt. A succession of brief governments followed, but on 23 July radical political changes were inaugurated by a group of younger officers, headed by General Mohammad Neguib, who seized key points in Cairo. This was hardly a 'military coup' in the ordinary sense of the term, for those officers were by no means part of the traditional Egyptian military 'establishment'. Three days later King Farouk was forced to abdicate, and his infant son was proclaimed King Fuad II. A year later the country was formally constituted a Republic.

Discussions ran on between the British and the revolutionary regime of General Neguib on the two main issues of Farouk's time – the Sudan and the Canal Zone – but in a noticeably more concilatory atmosphere. No doubt the truculence of the old Egyptian regime had derived in part from a perceived need to rally domestic opinion against the foreign enemy, in order to deflect attention from the incompetence and corruption of the country's own government.

By the early part of 1953 the British and Egyptian Governments were approaching agreement on the Sudan, to the effect that the condominium would have a limited period more or less on its own, whereafter it would be free to choose between complete independence and union with Egypt. Suddenly the British Conservative Government ran into a sharp and unexpected dispute – not with the Egyptians, nor with the acknowledged opposition at home, but with their own backbenchers. As wind of the course of discussions reached MPs, tremendous protest arose. Churchill was obviously shaken by the extent of that protest, and showed considerable alarm in Cabinet. Eventually

Eden and the Conservative Chief Whip met the truculent back-benchers, and were able to report back with relief to an emergency late-night meeting of the Cabinet, to the effect that most of the critics now accepted the agreement as the least of available evils – though remaining uneasy.[2] Having damped down the revolt of their own followers, the government ran into new trouble with Egypt when a Parliamentary questioner was assured that if the Sudan became independent, it would be free to apply for Commonwealth membership, should it so desire. The Egyptians, regarding this as a piece of sharp practice, complained vigorously.

Despite such tribulations, agreement was reached. A Sudanese Constituent Assembly was to be elected, in whose hands the eventual decision would lie. Neither Britain nor Egypt had the least intention of leaving matters to the unfettered judgement of the Sudanese. The British tried without success to secure an early poll, convinced that this would be to their advantage; but they were frustrated, and voting was postponed until after the rainy season. Selwyn Lloyd, Minister of State, visited the Sudan to try to handle matters on the spot. As he explained to collegues on his return, the main purpose of the visit was 'to encourage the British officials not to lose heart and to stiffen the pro-independence Sudanese to stand up to the Egyptians'.[3] Various proposals were made for spending modest sums of public money to that purpose; whereupon Harold Macmillan, whose reputation was rising rapidly within the government, circulated a brief but sharp memorandum complaining that the scale of expenditure contemplated was far too modest.[4] The upshot in the Sudan was paradoxical. Elections held in November 1953 gave a small over-all majority to a party generally considered to be pro-Egyptian; but the British still did not despair, and eventually they prevailed upon the Sudanese to decide in favour of complete independence, which took effect at the beginning of 1956.

The matter of the Suez Canal proved more difficult. Foreign Secretary Eden's health tended to break down at times of crisis, and for a considerable part of 1953 he was indisposed. Not long before his illness Eden circulated a weighty memorandum to the Cabinet, pointing out certain unpalatable facts about the 1936 treaty, on which the British were relying as authority for the presence of their troops. 'We are ourselves in serious breach of it. It allows us to maintain not more than 10 000 troops in Egypt in time of peace; since 1936 we have rarely had so few there, and we now have nearer 80 000.' The Egyptians alleged that the number was substantially greater still. 'Moreover', added Eden, 'the treaty expires at the end of 1956, and it will take at least eighteen months to complete the withdrawal of our troops'.[5]

Even the British military authorities wanted an early agreement. The Commander wrote that 'If we do get an agreement, I believe that the present Egyptian Government will do their best to honour it. No alternative government is likely to behave better in this respect: on the countrary.'[6] The wrangling still continued for a long time, but eventually, in July 1954, the two governments reached agreement. British troops would be withdrawn from the Canal Zone within twenty months; but in event of attack upon any Arab stage, or upon Turkey, the British would be authorised to reoccupy the base. With that contingency in mind, the Egyptians would keep it in order for seven years.

The agreement ran into serious trouble. The rebellion among Conservative MPs which had arisen at the time of the Sudan agreement now reappeared in another and more dangerous form – the so-called 'Suez Group', headed by a backbencher, Captain Charles Waterhouse. At one point about forty government supporters intimated that they would vote against any treaty involving withdrawal of troops from the Suez base. At a time when the govenment's over-all majority was under twenty, such a revolt might prove catastrophic; but no doubt Ministers could ponder that the Suez Group and the opposition would scarcely make common cause on such a matter. Labour decided to abstain on the critical division, and the adverse Conservative vote – twenty-six – was less than had originally been feared. Nevertheless, it provided serious warning of the precarious nature of Parliamentary support for any policy of conciliation.

The Egyptian Government also ran into trouble. The new agreement was eventually concluded in October 1954, but in the following month Neguib fell; and the reins of power passed into the hands of the younger, more charismatic, and far more truculent Gamal Abdel Nasser. Nasser was deeply concerned with the idea of constructing a massive High Dam at Aswan, in the south of Egypt. This would create a vast lake (submerging, incidently, the dwellings of 50 000 Sudanese), and was designed both to control the Nile flooding and to provide a major source of hydro-electric power. To this project it will be necessary to return.

Political changes in Britain were also relevant to the general story of Anglo-Egyptian relations. In April 1955 Sir Winston Churchill, eighty years of age, at last decided to resign the premiership, and Anthony – by then Sir Anthony – Eden succeeded. The new Prime Minister took this as an appropriate occasion to call a General Election, and won an over-all majority of nearly sixty. This reduced the Conservative Government's vulnerability to rebellions from the Suez Group and from similar malcontents. Indeed, the whole political atmosphere in Britain appeared to have softened considerably. Eden still retained considerable prestige on the 'left' for the circumstances (or rather, for what were imagined to have been the circumstances) of his celebrated resignation in 1938, and for his supposedly intransigent opposition to 'Appeasement' thereafter. The Chancellor of the Exchequer, R. A. Butler, whom Eden inherited from Churchill, was pursuing very conciliatory economic policies which largely disarmed opposition criticism. Labour also had acquired a new leader, Hugh Gaitskell, and he was seen to stand well to the 'right' within his party. So close did the views of the two men seem that the term 'Butskellism' was coined to signal their apparent agreement on essentials. Thus Eden presided over a government which not only had won an unexpected accretion of public support, but which also stirred little implacable opposition even among people who voted for other parties.

While Britain enjoyed unwonted 'national unity', and Nasser of Egypt appeared preoccupied with works of civil engineering, diplomats were engaged in a different kind of engineering. Turkey was linked to the West through NATO, Pakistan through SEATO. It was considered necessary to stop the gap between them, and for that reason the 'Baghdad Pact' was concluded in stages during 1955: a military alliance between Turkey, Pakistan, Iran and Iraq, backed by Britain. The United States approved of the transaction, but did not involve herself as closely as the British desired. The authors hoped eventually to link Egypt as well – indeed, the germ of that idea could be perceived several years earlier, when Britain had sought to effect a compromise with the Egyptians over the occupation question by offering them a somewhat less extensive military alliance as inducement.

The Baghdad Pact was designed largely to contain Soviet influence, but its most conspicuous effect was to cut across the internal politics of the Middle East. 'Pan-Arabism' – the idea that all Arabic-speaking peoples had an essential identity of interest – had been a growing force for years; but for pan-Arabism there were two possible centres – Egypt and Iraq. Thus a natural rivalry existed between the two countries, and now that Iraq was about to receive further backing from the West, it was tempting for the Soviet bloc and Egypt to seek to exploit the situation, though in different ways. To the Soviet Union there opened the prospect of building an aggrieved and ambitious Egypt as counterpoise to pro-western Iraq; to Egypt there was a prospect of playing off the cold warriors against each other, to her own advantage. There were also numerous cross-currents flowing: rising hostility between Israel and her Arab neighbours; dynastic rivalry between the Hashemite Kings of

Jordan and Iraq on one side and the Saudi dynasty in Arabia on the other; the internal politics of Syria and Jordan – the list is endless. All played their part in the compex web of Middle Eastern affairs; and it is important to remember that to everybody involved, events in his own immediate area of concern transcended all others in their importance.

Although Egypt showed considerable interest in the idea of obtaining arms from Soviet sources, the governments of Britain and Egypt remained on quite good terms for some time to come, and arrangements for the evacuation of the last British troops from the Canal Zone proceeded according to plan. Massive financial aid was necessary for the construction of the Aswan Dam, and proposals were made in December 1955 under which Britain, the United States, and the World Bank would all make substantial loans and grants. Nasser, however, was equally interested in the idea of winning aid from the Soviet Union, which was prepared to offer help on very favourable terms. This disposition to turn to such sources for assistance amounted to mortal sin in Dulles's eyes, and on 19 July 1956, under the strong influence of the Secretary of State, western support was withdrawn. Dulles's anger would have been even greater had he known that the Egyptian Government was also negotiating a secret agreement – published a couple of months later – under which Czechoslovakia was to supply quantities of arms.

On 26 July 1956 Nasser delivered his riposte to the West at a great mass-demonstration. To obtain funds for building the Aswan Dam, Egypt would nationalise the Suez Canal Company. Investors would receive what had been the market value of their shares immediately before announcement.

The legality or otherwise of this action was open to some debate. The British contended that it breached the 1888 Convention of Constantinople, which guaranted the international character of the canal. The Egyptians could argue that the Company was legally Egyptian, even though its headquarters were in Paris and only five of its thirty-two directors were Egyptian. In any event, the Canal Company's concession was due to expire in 1968, so the parties were concerned only with a limited period of use. The atmosphere of the announcement, however, and the rhetoric which accompanied it, left no doubt in anybody's mind that the action was conceived in a spirit of deep hostility to the West, and was designed to whip up public support for Nasser both in Egypt and in other Arab countries, with Britain as the particular target of execration. To all this Eden reacted with extreme sharpness, and thereafter plainly visualised Nasser as a latter-day dictator of the 'Thirties vintage. This view was simplistic, but there was superficial justification for it. The internal regime in Egypt was rapidly developing familiar attributes of a totalitarian state, complete with suppression of civil liberties, persecution of opponents, xenophobic rhetoric, (spiced at times with plain lies), organised subversion in other countries, and visible designs for greatly extending the area of domination. Eden's view of Nasser, and of the need to 'stop' him, had considerable appeal to people subscribing to the widespread view that 'the dictators' could, and should, have been 'stopped' at an early stage and with little cost by 'the democracies'; that failure to do so proved of critical importance in permitting the drift of events which led to the Second World War. At a lower level one must record that wartime relations between occupying British forces and the local population had often been bad, and there was much anti-Egyptian feeling among ex-servicemen. Thus 'strong action by Britain' had a powerful appeal not only to old-style imperialists but also to people whose politics were of a very different stamp.

The Prime Minister's own book, written years afterwards, leaves no doubt in the reader's mind as to the real hatred he felt for Nasser. Others have confirmed the picture. Anthony Nutting, who later resigned from the government, tells how Eden riposted to a Foreign Office document. 'I want [Nasser] destroyed, can't you understand . . . And I don't give a damn if there's anarchy and chaos in Egypt'.[7] The Prime Minister's public utterances, however, were at this time more measured, while Gaitskell and other Labour spokesmen condemned Nasser's action as vigorously as did Eden.

There was wide international concern lest a side-effect of canal nationalisation should be to block passage of shipping, and in mid-August a conference of interested nations was convened in London. Only Egypt and Greece – currently aggrieved over Cyprus – refused to attend. About 95 per cent of the Canal users were represented by their governments. Eighteen of the twenty-two governments supported an American plan that the Canal should be run by an international body – a 'users' association' – which would include Egypt; the remaining governments, which included those of the Soviet Union and India, favoured an alternative plan under which the users' association should possess only advisory powers, and control would remain with Egypt. At a second conference, in September, the majority group worked out more detailed plans for the users' association, which was set up at the beginning of October.

The majority group itself soon began to fragment. Even before the users' association came into being, the British and French argued over the tactical wisdom of referring the Suez issue to the United Nations. France reluctantly accepted the British proposal to make the reference. Predictably, a majority of the Security Council supported the substantive view of the British and French; equaly predictably, the Soviet Union interposed its veto, and no effective action was possible. The Americans, perhaps in part through preoccupation with Cold War issues, were exceedingly anxious that the dispute should not be resolved by force. President Eisenhower sent a very explicit letter to that effect to Eden on 2 September. Gaitskell felt similar anxieties, and asked a pointed question of the Prime Minister, seeking in vain an assurance that the government 'will not shoot their way through the Canal'. Thereafter Eden's unbridled rage against Nasser was paralleled by a milder, but still considerable, animus against the American and Opposition leaders: a state of affairs which made close co-operation difficult. It was a fair guess that what unity yet remained within and between the various countries which had been aggrieved by Nasser's initial pronouncement would be eroded further as time went on.

As for the three countries most deeply involved at this stage, it is important to remember that for each of them there were issues latent in the dispute which ranked a good deal higher than the fate of the Suez Canal revenues, or even perhaps the Canal itself. No doubt Nasser was anxious to build the Aswan Dam and to use the Suez Canal revenues in order to do so; he was even more anxious to secure his position at home and to establish himself as the supreme leader of all Arabic-speaking peoples. For both of those purposes, he required the prestige of a resounding diplomatic victory over the British and French. By the same token, it was vital for Britain's prestige with the Arabs who still looked to her leadership, that Nasser should fail in that object. Earlier in 1956 Britain had received a sharp rebuff from Jordan when King Hussein dismissed Glubb Pasha, the British soldier who had commanded the Arab Legion for many years; and for this event Nasser's influence was widely blamed. Britain still retained influence elsewhere, notably in Iraq; but this could easily be undermined. A rebuff to Nasser was no less vital to the French, who were disposed to blame him for their existing bad relations with Syria; but their main concern was elsewhere. Nasser was suspected of fomenting trouble among Moslems in Algeria – a country which was regarded, not as a colony, but as an integral part of metropolitan France. Nasser must not be permitted to radiate his dangerous appeal across the whole of North Africa. Britain and France alike were conscious that moral defeat at the hands of Egypt could have indirect repercussions much further afield.

In the Iranian oil dispute time had been on the side of the British. In the current dispute, where the prospect of defeating Nasser turned on keeping a lot of nations and a lot of disparate politicians in line, time was on the side of Egypt. Thus the British and French had every reason to force the issue as soon as possible. The occasion for so doing came swiftly enough. Another element of Nasser's plan to build up prestige among his fellow Arabs was his campaign against Israel. If Egypt could be seen as the champion of all Arabs, who would lead them to victory against Israel, then this would represent a gigantic step forward in the design. Israeli vessels had long been excluded from the Suez Canal. More recently, Egyptian commandos, the Fedayeen, had been mounting attacks on Israel from bases in Sinai. Neither Israel nor Egypt was likely to show any compunction in attacking the other at any moment when it seemed propitious to do so; but Israel had some reason to fear the Egyptian air force.

The British, French and Israeli Governments all had plenty of causes for desiring the collapse of Nasser, and none of them was over-meticulous as to the means by which that effect should be brought about. No doubt many details of the next part of the story are still unknown, and probably some features which now seem accurate will later need to be revised; but the essential outline appears fairly clear.[8] In mid-August, preliminary plans were drawn up for an Anglo-French assault on Alexandria. In the following month Franco-Israeli staff talks prepared for the neutralisation and possible destruction of the Egyptian air force, accompanied by land action from the western powers to draw the heat off Israel. In October a series of highly secret meetings, involving leading Ministers of all three countries, took place; and by the 24th of the month plans had been worked out in considerable detail; though to what extent even all of the senior members of the British Government knew of the arrangements is not at the moment clear. Israeli forces were to enter Egypt with the object of liquidating Fedayeen strongholds; but the nature of their attack would create an apparent threat to the Canal. The British and French would use this threat as a pretext for their own actions in the area. One may guess that the parties had not excluded from consideration the knowledge that their main operations were likely to take place in the immediate run-up to the American Presidential Elections. Perhaps the United States would be too preoccupied to react effectively; furthermore, the administration would not wish to behave in a manner hostile to Israel at that juncture, lest it should alienate the large Jewish vote in critical locations like the marginal State of New York.

On 29 October Israeli forces attacked Egypt in strength. Next day the British and French Government issued ultimata to Egypt and to Israel, requiring each of them to cease warlike action and withdraw to positions ten miles clear of the Suez Canal. Egypt was further required to allow Anglo-French forces temporarily to occupy positions at Suez, Port Said and Ismailia. The belligerents were given twelve hours to comply, with the threat that Britain and France would otherwise intervene by force. Israel, who had no occasion to approach the Canal, naturally agreed. Egypt, through whose territory the Canal actually ran, equally naturally refused. On 31 October British and French bombers attacked military targets in Egypt. By 2 November the Israelis had achieved a decisive victory in Sinai, and Anglo-French bombardment had largely wiped out the Egyptian air force on the ground.

By this time an enormous furore had commenced. On 1 November an Opposition motion of censure was brought in the House of Commons. The Government won its inevitable majority, but there were notable abstentions. Two junior Ministers, Anthony Nutting and Sir Edward Boyle, resigned from the Government. A few weeks later Stanley Evans, a Labour MP who approved of the Government's action, resigned from his party and from the House of Commons. Eden derived some comfort from a letter of approval under the hand of Churchill.

The British Government's official view was that action over Suez would be stopped as soon as the United Nations agreed to constitute a peacekeeping force, and the two belligerents agreed to accept it. In the meantime Anglo-French forces must be stationed between the two armies. At dawn on 5 November airborne forces were landed near Port Said. A full week had already elapsed since the original occasion for intervention, and ample time was thus afforded to the various critics to mobilise political and diplomatic opposition.

Meanwhile the United Nations was moving into action. On 30 October the United States and the Soviet Union joined in proposing a resolution to the Security Council, which called for a cease-fire and Israeli withdrawal. Britain, for the first time, used her veto to block it. Four days later Canada submitted a proposal to the General Assembly – where no veto could be applied – recommending the urgent establishment of an international force to separate the combatants. The proposal was carried with no dissentient votes; but Britain was among the minority who abstained.

Inherent international difficulties attending the Suez crisis were compounded because that crisis coincided with another which was in many ways more dramatic and poignant. Hungary had been in a state of considerable turmoil for some time, and for a variety of reasons, both ideological and economic. On 23 October a great demonstration occurred in Budapest, and the authorities called in soldiers to suppress it. Soldiers and workers fraternised with the crowd, and on the following day Imre Nagy, whom the demonstrators favoured, was appointed Minister-President. In the next two or three days revolutionary committees, organised more or less spontaneously, took power all over the country. Here, one might say, was the classic pattern of Marxist revolutions, with the variation that the primary object of this particular revolution was to overthrow, and not to establish, a putatively Marxist Government. To add to the drama, the same Imre Nagy had played a leading part in events which led to the communist take-over in Hungary less than a decade earlier.

For a time Soviet tanks were much in evidence, but in the last few days of October those tanks seemed to be withdrawing, in response to Nagy's request. The President called on the powers to recognise Hungarian neutrality. Then the Soviet tanks returned, and on 4 November attacked the insurgents. A new government was set up under Soviet auspices, and headed by Janos Kadar – who at an earlier stage had seemed to be one of the insurrectionaries. For a considerable time to come resistance continued in many parts of the country. The resisters had scant sympathy for 'reactionary' elements who had governed Hungary in the past. To many people living through those events, the fate of Hungary appeared a matter of incomparably greater importance than who won at Suez. There were elements in the Hungarian uprising, one might say, which could have led to a synthesis between the philosophies entrenched in the two halves of Europe, and also to a profound relaxation of military tensions throughout the world.

For disparate reasons, most governments in the world were anxious to suppress the three-power invasion of Egypt at the earliest possible moment. The Americans were conscious that any disturbance of peace, particularly in the Middle East, might redound to the benefit of communism. The Soviet Union saw merit in lambasting 'imperialists', in appearing as protector of an Arab country, and in diverting attention from Hungary. The emerging 'Afrasian' group of unaligned states, most particularly the Moslems among them, had fellow-feeling for Egypt. On top of all this there was a general view that if the United Nations failed to act against such a palpable breach of its Charter, the organisation would be universally discredited – and not least because of its simultaneous failure to help Hungary. No doubt the British and French could argue that their own action in Egypt and the Soviet action in Hungary were not similar in character. Perhaps that was true; but it did not derogate from the international risks which would arise if the United Nations should prove ineffectual in both places.

An element of immediate menace now entered the crisis. On 5 November the USSR issued threats hinting at the possible use of Soviet 'missiles' to drive out the invaders. However anxious the United States might be that the conflict should come to an end, they were even more concerned that its termination should not seem attributable to intervention of that kind; and a very chilly retort was issued to the effect that Soviet intervention in the area would provoke American reaction. The Canadian proposal to establish a United Nations peacekeeping force provided a far more acceptable occasion for the British and French to climb down.

On 6 November Egypt and Israel accepted a ceasefire. Each had good reason to do so. The Israelis had achieved their military objectives; the Egyptians had no prospect of disturbing them by military force, but might have better luck with an international tribunal. This removed all pretext for the Anglo-French invasion. At the same moment an enormous run on the pound took place, but was balanced by an American offer of a large supporting loan as soon as a decision had been taken to withdraw British forces. Eden capitulated. For a moment there was some pressure in France for independent action, but this was almost immediately seen to be impracticable for military reasons, if for no others. That night the Anglo-French expeditionary force at Suez came to a halt. The Canal, for whose protection the expedition had been ostensibly launched, was by this time out of action, for the Egyptians had sunk blockships which made passage impossible.

The world owed much to Lester Pearson, Liberal Prime Minister of Canada. It was his initiative which led to the United Nations resolution, and thereafter to the feverish diplomacy of the next few days, which ended in a halt to military operations. The Egyptians and the Israelis were both preserved from unnecessary carnage. The faces of the British and French had been saved, just as far as they could be saved. The risk of really dangerous altercations between the United States and the Soviet Union had been averted. The United Nations, which appeared on the point of breaking down, had instead been triumphantly vindicated as the most hopeful instrument of world order.

In Britain the turmoil gradually subsided. The crisis had been a bitter one, and feeling had run high. No party was completely united, and divisions among the Press also did not correspond exactly to the ordinary lines of party cleavage. On 19 November it was announced that

Eden was suffering from severe overstrain, and two days later he departed for a sojourn in Jamaica. The Anglo-French withdrawal was formally announced on 3 December, and a couple of days later there was debate on the matter in the House of Commons. Many condemned the invasion, while the 'Suez Group' made its last stand by maintaining the opposite proposition: that the government had been right to invade but wrong to withdraw. Eden's health was certainly not good, and there was much evidence to suggest that his judgment was seriously impaired either by his illness or by the medication he received. At the end of the year it deteriorated further, and soon unambiguous medical evidence established beyond doubt that he could carry on no longer. On 9 January 1957 the Prime Minister resigned. In form at least, and probably in fact as well, that resignation was necessitated by failure of his health, not by failure of his policy. On the following day Harold Macmillan succeeded Eden.

The diplomacy of the aftermath of Suez was complex. By the end of 1956 British and French troops had left Egypt, and the United Nations were in occupation. It took rather longer to evict the Israelis, but in March 1957 they too withdrew from Egyptian soil. In April the last physical obstructions were removed from the Canal. Later in the same month, arrangements were concluded for its future management and operation, which were tolerable both to Egypt and to the various 'users'. In the following month international shipping was again moving. Thus ended the last serious attempt by either Britain or France to cut a great international figure on her own.

19 Reflections

The period between the arrival of the 'Great Depression' in 1929 and the Suez expedition of 1956 covers barely a generation. At the beginning of that period Britain was head of the greatest Empire the world had seen; the acknowledged leader in world diplomacy; and in the first rank of economic power and influence. At the end the Empire was falling apart; nobody ranked Britain among the 'Super Powers', and her economy was largely dependent on the United States. In a sense there is nothing particularly remarkable in such developments. Other Empires have fallen as fast, or faster, yet their collapse has usually been occasioned by military defeat. Britain, so far from being defeated in war, had emerged victorious from the Second World War: indeed, she was still universally acknowledged in 1945 as one of the 'Big Three' who were to determine the world's future. Nor is there much to show that the government either of the United States or of the Soviet Union was disposed to take positive action to undermine her position.

In the nineteenth and early twentieth centuries people had often spoken of Britain as a 'Great Power'. Before we consider the manner of Britain's decline further, it is appropriate to examine the meaning of this term, since it casts some useful light on the part which Britain was 'authorised' – and, indeed, expected – to perform when she held the status of a 'Great Power'. An understanding of custom in relation to 'Great Powers' also helps to explain features of international behaviour during the period of study which might otherwise appear surprising.

The cynic may be disposed to describe a 'Great Power' as a country which is strong enough to behave unpleasantly towards others, or to compel them to do things which they do not wish to do. Yet this is not the whole of the story; for an essential 'right' of a Great Power was the right to consultation. Failure to consult a Great Power which wished to be consulted was a hostile act – a sort of slight on its status.

The point about a Great Power's right to consultation was brought out with especial clarity by several features of the Czechoslovak question in 1938. When Britain began to intervene in the affairs of Czechoslovakia with the object of bringing the country's government and the Sudetendeutsch to an agreement, neither party retorted that these matters were no business of hers, even though Britain was under no special obligations to Czechoslovakia, and had no capacity to intervene directly in the country's affairs. Yet nobody suggested that Hungary, who was not a Great Power, had a similar right to have her views considered – even though Hungary had a direct interest in the affairs of Czechoslovakia and the power – in certain circumstances – to intervene there by force. The eventual Munich settlement was, in form at least, an amicable agreement between European Great Powers. Thus there was nothing inherently surprising in Britain and Italy, neither of whom had special interests in Czechoslovakia being invited to attend.

Yet there was another important side to the diplomacy of the Czechoslovak crisis, and that was the failure of the four Great Powers to consult the Soviet Union, even though she plainly desired consultation. It may well have seemed to Russia that, by received Great Power etiquette, the four were refusing to treat her as a full member of their 'club'.

The behaviour of the United States and the Soviet Union at the time of Suez looks like a not dissimilar assessment of Britain by the new 'Super Powers': that she was no longer in the first rank, and was therefore not entitled to the kind of treatment which goes with Great Power status. Britain was not so much 'negotiated out' of Suez as ordered out. Any similar treatment of the Soviet Union in the Hungarian crisis of the same year, or of the United States in the renewed Vietnam conflict a few years later, would have amounted virtually to a declaration of war. Indeed, it would have been unthinkable that Britain should be so treated even ten years earlier.

There is no single point in those ten years at which we can say that Britain ceased to be a Great Power – or, indeed, where Britain had a real choice between conflicting courses of action such that if she had behaved differently her loss of Great Power status and subsequent decline could have been averted or postponed. Certainly Suez was not such an occasion. It was undoubtedly a time of particularly bitter controversy in Britain. That controversy centred on the morality or otherwise of the enterprise. Today the point which stands out most clearly is that the whole venture was a profound miscalculation, a gross over-estimate of the power and influence which Britain and France possessed in the mid-1950s. In a sense Suez did not really change anything much. With or without it, the general pattern of disintegration of British overseas power would doubtless have continued, for the world balance of economic and military might so prescribed. At most, Suez may have accelerated the process by a few years. The main interest of the expedition today lies in its symbolism, in the fact that it proved beyond doubt what many people had long guessed. The British and French failed absurdly in an enterprise which, in parallel circumstances before the war, they could probably have carried through without difficulty. In the climate of 1956 their behaviour was a complete anachronism.

It is arguable that the changing weapons of war had played a substantial part in Britain's decline. In the nineteenth century, and for much of the twentieth, Britannia really did rule the waves, and on that thalassocracy her Empire and her international authority were largely founded. The British navy was still one of the world's greatest in 1956; but ships had been declining in importance for a long time, and were now being rapidly outclassed by vastly more expensive weapons, far beyond Britain's means. In fact she was still attempting to keep up with those weapons; but whatever continuing military power they afforded was more than counterbalanced by the economic burden imposed. In more peaceful fields the gigantic impetus which Britain had received from early industrialisation had turned from a great asset into a liability; for Britain was still cumbered with old equipment and – more serious – archaic organisations and archaic attitudes among both capital and labour, operating in a milieu of obsolescent industries; while the rest of the world was building afresh to meet requirements of the second half of the twentieth century. The great overseas investment which had helped maintain Britain's economic and financial primacy for so long had largely been sold to pay for two world wars. The measure of Britain's loss was brought out sharply at the time of the American loan debate of 1945–46, and the frantic need to cut overseas commitments which was suddenly appreciated in 1947.

British power had long turned on the existence of the British Empire, and of weapons designed primarily for the protection of that Empire. Before 1939 there had been little to suggest that the British Empire was close to the point of final disintegration. Children in British schools were taught, and teachers evidently believed, that the British Empire possessed qualities of permanence which even Rome had lacked. In recognition of this, 24 May, the birthday of Queen Victoria, was widely celebrated as a half-holiday down to the Second World War – as 'Empire Day'.

Yet that Empire had, from its very inception, certain fundamental weaknesses. Most historic empires, and both of the modern 'Super Powers', have grown by territorial expansion at the margins – assimilating, subjugating, expelling or exterminating other peoples who stood in the way of that expansion. Britain, as an island, had no such opportunities, although her insular status did give her considerable advantages. As Britain forged ahead economically, particularly during the nineteenth century, she naturally looked for expansion, and that expansion could only occur overseas. The strength of the British Navy made expansion easy – too easy, we may perhaps decide today. In time she amassed that enormous Empire which was the source of so much pride. The Empire, however, was so scattered that the only possible way of preserving it from external attack lay in the maintenance of complete domination at sea.

Even in the late nineteenth century that domination was coming under challenge, and by the early twentieth century Britain could no longer maintain a clear naval lead over possible combinations of hostile powers without full-scale co-operation from other countries. The trouble with alliances is that allies never share identical interests. Britain could only persuade others to underwrite her interests by being prepared to underwrite theirs. In the 1914 war, however, Britain's survival was ensured because the allies preserved naval domination; and the geographical distribution of those allies was such that no part of the British Empire came under serious threat.

Yet by 1918 there were already plenty of signs which, we may reflect with the benefit of hindsight, presaged the likely doom of the British Empire and British power before many decades should pass. Britain still had a naval lead; but several of her recent allies had naval forces not so very much smaller than her own. The strains of war had imposed a huge economic burden which made the maintenance of naval domination increasingly difficult. The new dimension of warfare, the air, represented a region of such rapid technological development that there was no way by which any particular power or combination of powers could preserve certain domination for very long. At the same time, that political instability of which communism and fascism were both expressions, made all governments nervous and insecure; while nationalism grew apace among the educated classes in colonial lands. Whatever happened, the British Empire in the old sense of the term was doomed.

There did remain one possible means of preserving British power in a changed form. Given time, it was not unrealistic to envisage the gradual evolution of that Empire into a 'real' Commonwealth of like-minded countries, autonomous in their internal affairs and freely co-operating in matters of international importance. Whether this system would have proved durable, or whether the component countries would soon have discovered conflicting interests, is open to debate. But if the apologists of 'Commonwealth' were right in contending that Britain had a function of peculiar value to perform in the interest both of herself and of her dependent territories, then it was a matter of overriding importance that she should keep out of a major war. It is surely a great paradox that Chamberlain and Churchill who – for all their differences – were both soaked in the imperial tradition, each played a crucial role in committing Britain to courses of action in Europe which made the destruction of that Empire inescapable. It would be wrong, however, to set the responsibility exclusively or primarily upon either or both of them.

'Appeasement' was widely condemned at the time, and afterwards, but usually for the wrong reasons. The idea of Britain playing an active part in the pacification of Europe was, at first sight, a splendid one – wholly consistent with British interests and with the interests of people living on the Continent. Yet when she began to play that part, Britain became responsible for the settlement which she was attempting to engineer. In February 1938 Central Europe was generally regarded, and rightly so, as an area outside British control and influence. How could a country with a great navy but a tiny army and air force, determine events in a landlocked area? Yet, long before the 'Munich' crisis of that September, it was already widely assumed that Britain had special responsibilities for the fate of Czechoslovakia; and in March 1939 very few voices were raised against the Polish guarantee which effectively selected the *casus belli* of the Second World War. Perhaps Hitler really did think that Britain was bluffing – not so much from an assessment of the Prime Minister's personality or record, but because it seemed self-evident that central and eastern Europe was not a 'vital interest' for Britain, while her Empire was. If Britain was engaged in war in Europe, how could she expect to defend her interests elsewhere? Chamberlain's critics were no whit wiser than the Prime Minister. They wrongly blamed him for pusillanimity; he could be blamed far more justly for engaging his country in international commitments which were impossible to fulfill.

That point came home later, when Chamberlain was no longer Prime Minister. To Churchill, the overriding aim was not to restore Poland in fulfilment of Britain's guarantee, or to preserve British influence for the future, or to establish any particular kind of political system on an international scale, but to defeat Germany. In mid-1940, when France had collapsed and there was no prospect of Britain achieving that object without massive help, he conceived the vision of a 'Grand Alliance' involving the United States and the Soviet Union as the vehicle for so doing. By the time of Yalta he had nothing but the word of Stalin as assurance that Poland would be restored at all; while the fate of the British Empire had already been sealed long before that. The first few months of the war against Japan destroyed British prestige in Asia irrevocably. Thereafter Churchill, arch-enemy of Indian nationalism in the 1930s, despatched the Cripps mission to India with its contingent offer of complete independence. To add to the paradox, that offer was in fact refused, and had no discernible effect on the course of the war. With or without the Cripps mission, nothing could have saved the British Raj in India from destruction in the aftermath; and Britain was very lucky to slide out of the commitment as easily as she did in 1947.

It is necessary to look further back to see how such contradictions of policy arose. Around 1930, when the process of international disruption leading to the Second World War was just commencing, Britain's defences and her foreign policy both seemed designed to avert any serious change in the status quo. Britain appeared well able to protect territories and interests which she already possessed; there was no question whatever of her seeking to acquire more. The 'Ten Year Rule' seemed reasonable. Foreign policy turned on the League of Nations, whose leading members were Britain and France, Japan and Italy – all of them victors of the First World War, who had gained at the expense of the vanquished enemy. The major international treaties of the previous decade – the Washington agreements of 1921, the Locarno agreements of 1925 – seemed to have tied up international affairs so well that war involving major countries was impossible; while the League was well able to control disputes between minor ones.

Tensions of the 1930s made it increasingly apparent that this seemingly secure world was breaking down, and that the apparently complementary lines of defence policy and foreign policy were pointing in very different directions. The Manchurian crisis of 1931–32 brought out several sombre facts at once. First, in a complex affair with deep historical roots, it was not always easy to apply League of Nations principles and decide who was the 'aggressor' and ought to be restrained. Secondly, if Japan was in fact the more 'guilty' party (as later became apparent), the international apparatus of diplomacy and defence could do little to restrain her. The third implication was that if one fixed point in international assumptions could dissolve so easily – in this case the assumption that a major victor of the First World War would not disrupt the peace – then other fixed points might also disappear.

So Japan turned very quickly from a certain friend to a possible enemy. As for Germany, there had long been an undercurrent of British opinion which held that she would – sooner or later – seek to reverse the military decision of 1918. Yet there were many British people who felt that Germany had been wronged; and such people were by no means all on the political 'right'. When Hitler took office in 1933 – long before Germany had transgressed frontiers or openly violated international treaties – some influential people began to contend with great force that Nazi policies would lead to war if active steps were not taken to check them. Sir Robert Vansittart, civil service head of the Foreign Office, argued that view from the start. The very pointed question which MacDonald asked of his Cabinet colleagues early in 1934 – whether Germany should be taken 'as the ultimate potential enemy against which our long-range policy must be directed'[1] – was never properly answered; but the fact that it was asked suggests that the Prime Minister of the day took the same view. The gravity of the Japanese challenge derived from the fact that nobody had anticipated any challenge at all from that particular direction. The German challenge was, in a sense, anticipated; but Britain had no great land army to meet that challenge, and even if she had possessed one there was no means of deploying it against Germany without the closest co-operation from France. There was little sign of any spontaneous demand for the creation of such an army, either from the public at large or from the government's critics in particular.

When Italy was at loggerheads with Britain and France over Abyssinia in 1935–36, the British predicament was very similar to that in which Britain found herself over Japan four years earlier. Her defence preparations were organised on the assumption that Italy was a firm friend; and it was inordinately difficult to adjust quickly to the contrary view. One matter admitted of no dispute: that Britain and France could not face the three challenges simultaneously and alone, with any prospect of surviving the experience.

Granted the perception that Germany, Italy and Japan were all potential enemies; and granted the near-certainty that Britain's Empire and Britain's economic authority could not withstand the impact of a long war, why did not Britain attempt to fend off actual or potential challenge through the traditional means of international diplomacy? This was the line of conduct which the Chiefs of Staff were inclined to recommend, although they preferred to put it somewhat more euphemistically: increasing the number of Britain's friends and reducing the number of her enemies. If the identification of Germany as the principal enemy had been made when MacDonald suggested it, then lines of foreign and defence policies would have been clear. Britain would not have risked driving Italy into Hitler's arms over Abyssinia, and would have worked actively for an accommodation with Japan. Such policies would doubtless have infuriated enthusiasts for the League of Nations. The original vision of the League as the instrument of international order, enforcing a moral law among states, had been honourable and worthy; what was less creditable was the disposition on the part of League enthusiasts to demand gestures which were bound to prove futile, or to pretend that the League still possessed power to act, in circumstances where all evidence supported the contrary view.

In the late 1930s critics of the government's foreign policy were still showing little disposition to identify Nazi Germany as something egregiously evil and dangerous. They were much more disposed to see international affairs as a struggle against all 'fascists' or 'aggressors' – which meant in effect perceiving Germany, Italy and Japan as equal enemies. Any compromise with the 'enemy', any attempt to drive wedges between aggressors, amounted to unforgiveable sin. This outlook was by no means confined to young idealists with 'left-of-centre' opinions and no political responsibility. As time went on it came largely to influence policy at the highest levels of government.

It was generally taken for granted that France was the major power which shared most closely Britain's international aspirations and interests; yet, as we have seen, those two countries by themselves could not contain all the various threats to international order. Might they bring others into the alliance? That question arose particularly after 1934 when the Soviet Union, justly fearful of German aggression, was admitted to the League. The Soviet Union was apparently eager to participate in schemes of international defence, to which the name 'Collective Security' came to be applied. In 1936, for example, she concluded a mutual assistance pact with France, and in the same year undertook to go to the aid of Czechoslovakia should France do the same. Yet there was deep suspicion between the Soviet Union and the democracies, fostered to no small extent by mutual incomprehension. Furthermore, while both sides had every reason for desiring to stop Germany moving either eastwards or westwards, each naturally hoped that, if she did move, it would not be in their own direction. In such circumstances full co-operation was probably out of the question; but even if this could be achieved, it is difficult to believe that the combination would have been adequate to hold back Germany if she formed a close alliance with Italy and Japan. Effective Collective Security probably implied support from the United States as well; but for historical, geographical and constitutional reasons there was no practical way of procuring American participation in those international engagements which were a necessary prerequisite.

When Appeasement collapsed in March 1939, most people in Britain turned eagerly to Collective Security, not so much out of confidence that it would succeed, but out of desperation. The theory, of course, was that war could be averted altogether by the mere threat of collective action by such a powerful combination; but many people probably guessed that any sort of alliance would, sooner or later, be put to the test. Whether true Collective Security, an alliance involving, at the very least, Britain, France, Poland and the Soviet Union – was ever possible, even against the single enemy Germany, is open to much doubt; but the guarantee issued to Poland as a stop-gap in March 1939 effectively blocked any further developments in that direction.

The atmosphere in Britain during the period between March 1939 and the outbreak of war in September was certainly not pacifistic. Critics blamed the governments for not working harder to bring Russia into the alliance; but few people challenged the view that an attack on Poland should constitute a *casus belli*. One of the most difficult moments in Chamberlain's political life came when he met the House of Commons on 2 September, and critics suspected – quite wrongly, as it turned out – that he was trying to duck the challenge of war. The same spirit remained thereafter. Anti-war candidates of very different political complexions appeared at early by-elections; their performance certainly did not suggest that the opinions they maintained carried any wide measure of public support. In the latter part of 1940, all evidence shows that public morale was everything that the Churchill Government could wish, and there was no audible voice calling for peace negotiations of any kind. No British Government could have averted war in September 1939, or conducted successful peace negotiations with the enemy once war had started.

Although the British people had taken a long time to identify Nazi Germany as their principal enemy, yet once that identification was made there was no disposition to 'second thoughts', and the public at large had little interest in other potential enemies. Italy, perhaps, was never taken too seriously, despite real or feigned Service apprehensions of a 'mad dog act' at the time of the Abyssinian conflict. Japan, however, was a very different proposition; for no informed person doubted from 1931 onwards that she had the power to inflict enormous damage on the British Empire. Yet to the ordinary Briton, Japan – like Italy – was a peripheral problem. The 'real' war, as he saw it, was the war against

Germany. Whatever the ideologists might have thought, the mass of the British people probably cared little what policies were pursued towards Japan, provided only that the British Empire, and most particularly Australia and New Zealand, was left unscathed. If the politicians and diplomats could somehow have kept Japan out of the war, the main-in-the-street would have been well pleased.

On the face of it, there were many opportunities to fend off Japan. The Japanese were deeply outraged by the Soviet-German Non-aggression Pact of August 1939 – although, of course, this did not prevent them making their own Non-aggression Pact with the Soviet Union a year and a half later. Japan's primary concern was with her war against China, and if the western countries had not intervened against her in that war, there is little reason for thinking that any action would have been taken against them. But after Britain and the United States began to impose really severe economic pressure by freezing Japanese assets in July 1941, the situation changed. In the view of the British Ambassador in Tokyo, 'War could only be a question of time unless some method could be devised for bringing abut a *détente*'.[2] Thereafter, Japan began to give increasing attention to the idea of a major attack on the Anglo-Saxon powers. Even then, conversations continued at Washington; and there is reason for thinking that the Japanese were considerably more anxious than the allies to achieve a settlement. Only when serious Japanese proposals were more or less rejected at the end of November 1941 was the die cast. The Japanese, we may reflect today, had no real choice.

The lead in these events was very clearly taken by the United States rather than by Britain. If Britain could have cut free, she would have had a good chance of buying off Japan and avoiding participation in war in the Far East. Yet Britain, too, had no real choice. Granted that it was all-important to fight Germany to the end, granted Britain's immediate dependence on the United States for continuing the fight, and granted the judgement that full American involvement was a *sine qua non* for eventual victory – then Britain, like Japan, had no real choice.

From the point of view of Britain's future world role, the Far Eastern war was in some ways more crucial than the war in Europe. The rapid capitulation of allied colonies sent a shock through Asia which persuaded the indigenous peoples that Europeans were not invincible. Yet these Far Eastern disasters were part of the price of a European victory. Pearl Harbor was essential to bring the United States into the war; and Pearl Harbor implied parallel catastrophes for Britain's Asian Empire from which – unlike the Americans – Britain could not hope for eventual recovery. Did Churchill and Roosevelt resolve to force Japan's hand in order to overcome opposition to war within the United States? We shall probably never know; very likely there was no sort of explicit agreement on the matter at all.

If indeed some plan, express or tacit, existed in the minds of the two leaders, there was a tremendous risk that it would miscarry. Britain and the United States could easily have become allies in the Far East but not in Europe, just as Britain and the Soviet Union were allies in Europe but not in the Far East; and the more deeply and calamitously the United States became involved in war against Japan, the more difficult it would have been to persuade Americans to interest themselves deeply in Europe. It was Hitler's own folly in declaring war against the United States, a few days after Pearl Harbor, which resolved the issue. Even then it was not a foregone conclusion that the Americans would give priority to the European war, and a President with roots in the Pacific States rather than New England might have seen matters differently from Roosevelt. Churchill was far from certain about even Roosevelt's military priorities until the two men met, shortly after the United States entered the war. It is chilling to contemplate what would have happened to the course of the war, and to Britain, if Hitler had not gratuitously intervened, or if the gamble that America would give priority to the European war had not come off.

Yet the Anglo-American plans – and, for that matter, most of the British 'grand strategy' from mid-1940 onwards – certainly did come off. Such events represented astonishing strokes of luck; and in the aftermath of the European war this luck remained. The prospect of a long-drawn out war in the Far East, very likely entailing far heavier British casualties than the war in Europe, was daunting, and it is far from certain how the British people would have responded in that event. The European scenario was even more alarming. The picture which Churchill drew in his message to Truman a few days after VE Day, showing the Soviet Union armed to the teeth in Europe, while the Anglo-American armies 'melted away', was not unduly alarmist. Perhaps the Russians had no hostile intent towards the Anglo-Saxon powers; but whether that was true or not, the balance of 'conventional' forces which was likely to develop in Europe within a short time of the end of the war was unnerving for the West. In the short run, the fearful bombs dropped on Hiroshima and Nagasaki provided a kind of answer to these two problems. They certainly discouraged the Japanese from haggling delays. Their effect on relations between the West and the Soviet Union were far more complex. The British and Americans appreciated from the start that the Russians were well on the way to nuclear weapons of their own, and there could be no question of using the brief western monopoly in order to coerce the Soviet Union. Yet the existence of such weapons made it impossible for the Russians to employ their preponderance in 'conventional' weapons to overawe the West.

Britain still faced enormous risks. American commitment to western Europe was by no means a foregone conclusion; and without that commitment the economic prospects for the aftermath of war – to say nothing of the military perils – would have been fearful. Economic collapse was quite likely in many places; and in those circumstances political chaos leading to communism would have been a probable development, even without active Soviet encouragement. But in 1945 'communism' and 'Soviet influence' were for most purposes practically synonymous terms. The influence of George Marshall's two-year period as Secretary of State upon the whole future of Britain and Europe was incalculable. Other great events in the late 1940s and early 1950s worked astonishingly well for Britain. As we have seen, the withdrawal from imperial commitments was smooth and easy, from Britain's point of view at least. No less fortunate was the course of the Korean war, which might easily have led to one of two equally perilous consequences: extirpation of the South Korean state by force, which would set most dangerous precedents for the future; or full-scale American commitment to eastern Asia, which would have left western Europe practically undefended. Yet nobody could be sure whether the United States would always regard Europe as its primary area of concern; and it would seem likely that the British decisions to manufacture first atomic bombs and later thermonuclear bombs were influenced at least as much by worries over future United States commitment to Europe as by apprehensions over Soviet policy.

Thus on balance Britain was permitted to withdraw from the first rank of world powers with remarkably little trouble. Her wartime casualties were heavy indeed in all ordinary terms; but by comparison with those sustained by the Soviet Union, or Poland, or Germany, or Japan, they were remarkably light. The social transitions at home in the aftermath of Empire were very smooth; most acts of withdrawal were conducted at wise moments; while the whole process coincided with a period of technological innovation which ensured that the British people at no point suffered severe economic privation; and for most of the time most of the population was experiencing a rise in living standards.

If we attempt to draw lessons from the exceedingly narrow squeaks which Britain experienced during the war and its aftermath, those lessons are likely to be very different from the ones which were generally drawn twenty or thirty years ago. It is perhaps a caricature of the general judgement at that time to say that Britain's troubles were largely attributed to her failure to 'stand up to' Germany, Italy and Japan in the 1930s. This assessment was originally a political criticism levelled at the National Government in the second half of that decade: a criticism designed to produce a change in current policy. That criticism appeared largely valid at the time when it was made; but today it is far less credible. The underlying assumption on the part of many critics was not just that errors of judgement had been committed, but that there was moral turpitude involved as well: at best, cowardice; at worst, clandestine sympathy with 'fascists'. Now that most of the important documents which are ever likely to become available have been opened, the picture begins to look very different. Did Britain fail to resist Japan in the early 1930s? If she had acted, she would have been almost alone. The price would have been enormous, and the outcome uncertain. Did Britain fail to resist Italy adequately in the middle of the decade? Only France gave much useful assistance in the very moderate measure of resistance which did take place, and the French were disposed to drag their feet – not because they approved of what Mussolini was doing, or because they were afraid of him, but because they had no wish to drive him into the arms of Hitler. Did the British fail to 'stand by the Czechs' in 1938? There was the greatest doubt as to how the Czechs, the French, the Russians, the British Dominions – and perhaps even the British people themselves – would have reacted if set to the test; and it is excessively unlikely that Czechoslovakia could have been 'saved' even if they had all stood together, in a common determination to 'save' her.

But it is no part of the author's purpose to argue that the decisions of the 1930s were necessarily the 'best' ones – still less that they were 'inevitable'. It was quite possible for the British Government to adopt very different courses of action at several important points. There is, for example, quite a lot to be said for the view that in the spring of 1935 Britain should have faced France with a simple choice. Either France would stand up resolutely to any challenges to the international order in Europe – in which case Britain would back her, if necessary, to the point of war – or, if France was not prepared to act in that manner, then Britain would wash her hands of European commitments. At Stresa France might perhaps have been coerced into entering Germany through the still-vacant Rhineland, while Italy would probably have required little encouragement to send troops through her satellite Austria, in order to compel Hitler to forego rearmament and any other unilateral defiance of Versailles. It is possible – though far from certain – that France both could, and should, have been coerced into a stronger line against Italy over Abyssinia, and that such action would have delivered a message to Hitler which would have stopped him in his tracks. It is also possible that the very opposite policy would have been more expedient – avoiding any antagonism to Mussolini which might drive him into the arms of Hitler. It is arguable that Chamberlain could have stopped the Hitler-Mussolini association from developing by overruling the British Foreign Office in the course of 1937; that more positive diplomacy towards Italy and Japan even after the Second World War commenced might have isolated Germany. Many people were arguing in the 1930s, and many people have gone on arguing to this day, that different attitudes towards the Soviet Union during the run-up to war would have been effective in 'stopping Hitler'.

These things are possible; but they are far from certain. The British Government may have had real freedom of choice; and it may be that the exercise of that choice in a different manner would have averted the Second World War. But it is also possible that there was no real freedom of choice at all; or that the exercise of choice in a different way would not have averted the war – or even that the war would have broken out in different circumstances and ended in Britain's defeat. Whether the behaviour of the British Government in the middle and late 1930s was right, wrong or inevitable, it was certainly not absurd, as many people suggested during the war and for several decades afterwards. The possible exception to this statement was the Polish guarantee of March 1939 – the one spectacular example of a major decision whose implications do not appear to have been thought through; but that guarantee came under so little criticism at the time when it was given that it hardly lies in anybody's mouth to curse the government for it in later days.

If blame must be delivered, it appears to belong in different places. The whole process of international disruption in the 1930s ties up so closely with the impetus of the Great Depression that it is difficult to escape the view that a close causal relationship existed. The Depression, in its turn, was perhaps caused, and was certainly exacerbated, by policies of economic nationalism pursued by countries great and small in the 1920s: policies which became far more intense in the succeeding decade. There were spectacular instances of such policies during the worst period of the Depression: the Smoot-Hawley tariffs in the United States in 1930; French financial pressure against an Austro-German Zollverein in 1931; and the British adoption of protection in 1932. It is arguable that the direct economic effects of these policies on the world economy was slight. Perhaps so; but the indirect and moral effect was enormous, for others took them as a cue to pursue restrictionist policies of their own. Worse still were the long-term effects of economic nationalism, and the general ill-will which they generated, which made co-operation difficult even between countries with essentially similar interests in preserving peace. The misery of Austria paved the way to the Anschluss; the differential impact of the Depression on Slav peasants and German industrial workers pointed to Czechoslovakia's disruption later in 1938. If some frontiers could be changed with impunity, then all frontiers became uncertain. Yet why – we ask ourselves today – did people ever wish to cross each other's frontiers? The judgement that armies crossed because goods could not do so, is inescapable.

That assessment must be qualified, or at least explained. By the late 1930s international trade had largely recovered, tariffs notwithstanding, and most people in most industrial countries were perceptibly better off than they had been before the Depression began. Yet the Depression had put Hitler in power in Germany – and it really had been touch-and-go that he was ever able to take power. A small margin of extra prosperity in Germany in 1932 would have sufficed to avert that unspeakable catastrophe. Tariffs were enough to turn the scale.

People notice a problem not when it first appears and is still tractable, but when it becomes acute; by which time it is often no longer amenable to any satisfactory solution. Yet when the disaster occurs, there is usually a tacit assumption that some alternative existed right up to the last moment, which would have averted the disaster if leaders had been wise enough to take it. Perhaps some alternative did exist at one time, but there is no good reason for assuming that it was still available at the moment of crisis. The more closely we look at the various crises which presented themselves from the spring of 1938 onwards, the more difficult it becomes to visualise courses of action open to British statesmen which could have been expected to lead to the destruction of the three chief enemy powers at a lesser cost to Britain. It is a profound paradox, for example, that Chamberlain's critics have deeply reviled him for his part in the Munich settlement, where he probably played an appalling hand about as well as it could be played, and yet have said far less concerning his part in the economic policies pursued in the early 1930s, where he exercised a strong influence in encouraging the world-wide movement to autarky. Economic barriers are less visibly destructive than armaments; far less noteworthy than a 'cliffhanger' crisis like that of September 1938; but they are no less important in the genesis of war.

By the time of the Austrian Anschluss, the choice before Britain was between 'disinterest' in the politics of central and eastern Europe, and a war into which she would assuredly be drawn. That war might have started at a different date; it could easily have followed a radically different course; the alliances could have been different; even the final upshot could have been dramatically different; but conflict was inevitable. 'Inevitable' is a strong word for a historian to use, but it is appropriate here. Whether even 'disinterest' was possible from a long-term view is dubious. Prolonged war tends to drag countries which desire to be neutral into its vortex; and in Britain's case there were powerful forces at work pressing eagerly for policies which would necessarily lead to involvement.

To understand the disruptive processes set in motion during the 1930s, in order to derive lessons which may help avert catastrophe in future, it is necessary to look well back into the apparently secure world of the late 1920s – when it looked as if general war was not merely unwise or wicked, but flatly impossible. The post-1918 treaties have been criticised on many counts, and with good cause. Existing European frontiers could be shown to be absurd from a variety of angles; the reparation and war-debt arrangements were unsatisfactory for all concerned; the disposition of national armaments was objectionable. It was easy to argue that the peace treaties should have been either less, or more, severe on the vanquished. Yet by 1928 nearly everybody had decided that the settlement, bad as it was, was incomparably preferable to any attempt to disrupt it by force. Indeed there had been a number of recent examples which showed that it was possible to adjust objectionable features of the settlement by peaceful means.

In the late 1920s – indeed, right down to the outbreak of war – there was little reason for thinking that anybody was disposed to launch an attack whose prime aim was to seize parts of the British Empire – or, indeed, of the possessions of other 'satiated' powers like France and the United States. No doubt there were plenty of people who were ready to fall on parts of the British Empire if for some reason it happened to collapse; but there was little sign that any of them was preparing to take serious and unprovoked action to bring about that collapse. The Italian hostility to British interests in the Arab lands during the late 1930s was designed primarily to compel the British to come to terms with Italy on other matters, notably Abyssinia. The Japanese attack on British Asian possessions in 1941–42 did not take place mainly because Japan sought to acquire those territories, but because Britain was seen in Tokyo as part of a hostile alliance against Japanese interests in China. The German preparations for invasion of Britain in 1940 had all the appearance of last-minute arrangements, never properly thought through, designed to deal with the unexpected British reluctance to accept the continental *fait accompli*. The Germans, the Italians and the Japanese were all attempting in different ways to establish large areas within which goods could move. They sought other things as well – that those areas should be dominated by the new imperial power; and – particularly in the German example – application of bizarre doctrines of ethnic superiority. The means used to achieve these ambitions were appalling, and because they were so appalling the rest of the world eventually united against the three countries. Yet in the aftermath of the Second World War this one brief, constructive, achievement was resurrected in a new form. From the General Agreement on Trade and Tariffs onwards, a wide variety of means has been devised to break down trade barriers, either universally or at least over substantial areas. Some of these devices, we may decide, have done more harm than good to the cause which they were invented to serve; but, for all their faults they do signal a general recognition in the post-1945 world that small autarkic units are harmful all round. In a world where advancing technology is rapidly making all political frontiers a dangerous anachronism; where national barriers against trade are a palpable absurdity; where extreme disparities of wealth and poverty are no longer taken for granted – in that context, at least lip-service is generally paid to the idea of 'one world'.

By 1956 it was plain enough that the remains of the British Empire would eventually be dismantled, and perhaps the visionary could discern, at some point in the remote future, the eventual establishment of 'one world'. What was far less plain was how Britain could fit herself into the international society of the intervening period. Not least of her problems was how to respond to the changing character of Europe The eastern side of the continent was already being integrated politically, militarily and economically with the Soviet Union. In the west the military alliance of NATO had taken shape, and negotiations were moving rapidly towards the economic association of France, Italy, West Germany and the Low Countries which would be the foundation of the European Economic Community.

Britain's international trading pattern was radically different from that of the continental EEC countries. During both World Wars, but particularly the Second, she had survived for several years with practically no European trade; but the German threat to cut off her non-European supplies was a threat to her very existence. British Governments of the 1950s, whether Labour or Conservative, did not wish to see an exclusive economic involvement with western Europe which would deny or curtail access of domestic consumers to cheaper goods from elsewhere. Reciprocal free trade with western Europe was welcome; obligations to impose barriers against trade with non-Europeans were most unwelcome.

It is easy to state the British reservations, and the reasons for them. Those reservations were to produce that deep uncertainty over attitudes to the EEC which persist to this day. The British, in fact, were losing out in all ways. It was impossible to integrate an economy which had turned on free importation from the whole world with economies whose directors aimed at a largely self-supporting Europe, without sustaining acute distress. Britain could not accept a position of leadership, or even of joint leadership, because she did not wish to go where others would follow her; while any arrangements which those others might make without Britain were likely to operate in her disfavour. Nor were Americans or Russians disposed to give her the role of 'honest broker' between the super powers, whether in economic, political or military matters. The aphorism made by Dean Acheson, sometime United States Secretary of State, a few years later, was already true: that Britain had 'lost an Empire, but not yet discovered a role'. Yet Britain could hardly be blamed for that state of affairs, and not many useful suggestions had – or have – been advanced as to how she might extricate herself from it.

In a variety of indirect ways Britain in the period of her greatness as a world power generated and propagated important ideas which remain of high importance in the present. Most people accepted, at least in theory, the idea that components of the British Empire should develop towards self-government: that the peoples living in those countries should be able, through some form of democratic process, to determine their own system of government; that member-states of the imperial group should co-operate closely in matters both political and economic which were of common concern. These important notions were not peculiar to the British Empire, but they were developed in that Empire to a very high degree.

The historian, like the journalist, becomes all too easily preoccupied with costly disasters and dramatic acts of folly; and the present story of the decline of British influence and power has necessarily made much of such features. Yet these spectacular events only represent one side of the story. For every costly fiasco like Suez; for every atrocity like Amritsar; for every instance like Palestine where Britain reaped, years afterwards, the harvest of earlier duplicity; for every example like South Africa where a brave beginning has led to disappointment and retrogression, there have been many cases where orderly progress has beem made; where power has been transferred easily and peacefully. The aftermath of the transfer has often been disappointing. In the successor states of British India, massacre and counter-massacre followed on a gigantic scale. Elsewhere the Parliamentary democracies left behind by the retreating imperial power have in many cases withered and died because the process of transfer of authority was too abrupt to permit democratic constitutions to strike deep roots. Yet – and despite the exigencies of the Great Depression, the Second World War and the Cold War which followed – in most places which were under British influence in 1929 the general quality of life had become markedly higher at the end of the story than at the beginning. Much has been lost, indeed, which might perhaps have been saved had Britain sought with greater determination to avoid participation in war. Many people extol the wrong preceptors: the flamboyant warriors rather than the men of peace. The builders and the destroyers of imperial power are remembered; the wise administrators who promoted gradual but durable transitions are largely forgotten. One day, perhaps, the balance will be restored; and when that day comes it will be possible to attempt a much better assessment of Britain's influence than any historian can make today.

Abbreviations Used in Notes and Bibliography

CM	Cabinet Minutes (record of particular meeting)
CP	Cabinet Paper (individual item)
CAB 23, CAB 65, CAB 128	
	Cabinet Minutes (volume series)
CAB 24, CAB 66, CAB 129	
	Cabinet Papers (volume series)
DA	Dean Acheson papers
DBFP	*Documents on British Foreign Policy 1919–1939*, Third Series
DDF	*Documents diplomatiques français 1932–1939*
DGFP	*Documents on German Foreign Policy 1918–1945*, translated
FDR	Franklin D. Roosevelt papers
FO 371	Foreign Office papers: correspondence with posts abroad
FO 800	Foreign Office papers: collections associated with particular individuals
FO 954	Foreign Office papers: (Sir) Anthony Eden (Earl of Avon) collection
FRUS	*Foreign Relations of the United States*
HST	Harry S. Truman papers
NC	Neville Chamberlain papers
PREM 1, PREM 3, PREM 8	
	Prime Minister's Papers
PSF	President's Secretary's File (Truman papers)
WM	War Cabinet Minutes (record of particular meeting)
WP	War Cabinet papers (individual item)

Notes and References

1 A KIND OF STABILITY

1. See comparative tables in *Liberal Year Book*, 1931, p. 161.
2. John Reed, *Ten Days that Shook the World* (New York; 1960) p. 190.
3. Geoffrey Shakespeare, *Lloyd George Liberal Magazine*, vi, 119.
4. League of Nations Yearbook figures, quoted in CID Defence Requirements report, 29 February 1934 (PREM 1/175), give comparisons between 1925–6 and 1929–30: France, 5543m francs to 10 968m; Italy, 4506m lira to 5015m; Japan, 444m yen to 495m; USA $585m to $701m; Germany 587.7m RM to 691.0m.
5. Statistical information based on tables in B. R. Mitchell, *European Historical Statistics 1750–1975* (1980), and US Department of Commerce, *Historical Statistics of the United States: Colonial Times to 1970* (1975).
6. See W. S. and E. S. Woytinsky, *World Commerce and Governments* (1955) pp. 276–7.
7. Figures based on comparison between government revenue and tax yield figures cited in Mitchell *op. cit.*
8. Woytinsky and *op. cit.*, p. 463.
9. Woytinsky and *op. cit.*
10. See Mitchell, *op. cit.* and US Department of Commerce, *op. cit.*

2 THE GREAT DEPRESSION

1. *Annual Register*, 1929, p. 307.
2. Unemployment figures from *Ministry of Labour Gazette*; trade figures for Britain and (see below) other countries, from B.R. Mitchell, *European Historical Statistics* (1980) and US Department of Commerce, *Historical Statistics of the United States* (1975).
3. See Lindsay to Henderson 31 December 1930, in C.P. 23(31). CAB 24/219.
4. Eugene Lyons: *Herbert Hoover* (Doubleday, 1964) p. 256.
5. Cabinet 29(31) 20 May. CAB 23/67.
6. *Annual Register*, 1931, p. 194.
7. See, for example, R. Bassett, *1931*.
8. Cabinet 69(31) 2 October, etc. CAB 23/68.
9. Ibid.
10. Cabinet 74, 76 (31) 10, 12 November 1931. CAB 23/69; C.P. 274(31). CAB 24/224.
11. Cabinet 80, 88(31). 20 November, 11 December. CAB 23/69.

3 THE DARKENING SKIES

1. C.P. 25, 31, 32(32) 18–19 January. CAB 24/228.
2. Cabinet 22(32) 18 April. CAB 23/71; C.P. 149(32) MacDonald, 4 May. CAB 24/229.
3. See *Annual Register*, 1932, p. 165.
4. Richard Storry, *Japan and the Decline of the West in Asia 1894–1943* (1979) p. 139.
5. Walter H. Mallory, 'The permanent conflict in Manchuria', *Foreign Affairs* 10 (1931–32), p. 220.
6. C.P. 104(32), 17 March. CAB 24/229; Cabinet 19(32) 23 March. CAB 23/70.
7. Cabinet 10, 11, 12, 14, 17 (33) 22 February–13 March. CAB 23/75.
8. François-Poncet to Herriot 10 November 1932. DDF ser. 1, i, 318.
9. C.P. 129(33) (Simon, 16 May). CAB 24/241.
10. Neville to Hilda Chamberlain 12 May 1933. NC 18/1/827.
11. Neurath to Nadolny 15 February; Köster to Neurath 21 May 1933. DGFP(C) i, 257, 26.
12. C.P. 68(34) (Simon, 9 March). CAB 24/248.
13. François-Poncet to Paul-Boncour 14 November 1933. DDF ser. 1, v, 10.
14. See, for example, C. T. Stannage, 'The East Fulham By-election of 25 October 1933', *Hist. J.*, xv, 1 (1971), 165–200.
15. Eden to Simon 18 February 1934. FO 800/289.

4 STRESA AND AFTER

1. C.P. 70(34) (Defence Requirements Committee, 12 March) CAB 24/248; Cabinet 10(34) 19 March. CAB 23/78.
2. C.P. 82(34) (Simon, 21 March) CAB 24/248.
3. Chilston to Simon 30 December 1933. FO 371/18297.
4. Directions of Dept. II to Minister in Austria. 15 March 1933. DGFP(C) ii, 328.
5. See, for example, François-Poncet to Barthou 27 September 1934. DDF ser. 1, vi, 387.
6. J. B. Duroselle, *La Décadence* (1979) pp. 136–7.
7. Hankey to Baldwin 12 December 1935. PREM 1/195.
8. Baldwin interview with League of Nations delegation 13 December 1935. PREM 1/195.
9. See MacDonald to Hoare 13 August 1935; Hoare to Chamberlain 18 August 1935. FO 800/295.
10. For details see list in FRUS 1935, i, p. 695 et seq.
11. Cabinet 50(35) 2 December; CAB 23/82; Eden, *Facing the Dictators*, p. 295.
12. Austen Chamberlain to Hoare 1 December 1935. FO 800/295.
13. Bingham to Hull 11 December 1935. FRUS 1935, i, pp. 700–1.
14. Cabinets 50, 51(35) 2, 4 December. CAB 23/82; Eden *op. cit.*, pp. 297–8.
15. Eden, *op. cit.*, p. 298.
16. Bingham to Hull, *loc. cit.*

17. C.P. 233(35) (Eden, 9 December); C.P. 235(35) (Hoare, 8 December). CAB 24/257; Bingham to Hull 16 December. FRUS 1935, i, p. 712 et seq.
18. See Cabinet 55(35), 17 December. It was later deleted, by agreement, from the French document as well. CAB 23/82.
19. Cabinet 52(35) 9 December. CAB 25/82; Eden *op. cit.*, pp. 300–303.
20. Gilbert to Hull 11 December 1935. FRUS 1935, i, p. 701 et seq.
21. Cabinet 56(35), 18 December. This part of the Minutes, which was not generally circulated, is out of regular sequence in the Cabinet files, in CAB 23/87.

5 POLARISATION

1. Dodd to Hull 7 March 1936. FRUS 1936, i, 207.
2. Note sur les répercussions possibles . . . (French War Department archives, 27 January 1936). DDF i, 106.
3. Flandin to Corbin 5 March 1936. DDF i, 283; J.-B. Duroselle, *La Décadence* (1979) p. 166.
4. Bullitt to Hull 7 March 1936. FRUS 1936, i, 212.
5. Cabinet 24(36) 25 March. CAB 23/83.
6. Cabinet 18(36) 11 March. CAB 23/83.
7. Eden to Foreign Office, 26 June, 2 July 1936. FO 954/8A.
8. Ingram to Foreign Office, 7 August 1936. DBFP 17, No. 69; Henderson to Hull 31 July. FRUS 1936, i, 1452; contrast 4 August, p. 461.
9. Appendix II to Cabinet 58(36). CAB 23/85.
10. Cabinet 37(37) 13 October. CAB 23/80.
11. Perkins, Bullitt to Hull 20, 30 April 1937. FRUS 1937, i, 284, 291.
12. See Douglas, Chamberlain and Eden 1937–38, *J. Contemp. Hist.* 13 (1978), 97–116.
13. Cabinet 43(37) 24 November. CAB 23/90A.
14. Eden to Chamberlain 31 January 1938. PREM 1/276.
15. Cabinet 6(38) 19 February. CAB 23/92.
16. Plessen to Foreign Ministry 11 March 1938; Hitler to Mussolini 11 March; Mackensen to German Diplomatic Missions 11 March; Altenburg memo. 12 March. DGFP (D) i, 350, 352, 357, 364.

6 APPEASEMENT

1. Wilson to Hull 6 May 1938. FRUS 1938, i, 492.
2. Cabinet 15(38) 22 March. CAB 23/93.
3. See CAB 53/10, CAB 53/37.
4. Cabinet 15(38) 22 March. CAB 23/93.
5. Bullitt to Hull, 9, 11, 16 May. FRUS 1938, i, 493, 495, 500.
6. See Halifax–Dawson correspondence of 15, 19 June 1938. FO 800/309.
7. Phipps to Halifax 14 September 1938. DBFP ser. 3, ii, 872, 874; Note du Ministre 13 septembre. DDF xi, 125.
8. Beneš, *Munich*, 223–7.
9. Cabinet 40(38) 19 September. CAB 23/95.

10. Meeting with delegation . . . 17 September 1938. PREM 1/264.
11. Note on whether . . . (Ismay, 20 September 1938). CAB 21/544.
12. Cabinet 47(38) 30 September. CAB 23/95.
13. Ogilvie-Forbes to Halifax 24 October 1938. FO 371/21658.
14. F.P. (36) 32nd meeting 14 November 1938. CAB 27/624.
15. Johnson to Hull 24 January 1938. FRUS 1939, i, 2.

7 INTO WAR

1. See E. Wiskemann, The *Drang nach Osten* continues, *Foreign Affairs*, 17, 764 et seq.
2. Cabinet 12, 13(39) 18, 20 March. CAB 23/98.
3. Georges Bonnet, *Quai d'Orsay* (1965) 234, 235.
4. Neville to Hilda Chamberlain 15 April 1939. NC 18/1/1094.
5. Cabinet 30(39) 24 May (Confidential annex). CAB 23/99.
6. F.P.(36) 58th meeting. 19 July 1939. CAB 27/625.
7. Cabinet 26(39) 3 May. CAB 23/99.
8. Ribbentrop/Schluenburg documents, 3, 4 August 1939. DGFP(D)vi, 760, 766.
9. Steinhardt to Hull 16 August 1939. FRUS 1939. i, 334.
10. Cabinet 41(39) 22 August. CAB 23/100.
11. *Ciano's diary 1939–1943*, ed. Malcolm Muggeridge, *passim*.
12. Cabinet 47(39) 1 September. CAB 23/100.
13. DGFP (D) viii, 157–160, and *passim*.
14. Neville to Ida Chamberlain 22 September 1939. NC 18/1/1122; Hankey to Halifax 12, 27 September 1939. FO 800/317.

8 ANNUS MIRABILIS

1. W.M. 122(39), 1(40) (Confidential annexes). 22 December 1939, 2 January 1940. CAB 65/4, 11.
2. See Chamberlain note 31 March 1940. PREM 1/419: W.M.78, 80, 82, 84 (40) and Confidential annexes. 1, 3, 5, 8 April. CAB 65/6, 12.
3. See W.M. 153(40) 3 June. CAB 65/13.
4. Hankey-Halifax Correspondence, 22–23 June 1940. FO 800/312.
5. W.M. 140(40) 26 May. Confidential annex. CAB 65/13.
6. W.P.(40) 559, 5 September. CAB 66/11.
7. G. H. Gallup, *The Gallup Poll*, i, 236.
8. Cripps to Halifax 2 August 1940. FO 371/24845.
9. See, for example, Himmler to Ribbentrop 3 July 1940; Zechlen to Foreign Ministry 5 July 1940; Ribbentrop to Schulenburg 25 June 1940. DGFP(D) x, 102, 113, 13.
10. Ribbentrop to Bucharest 27 June 1940. DGFP(D) x, 34.
11. Ribbentrop to Schulenburg 25 June 1940. DGFP(D) x, 13.
12. Schulenburg to Foreign Ministry 1 September 1940. DGFP(D) xi, 1.
13. Schmidt memo 13 November 1940. DGFP(D) xi, 328.
14. Weizäcker to Ribbentrop 17 January 1941; Ribbentrop to Weizäcker 21 January. DGFP(D) xi, 668, 681.

9 GRAND ALLIANCE

1. W.P.(41) 38, 39. 21, 24 February. CAB 66/13; Palairet to Eden 7 March. FO 954/11A: Cadogan to Halifax 17 March. Hickleton 2.A4.410.4.26.
2. OREM 3/403/3, 7, *passim.*
3. F.O. to Moscow 4 June 1941. CAB 65/18, fo. 163.
4. W.M. 60(41) 16 June. CAB 65/22.
5. Churchill to Alexander 10 July 1941. PREM 3/395/16 fo. 370s.
6. Eden to Cripps 16 July 1941. FO 954/24B fo. 342; Stalin to Churchill 19 July, *ibid.* fo. 346; Churchill to Stalin July 1941. PREM 3/403/3.
7. Craigie memo, 4 February 1943. PREM 3/158/4.
8. W.M. 10(41) 16 October. Confidential annex. CAB 65/23; Churchill to F.O. 12 August 1941. W.P.(41) 202. CAB 66/18. Dalton diary 26 August 1941.
9. See, in particular, views of Eden and Wood. W.M. 81(41) 12 August. CAB 65/19.
10. W.M. 90(41) 5 September. Confidential annex. CAB 65/23.
11. W.P.(41) 245 (Eden) 23 October. CAB 66/9.
12. Churchill note 4 December 1941 on Eden memo. PREM 3/170/1.
13. See Craigie memo. submitted 4 February 1943. PREM 3/158/4.
14. W.P.(42) 8. 5 January 1942. CAB 66/20.

10 STRAINS OF EMPIRE

1. Linlithgow to Amery 21 January 1942, circulated in W.P.(42)43, 20 January 1942. CAB 66/21.
2. W.P.(42)59 (Attlee, 2 February). CAB 66/21.
3. W.M. 21(42) 16 February 'no circulation'. CAB 65/25.
4. Cripps to Churchill 1 April 1942, circulated in W.P.(42)138. CAB 66/23.
5. See Eden, *Full Circle*, pp. 244–5.

11 THE COURSE OF WAR

1. Churchill to Eden 8 January 1942. PREM 3/399/6.
2. Churchill to Roosevelt 7 March 1942. PREM 3/395/12.
3. See FO 954/25A, *passim.*
4. Second meeting . . . 21 May 1942. PREM 3/399/8 fos 175–6.
5. W.M. 52(43) 12 April. CAB 65/34.
6. Churchill to Eden 20 December 1943. PREM 3/355/6; Dalton diary 21 December; Bohlen, *Witness to History*, p. 151.
7. Romer to O'Malley 20 June 1944. PREM 3/355/12.
8. See Eden to Clark-Kerr 18 May 1944; Churchill to Roosevelt 31 May; Roosevelt to Churchill 11 June. PREM 3/66/7.
9. Roosevelt to Churchill 29 March 1945. CAB 66/64.
10. Churchill to Roosevelt 8 March 1945. FDR, Map Room 31.
11. Churchill to Roosevelt 13 March 1945. FRUS 1945, v, 158.
12. Truman, *Year of Decisions*, p. 85.

13. Churchill to Truman 12 May 1945. PREM 3/495/7.
14. See Dalton's diary, *passim*; also report of Churchill-Stalin talk, 18 July 1945. PREM 3/430/6.

12   UNEASY PEACE

1. *Annual Register*, 1944, p. 388.
2. David Thomson, *England in the 20th Century* (1965) p. 202.
3. A. J. P. Taylor, *English History 1914–1945* (1965) p. 599.
4. Attlee to Truman 9 August 1945 (2.40 p.m.) FO 800/438.
5. See, for example, memorandum, 'The Atomic Bomb', 28 August 1945. PREM 8/116.
6. McNeill memorandum 2 December 1946. CAB 129/15.
7. C.M. 57(45) 29 November (Confidential annex). CAB 128/4; Dalton diary 7 December.

13   1947

1. See British Embassy to S.D. 18 June 1947. FRUS 1947, iii, 17.
2. Henderson note, 'The eastern Mediterranean' 28 December 1946. FO 800/475.
3. Memo. by Joint COS to State-War-Navy Co-ordinating Committee, with appendix. 12 May 1947. FRUS 1947, i, 734.
4. C.P.(45) 281. 14 November. CAB 129/4.
5. C.M. 7(46) 22 January; 22(46) 6 March. Confidential annex. CAB 128/5, 7.
6. C.M. 65(45) 5 July. CAB 128/6.
7. See, for example, Vincent A. Smith, *Oxford History of India* (1976) p. 831.
8. C.P.(45) 456. Indian policy. Attlee, 24 December. CAB 129/15.
9. C.M. 1(47) 8 January.(Confidential annex). CAB 128/11.
10. C.P.(47) 158. Indian Policy (Attlee) 22 May. CAB 129/19.
11. C.M. 38(45) 4 October. CAB 128/1.
12. See, for example, F.O. note of 24 January 1947. FO 800/476.
13. Truman to Attlee 24 (?) July 1945. FO 800/484.
14. C.M. 30, 38(45) 11 September. (Confidential annex), 4 October. CAB 128/3, 1.
15. Attlee to Truman 16 September 1945. FO 800/484.
16. Halifax to Bevin and Attlee 3 October 1945. FO 800/484.
17. See C.M. 91(46) 25 October. CAB 128/6: C.P.(47)49: Palestine (Bevin and Creech-Jones) 6 February. CAB 129/16, etc.
18. C.P.(47)49. Palestine (Bevin and Creech-Jones) 6 February. CAB 120/16.
19. See Attlee and Bevin memoranda 5, 9 January 1947, and Dixon memo. 10 January. FO 800/476.
20. C.P.(47) 259. Palestine (Bevin) 18 September 1947. CAB 129/21.

14 THE LINES ARE DRAWN

1. See Roberts memorandum, 26 February 1948. FO 800/502.
2. S.D. Policy Paper, n.d. FRUS 1948, ii, 61; Marshall to Truman 11 February 1948. HST/PSF 178.
3. Ismay to Attlee 23 October 1946. MS Attlee Dep. 42; Reading Copy 1 (Acheson 10–11 October 1953). DA 75.
4. C.M. 19(48) 7 June. CAB 128/12.
5. Murphy to Marshall 23 June 1948. FRUS 1948, ii, 915.
6. Caffery to Marshall 24 June 1948. FRUS 1948, ii, 916; C.M. 43(48) 25 June. CAB 128/13; Truman 'Memoirs' file 18 July HST/Post-Presidential 2; Policy Planning Staff 28 September. FRUS 1948, ii, 1194.
7. C.M. 31(49) 2 May. CAB 128/15.
8. See, for example, Attlee to Mackenzie King 16 March 1948; Bevin to Attlee 6 April. PREM 8/788.
9. See discussion in Geddis Smith: *Dean Acheson*, p. 59 et seq.

15 THE DEEPEST DANGER

1. Geddis Smith, *Dean Acheson*, p. 174.
2. Memorandum of conversation . . . (Butterworth). 5 January 1949. FRUS 1949, vii, part 2, 940.
3. C.M. 71(50) 6 November. CAB 128/18.
4. MacArthur, *Reminiscences*, p. 334; FRUS 1950, vii, *passim*.
5. See FRUS 1950, vii, 449 et seq., *passim*.
6. Substance of statements . . . 15 October 1950. FRUS 1950, vii, 948; MacArthur, *Reminiscences*, p. 362.
7. See C.M. 62(50) 28 September. CAB 128/18.
8. C.M. 73(50) 13 November. CAB 128/18.
9. Acheson to Embassy, U.K., 28 November 1950; MacArthur to JCOS 28 November. FRUS 1950, vii, 1249, 1237.
10. JCOS to MacArthur 29 December 1950. FRUS 1950, vii, 1625.
11. MacArthur, *op. cit.*., 382.
12. C.M. 13(51) 12 February. CAB 128/19.
13. Franks to F.O. 1 July 1952 gives State Department figures. Total held: 169 944. Resisting repatriation, 86 222; not resisting, 83 722.

16 WITHDRAWAL FROM EMPIRE

1. C.M. 58(47) 1 July. CAB 128/10.
2. Report by the Paymaster-General . . . 16 January to 9 March 1948. PREM 8/923.
3. C (52)306. Relations with . . . South Africa (Lyttleton, 24 September). CAB 129/55.
4. See C (52)407, Kenya (Lyttleton, 14 November) CAB 129/57.
5. C.P. (51)94. Political problems . . . (Morrison) 29 March. CAB 129/45.
6. C.M. 2, 12(47). 6, 27 January. CAB 128/9.

7. See note of Conversation . . . 15 January 1948. FO 800/477.
8. For a good account of this and later stages in the dispute, see J. P. Derriennic, *Le Moyen-Orient au XXè Siècle* (Paris: 1980).
9. C.M. 52(51) 16 July, CAB 128/21, contrasted with C.P. (51)212, Persia (Morrison, 20 July). CAB 129/46.

17 A CALMER WORLD

1. Saikal, A; *Rise and Fall of the Shah*, p. 41; Derriennic, J.-P., *Le Moyen-Orient au XXè Siècle*, p. 146.
2. Eden, *Full Circle*, p. 201.
3. C.C. (54)52 (Confidential annex) 23 July 1954. CAB 128/27, part 2.
4. C.C. (54)61 21 Septemberr. CAB 128/27, part 2.
5. See Eden, *Full Circle*, pp. 82–3.
6. Eden, *Full Circle*, p. 77.
7. C.C. (54)83 7 December. CAB 128/27, part 2.
8. C.C. (53)5, 27 January. CAB 128/26, part 1.
9. C.C. (54)83 7 December. CAB 128/27, part 2.

18 SUEZ

1. C.C. (52)102 4 December. CAB 128/25.
2. C.C. (53)9, 10. 11 February. CAB 128/26, part I.
3. C. (53)131. The Sudan (Lloyd, 18 April). CAB 129/60.
4. C. (53)135. The Sudan (Macmillan, 20 April). CAB 129/60.
5. C. (53)65. Egypt – the alternative (Eden, 16 February); and see C. (53)196 (Salisbury, 7 July). CAB 129/59, 62.
6. C. (53) 328 Egypt – defence requirements (Eden 20 November, quoting Robertson). CAB 129/64.
7. Nutting, *No End of a Lesson*, pp. 31–35; Eden, *Full Circle, passim.*
8. See Robert R. Bowie, *Suez 1956*, p. 53 et seq.

19 REFELECTIONS

1. Cabinet 10(34) 19 March. CAB 23/78; C.P. 64(34) 5 March. CAB 24/247.
2. Craigie memo. 4 February 1943. PREM 3/158/4.

Bibliography

SECONDARY WORKS (published in London unless otherwise indicated)

Acheson, Dean, *Present at the Creation: my years in the State Department* (New York: 1969)

Adamthwaite, A., *France and the Coming of the Second World War* (1977)

Alperowitz, Gar., *Atomic Diplomacy: Hiroshima and Potsdam (1966)*

Annual Register

Avon, Earl of, *The Eden Memoirs:* (1) *Facing the Dictators*, (2) *The Reckoning*, (3) *Full Circle* (1960–65)

Barnett, Correlli, *The Collapse of British Power* (Gloucester, 1984)

Bassett, R., *1931: Political Crisis* (1958)

Beloff, Max, *The Foreign Policy of Soviet Russia 1929–1941* (Oxford, 1947–49)

Beneš, E., *Munich* (Paris, 1970)

Bohlen, C. E., *Witness to History 1929–1969* (New York, 1973)

Bonnet, Georges, *Quai d'Orsay* (Paris, 1965)

Bowie, Robert R., *Suez 1956* (Oxford, 1974)

Bullock, A., *Hitler* (New York, 1962)

Butler, R. A. *The Art of the Possible* (1971)

Cadogan, Sir A., *The Diaries of Sir Alexander Cadogan* (ed. David Dilks) (1972)

Carr, E. H., *International Relations between the Two World Wars* (1947)

Carr, E. H., *German-Soviet Relations between the Two World Wars* (1954)

Churchill, Winston L. S., *The Second World War* (various editions, 1948–54 onwards)

Ciano, Count G., *Ciano's Diary 1939–43* (ed. Malcolm Muggeridge) (1947)

Cienciala, A. M., *Poland and the Western Powers 1938–1939* (1968)

Colvin, I., *The Chamberlain Cabinet* (1971)

Dalton, Diary (p. 264, note 14)

Derriennic, J.-P., *Le Moyen-Orient an XXè Siècle* (Paris. 1980)

Divine, Robert A., *Foreign Policy and US Presidential elections 1940–48* (New York, 1974)

Douglas, Roy, (1) *In the Year of Munich* (2) *The Advent of War 1939–40* (3) *New Alliances 1940–41* (4) *From War to Cold War 1942–48* (1977–82)

Duroselle, J.-B., *La Décadence 1932–1939* (Paris, 1979)

Duroselle, J.-B., *L'Abîme 1939–1945* (Paris, 1982)

Eden, (Sir) Anthony, See Avon Earl of

Erickson, John, *The Soviet High Command* (1962)

Erickson, John, *The Road to Stalingrad* (1971)
Feiling, Sir Keith, *The Life of Neville Chamberlain* (1947)
Ferrell, Robert H. and S. F. Bemis, (eds), *The American Secretaries of State and their Diplomacy.* Vols 12 and 13: Julius W. Pratt on *Cordell Hull* (New York, 1964); Vol. 14: Richard L. Walker on *Edward R. Stettinius jr.* and George Curry on *James F. Byrnes* (New York, 1965); Vol. 15: Robert H. Ferrell on *George C. Marshall* (New York, 1966); Vol. 16: Gaddis Smith on *Dean Acheson* (New York, 1972): Vol. 17: Louis L. Gerson on *John Foster Dulles* (New York, 1967).
Gallup, G. H., *The Gallup Poll: Public Opinion 1935–1971* (3 vols) (New York, 1972)
Gilbert, Martin, *The Roots of Appeasement* (1964)
Gilbert, Martin, *Winston Churchill, vol. 5: The Prophet of Truth, 1922–1939* (1976)
Grigg, John, *1943: The Victory that Never Was* (1980)
Hart, B. H. Liddell, *The Other Side of the Hill* (1948)
Keesing's Contemporary Archives
Kolko, Gabriel, *The Politics of War* (1969)
Laqueur, Walter, *Europe since Hitler* (1982)
Liberal Magazine
Liberal Year Book
Lloyd George Liberal Magazine
Lyons, Eugene, *Herbert Hoover: A Biography* (Garden City, New York: 1964)
MacArthur, Douglas, *Reminiscences* (New York, 1964)
MacLeod, Iain, *Neville Chamberlain* (1961)
Macmillan, Harold, *The Blast of War 1939–1945* (1967)
Maisky, Ivan, *Memoirs of a Soviet Ambassador: The War 1939–43* (1962)
Marwick, Arthur, *Britain in the Century of Total War* (1968)
Medlicott, W. N., *British Foreign Policy since Versailles* (1940)
Medlicott, W. N., *Contemporary England* (1967)
Ministry of Labour Gazette
Mitchell, B. R., *European Historical Statistics 1750–1975* (2nd ed., 1980)
Mitchell, B. R. and Phyllis Deane, *Abstract of British Historical Statistics* (Cambridge, 1962)
Mitchell, B. R. and H. G. Jones, *Second Abstract of British Historical Statistics* (Cambridge, 1971)
Nutting, Anthony, *No End of a Lesson: The Story of Suez* (1967)
Porter, B., *The Lion's Share: A Short History of British Imperialism, 1850–1970* (1975)
Porter, B., *Britain, Europe and the World 1850–1982: Delusions of Granduer* (1983)
Reed, John, *Ten Days that Shook the World* (New York, 1960)
Robertson, E. M., *The Origins of the Second World War: Historical Interpretations* (1978)
Roskill, Stephen, *Hankey, Man of Secrets, vol. 3, 1931–63* (1974)
Saikal, A., *Rise and Fall of the Shah* (1980)
Sherwood, Robert E., *The White House Papers of Harry L. Hopkins, vol. 2* (1949)

Simon, Viscount, *Retrospect* (1952)

Skidelsky, Robert, *Politicians and the Slump: the Labour Government of 1929–1931* (1967)

Smith, V. A., *Oxford History of India* (1976)

Storry, G. R., *Japan and the Decline of the West in Asia 1894–1943* (1979)

Taylor, A. J. P., *The Origins of the Second World War* (1961, etc.)

Taylor, A. J. P., *English History 1914–1945* (Oxford, 1965)

Taylor, Telford, *Munich: the Price of Peace* (New York, 1980)

Thompson, Kenneth W., *Cold War Theories, vol. 1: World Polarisation 1943–1953* (Louisiana, 1981)

Thomson, David, *England in the 20th Century* (Harmondsworth, 1965)

Thorne, Christopher, *Allies of a Kind: the United States, Britain and the War against Japan 1941–45* (1978)

Truman, Harry S., *Memoirs: (1) Year of Decisions, 1945 (2) Years of Trial and Hope 1946–1952* (Garden City, New York, 1955 etc.)

United States Department of Commerce, Bureau of the Census, *Historical Statistics of the United States: Colonial Times to 1970* 2 vols (Washington: 1975)

Vansittart, Lord, *The Mist Procession* (1958)

Watt, D. C., *Personalities and Policies: Studies in the Formulation of British Foreign Policy in the 20th Century* (1965)

Wheeler-Bennett, J. W., *The Nemesis of Power* (1954)

Wheeler-Bennett, J. W., *Munich, Prologue to Tragedy* (1966).

Wilmot, Chester, *The Struggle for Europe* (1952)

Wiskemann, Elizabeth, *Europe of the Dictators 1919–1945* (1966)

Woodward, Sir Llewellyn, *British Foreign Policy in the Second World War* 5 vols (1976)

Woytinsky, W. S. and E. S., *World Commerce and Governments* (New York, 1955)

Young, G. M., *Stanely Baldwin* (1952)

PUBLISHED COLLECTIONS OF PRIMARY DOCUMENTS

Documents diplomatiques français 1932–1939, Ministère des affaires étrangères, Paris

Documents on British Foreign Policy, 1919–1939, Third series, edited by E. L. Woodward and Rohan Butler, HMSO, London

Documents on German Foreign Policy 1918–1945, HMSO, London

Foreign Relations of the United States, Department of State, Washington

UNPUBLISHED PAPERS

Bodleian Library, Oxford
Earl (C.R.) Attlee
Lord Ponsonby

Churchill College, Cambridge
Ernest Bevin
Lord Hankey
Viscout (Earl) Halifax, Hickleton series (microfilm)
Sir Eric Phipps
Viscount Thurso (Sir Archibald Sinclair)
Lord (Sir Robert) Vansittart

House of Lords Record Office, London
Lord Beaverbrook (Beaverbrook Library collection)
Earl Lloyd-George (Beaverbrook Library collection)

Labour Party, London
Executive Committee minutes

Library of Congress, Washington
Cordell Hull (microfilm)
H. L. Ickes

London School of Economics: British Library of Political and Economic Science
Lord (Hugh) Dalton, diary

National Archives, Washington
State Department

Public Record Office, Kew, Surrey
Cabinet minutes: CAB 23, 65 and 128
Cabinet memoranda: CAB 24, 66 and 129
Cabinet Committee on Foreign Policy: CAB 27
Foreign Office memoranda: FO 371
Foreign Office: collections of paper in FO 800 series:
Viscount (Earl) Halifax
Sir Nevile Henderson
Viscount Runciman
Sir Orme Sargent
Foreign Office: Earl of Avon (Anthony Eden) papers: FO 954 (also copies at University of Birmingham)
Premier papers: PREM 1, 3 and 8

F. D. Roosevelt Library, Hyde Park, New York
Harry L. Hopkins
F. D. Roosevelt

Harry S. Truman Library, Independence, Missouri
Dean Acheson
C. M. Clifford
Harry S. Truman

University of Birmingham
Neville Chamberlain
Earl of Avon (as FO 954)

University of Iowa, Iowa City
Henry A. Wallace

University of Newcastle upon Tyne
Viscount Runciman

University of Virginia, Charlottesville
Edward R. Stettinius

Index